Biobehavioral Treatment of
Obsessive-Compulsive
Spectrum Disorders

Also by José A. Yaryura-Tobias and Fugen Neziroglu

Obsessive-Compulsive Disorder Spectrum:
Pathogenesis, Diagnosis, and Treatment

Over and Over Again: Understanding Obsessive-Compulsive Disorder

Also by José A. Yaryura-Tobias
The Integral Being

A NORTON PROFESSIONAL BOOK

Biobehavioral Treatment of Obsessive-Compulsive Spectrum Disorders

José A. Yaryura-Tobias, M.D., FACPM

and

Fugen Neziroglu, Ph.D., ABBP, ABPP

W. W. Norton & Company
New York • London

DRUG DOSAGE

The authors and publisher have exerted every effort to ensure that drug selection and dosage set forth in this text are in accord with current recommendations and practice at the time of publication. However, in view of ongoing research, changes in government regulations, and the constant flow of information relating to drug therapy and drug reactions, the reader is urged to check the package insert for each drug for any change in indications and dosage and for added warnings and precautions. This is particularly important when the recommended agent is a new and/or infrequently used drug.

Library of Congress Cataloging-in-Publication Data

Yaryura-Tobias, José A. , 1934–
  Biobehavioral treatment of obsessive-compulsive spectrum disorders / José A. Yaryura-Tobias and Fugen A. Neziroglu.
      p.   cm.
  "A Norton professional book"
  Includes bibliographical references and index.
  ISBN 0-393-70245-6
  1. Obsessive-compulsive disorder—Treatment.   I. Neziroglu, Fugen A., 1951–   . II. Title.
RC533.Y365   1997
616.85'22706—dc21   97-8664 CIP

W.W. Norton & Company, Inc., 500 Fifth Avenue, New York, NY 10110
http://www.wwnorton.com

W.W. Norton & Company Ltd., 10 Coptic Street, London WC1A 1PU

1 2 3 4 5 6 7 8 9 0

To all our patients

Contents

Acknowledgments

We would like to thank Michael S. Grunes and Esteban Toro Martinez for their scientific assistance. We are also grateful to our professional staff, who have shared with us their opinions on the biobehavioral treatment approach. Last but not least, we would also like to thank Fran Noone, Lauren O'Connell, and Allen Pabo.

Introduction

For most people, spending their fortieth birthday doing laundry at a laundromat would be considered mundane, perhaps even depressing. For Sharon C., it was a dream come true. Just two months before, she was living in the same filthy clothes she had worn for months, trapped in a basement apartment that she had not left for almost 20 years. Her captors were obsessive-compulsive disorder (OCD) and panic disorder with agoraphobia.

"I never thought that life could be like this. If you told me three months ago that I'd be walking around outside, eating take-out food, shopping and living in the world, I would have said you were crazy."

Sharon first experienced panic symptoms at the age of seven, not long after being sexually molested by a man who was doing work on her house. The panic symptoms became incapacitating when Sharon was 19, after she collapsed at a dance club. She experienced extreme panic symptoms and kept collapsing over a period of several hours. After extensive medical tests at a local hospital, physicians concluded that there was nothing wrong with her. Sharon threw out everything she was wearing that night, because it represented "bad luck" to her, and she refused to leave the house.

Her OCD began when she was about 32 years old, although she states she had traces of it all her life. At this time, she was having an affair with a married man and believed she was pregnant. Even though she was not pregnant, she became obsessed with sperm and came to believe that she could get pregnant by brushing against objects that were previously touched by men. She became very withdrawn and would see no one, particularly her father, who "had a disgusting habit of masturbating in the living room." As her symptoms increased, she could no longer use toilet paper or wear underwear. She began wearing diapers in order to avoid using toilet paper and as a protective shield from the world.

Another obsessive-compulsive fear of Sharon's is that she might ingest food or substances that would alter her state of consciousness. Particularly, she refused to take medications of any kind and until recently would not combine certain foods for fear that they would ferment in her system and cause her to become incapacitated. Recently, she threw away food that touched a case of beer in a supermarket. Although she recognized the ridiculousness of her compulsions, at times she had little control over them and impulsively threw away food or engaged in a ritual.

Over the years, Sharon became more and more incapable of functioning. When the OCD hit, she refused to see anyone but her mother, because others could not be trusted "not to touch anything in the apartment, lean on anything, or brush up against anything." Sharon saw no one but her mother for eight years. Even today she becomes tearful when explaining how the condition rendered her almost completely helpless and how she controlled her mother in order to survive.

"I almost died and took my mother with me. I would sleep all day and stay up all night. Because I was so scared, I made my mother stay up with me and I would question her all night about the things that she did for me. I made her wash with bleach. I made her shop with one hand and pay for the food with the other hand. I questioned her about how many items were on the shelf, and if they were touching one another and in which store she bought my food. Things would get so detailed that I would forget what she said and then I would have to ask her all over again. This would sometimes take all night."

It is often interesting for therapists to discover the reasons that patients choose to enter treatment when they do. Sharon had phone visits with Dr. Neziroglu during the year 1987. At that time, the doctor had offered to come to the house and work gradually with her, to the point where she could tolerate the doctor entering the house and eventually even her basement apartment. She said, at that time, "I just can't let you in. I just can't do that."

Hospitalization and medication were recommended but she refused. Not making sufficient progress with our phone visits, we agreed to stop all treatment until such time as she was ready to accept professional recommendations.

Seven years later, Sharon's mother called indicating that it was an emergency. She said, "Sharon wants to be hospitalized. She is desperate for help."

We agreed to hospitalize her the next day. It is not uncommon for patients to seek help periodically in their lives. Whether it is family pressure, desperation or a crisis that gives the impetus to seek help, patients may go in and out of therapy. At times, they are more motivated than other times.

Sharon explained her motivation as "a matter of life and death." Her rituals had become so elaborate, they were impossible to complete. It literally took her hours to eat one meal and drink one glass of water. She had to be absolutely certain that the food was uncontaminated and that the plates were clean. This meant hours of washing and eating in a painstakingly slow manner so she could be sure that "nothing touched what it wasn't supposed to."

It was 5 A.M. the day before she decided to be admitted to South Oaks Hospital. She had been up all night, as usual, and was preparing a meal of pasta and beans, the only thing she was not afraid to eat.

"I thought the food touched the rim of the pot and I ended up throwing the whole thing away. I was sleep deprived and starving. The thought came to me, "You are going to die here. I knew I had to get help."

In getting to the hospital, Sharon had to confront one disorder to get treatment for the other. Sharon had not been out of her house in nearly twenty years and was terrified of being far away from home and having panic attacks. She was driven to the hospital by Dean McKay, Ph.D., one of her psychologists. At one point, three blocks from home, she wanted to turn back, but she was persuaded by Dr. McKay that she would be disappointing many people and making a big mistake.

At South Oaks, Sharon was very motivated in her treatment. Instead of avoiding the things she was afraid of, she confronted them with the help of an understanding staff and her psychologists. She took a shower for the first time in eight years. She sat where other patients had just been sitting. She did not stop other patients from comforting her with a touch on the arm or a pat on the back.

Sharon describes the whole experience of being hospitalized as "a shock to my system." At home, she was sensory deprived, without adequate food or sleep. Furthermore, she was in almost complete isolation and the obsessions and compulsions "just took over." Being around people again, Sharon was exposed to "what is normal" and often asked questions about whether or not her behavior was normal. The desire to be normal is what often sets success stories apart from treatment failures.

It is interesting that Sharon was able to do certain things while in the hospital that have again become "off limits" since her discharge, such as showering and being touched by other people. Her difficulties appear to mount when she is in an environment which is under her control. Loneliness and isolation also play a major role and make it difficult for Sharon to resist engaging in avoidance or rituals aimed at decreasing anxiety. Her discharge, after one week in the hospital, was premature. Unfortunately, none of us treating her could convince her of that and we could do no more than agree to treat her at home.

Fortunately, at home she has accepted many deviations from her former OCD "rules." For example, she will now eat take-out food even though she doesn't know how it is prepared. Furthermore, she will accept food from someone who has just touched money, something that was unthinkable previously.

"That is the way they do things in the world and, if I'm going to live in the world, I have to accept it."

She is able to buy clothing and wear it without washing first. In order to overcome panic symptoms, she goes out on a daily basis. If she feels dizzy or depersonalized, she walks further away from home, instead of returning immediately.

"It is unbelievable to me that I can do this," she says.

Needless to say, Sharon's difficulties have created problems for her entire family. Sharon's mother is so accustomed to reassuring her constantly that she continues to do so automatically, even when Sharon does not ask. Mrs. C. needs to be reminded that it is not therapeutic to provide constant reassurance and is encouraged not to do so, even when Sharon asks questions.

Mrs. C. looks worn out and has an expression of continual worry and fatigue, even when she smiles. In addition to helping Sharon, she also cares for her 80-year-old husband, who is in poor health and whom Sharon has not seen in eight years.

"My mother tells me that he is sick and that he cries every day because he thinks that what happened to me is his fault."

While to her therapists Sharon is making remarkable progress, given the severity and duration of her symptoms, family members are often impatient, expecting a quick and complete recovery.

"My sister gives me no credit. She only looks at what I still can't do rather than all the things that I can do."

At times, Sharon is regretful about the years that were wasted, saying, "It could have been a whole different life." It is also difficult at times for her to accept her own rate of recovery. While she has improved by anyone's standards, there are still so many things that seem impossible to her. She still cannot touch her own front door, touch anything her mother just touched, see her father, or take a shower. She is also unable to be touched by another human being.

As is often common with those who show some improvement from incapacitating symptoms, Sharon's motivation has waned since she was first hospitalized. Because exposure and response prevention are anxiety provoking at best (Sharon calls the process "brutal"), persons who have made enough improvement to lead semi-independent lives may suddenly find themselves unwilling to continue with behavioral exercises that are necessary for more complete recovery. Sharon is no exception; at times she says, "I am not as willing as I should be." She stays motivated by thinking of the horrors of her not-too-distant past.

"I never want to live like that again. I never want to be that sick again and, also, I can't give up shopping," she adds, laughing.

Sharon's life experiences as a person suffering the consequences for OCD reflect the devastating effects of this illness. OCD afflicts about six million Americans. The magnitude of this condition is comparable to that of other major psychiatric disorders, such as affect disorders or the schizophrenias. OCD is found around the world, without cultural or socioeconomic exceptions. The presence of OCD has been traced back to biblical times.

Clinicians working at the end of the nineteenth century and at the beginning of the twentieth century provided a thorough description of the illness. Since then, we have acquired a solid concept of what OCD is, robust evidence that it exists, and a series of specific treatments, indirectly reinforcing the presence of an independent nosology. However, OCD's vast symptomatology may overlap with conditions having prominent obsessions and compulsions, called spectrum disorders. This overlapping may bring about diagnostic difficulties, leading to the wrong treatment.

The purpose of this book is to share our experience of more than 25 years of treating this population within a biopsychosocial frame of reference. OCD seriously impinges on the lives of both the patients and their relatives, who share their suffering. We have sometimes felt impotent and overwhelmed by our inability to treat OCD successfully and by our sense of failure as therapists. This book was conceived knowing that our fellow colleagues have also, at times, walked the pathway of frustration.

Biobehavioral Treatment of Obsessive-Compulsive Spectrum Disorders is divided into 10 chapters. The first two discuss the clinical aspects and the tools available to diagnose OCD and its spectrum. The next eight chapters are dedicated to treatment management. An appendix contains various assessment scales considered to be useful aids for diagnosis and evaluation of treatment interventions. We have included a minimum number of references to avoid interrupting the teaching flow of the text; for those interested in delving into more detailed information, a list of suggested readings is provided.

Biobehavioral Treatment of
Obsessive-Compulsive
Spectrum Disorders

1

Obsessive-Compulsive Disorder and Its Spectrum

O CD WAS FIRST ADDRESSED in a scientific and clinical manner during the fourth quarter of the nineteenth century. Distinguished scholars such as Westphal, Tucke, Burton, Morel, Charcot, Gilles de la Tourette, Esquirol, Buccola, Morselli, Falret, Donnath, du Saulle, and Luys made clinical contributions to the understanding of this grave disorder. Janet, Freud, and Pollit have added to that research during this century. From this prolific source of clinical information, hundreds of research papers were born.

Current advancements in the study of OCD have offered important findings in the areas of classification, epidemiology, phenomenology, pathology, and treatment. The phenomenology of obsessive-compulsive disorder (OCD) and its spectrum is vast and mosaic, with symptoms sometimes taken from areas indirectly related to psychiatry, including magic and religion.

> Marion came to see us about 20 years ago, accompanied by her mother. She was 30 years old, recently married, with a degree in accounting, but currently taking care of her house. As far as she recalls, Marion has always suffered from OCD. It was not until she saw a television program on the subject that she realized her condition was OCD. Her symptoms were severe double checking, prolonged washing rituals, and morbid obsessions that controlled a great part of her daily life. Only her mother was aware of her terrible burden. Her husband was ignorant of her disorder, because she kept her symptoms secret. As soon as her husband would go to work, mother would walk in to assist her. Marion could not defecate and clean herself or take a shower without her mother's help. In fact, during her menses mother had to insert her tampons. At lunch time, Marion might require spoon-feeding. All these rituals would take place during the daytime, day after day, month after month, year after year. When her mother left, Marion would engage in intense obsessionality accompanied by rituals and magical thinking that required no assistance by her mother.

This case shows important dynamic characteristics of severe dependence and regression, to the point of a strong symbiotic relation, emerging during an arrested anal phase and communicated through an obsessive-compulsive language. Or, if you may, this case is characterized by severe obsessions and compulsions accompanied by rituals and magical thinking, in a borderline personality with histrionic features and dependence. This case synthesizes the OCD symptomatology with additional symptoms from personality disorders and with an analytical substratum with strong mother-daughter dynamics.

The symptoms of OCD are protean, and therefore OCD therapists must have an excellent understanding of the phenomenology of this condition and of any other condition that may obscure or overlap its diagnosis. And it is precisely for this reason that a slow and skillfull clinical examination of a patient suspected of having the disorder must be preformed. In-depth clinical observation of the patient was the basis of the research by clinicians of the last century who passed onto us their valuable heritage.

Definition

Obsessive-compulsive disorder is a complex neuropsychiatric process comprising a homogenous core of three major symptoms:

1. intrusive, forceful, and repetitive thoughts, images, or sounds that dwell in one's mind, without the possibility of rejecting them
2. imperative needs to perform motor or mental acts
3. doubting, that is, chronic questioning about great or minor matters

The *DSM-IV* criteria are set forth in table 1.1.

Besides the *DSM-IV* classification, the *International Classification and Diagnostic Manual* (ICD-10, 1995) classifies OCD into three subcategories: predominantly obsessions, predominantly compulsions, and mixed obsessions and compulsions. In the *DSM-IV* field trial it was found that 91.0% fell into the mixed category, only 8.5% percent fell into the predominantly obsessions classification, and 0.5% fell into the predominantly compulsive class.

Symptomatology

Knowledge of the patient's symptoms and behaviors is the base of a biobehavioral treatment program. A *symptom* is a subjective or objective feeling that conveys the occurrence of an event; it is the body's message, a signal,

TABLE 1.1   *DSM-IV* diagnostic criteria for obsessive-compulsive
disorder

A. Either obsessions or compulsions:

Obsessions as defined by (1), (2), (3), and (4):

    (1) Recurrent and persistent thoughts, impulses, or images that are experienced, at some time during the disturbance, as intrusive and inappropriate and that cause marked anxiety or distress.

    (2) The thoughts, impulses, or images are not simply excessive worries about real-life problems.

    (3) The person attempts to ignore or suppress such thoughts, impulses, or images, or to neutralize them with some other thought or action.

    (4) The person recognizes that the obsessional thoughts, impulses, or images are a product of his or her own mind (not imposed from without as in thought insertion).

Compulsions as defined by (1) and (2):

    (1) Repetitive behaviors (e.g., hand washing, ordering, checking) or mental acts (e.g., praying, counting, repeating words silently) that the person feels driven to perform in response to an obsession, or according to rules that must be applied rigidly.

    (2) The behaviors or mental acts are aimed at preventing or reducing distress or preventing some dreaded event or situation; however, these behaviors or mental acts either are not connected in a realistic way with what they are designed to neutralize or prevent or are clearly excessive.

B. At some point during the course of the disorder, the person has recognized that the obsessions or compulsions are excessive or unreasonable. (Note: This does not apply to children.)

C. The obsessions or compulsions cause marked distress, are time consuming (take more than 1 hour a day), or significantly interfere with the person's normal routine, occupational (or academic) functioning, or usual social activities or relationships.

D. If another Axis I disorder is present, the content of the obsessions or compulsions is not restricted to it (e.g., preoccupation with food in the presence of an Eating Disorder, hair pulling in the presence of Trichotillomania; concern with appearance in the presence of Body Dysmorphic Disorder; preoccupation with drugs in the presence of a

continued

TABLE 1.1   *continued*

Substance Use Disorder; preoccupation with having a serious illness in the presence of Hypochondriasis; preoccupation with sexual urges or fantasies in the presence of a Paraphilia; or guilty ruminations in the presence of Major Depressive Disorder).

E. The disturbance is not due to the direct physiological effects of a substance (e.g., a drug of abuse, a medication) or a general medical condition.

Specify if:

With Poor Insight: if, for most of the time during the current episode, the person does not recognize that the obsessions and compulsions are excessive or unreasonable.

From American Psychiatric Association, 1994, *Diagnostic and statistical manual of mental disorders* (4th ed., pp. 422-423), Washington, DC: Author.

a warning that something is wrong with the body. A subjective symptom is inwardly expressed, such as sadness or paranoia, and behaviorally manifested by, for example, tears or withdrawal. An objective symptom is one that is outwardly observed by others, for example, vomiting, limping, twitching. Symptoms can be grossly classified as physical or mental, although neuropsychiatric illnesses may present a combination of physical and mental symptoms.

OCD has a plethora of symptoms that may overlap with symptoms observed in other neuropsychiatric disorders. The practitioner should keep this in mind to establish a correct diagnosis.

A *behavior* is the response to an internal or external stimulus. This reaction is social because it is recorded or observed by the external milieu. In OCD the elicited behaviors are basically the expression of obsessions, compulsions, and doubting. Behaviorists may interchange the concepts of symptom and behavior, that is, a behavior is a symptom, but others, such as psychiatrists, believe a behavior is the final external expression of a symptom. Regardless of the wisdom of either choice, we assume and accept that in OCD one may treat symptoms and/or behaviors. Finally, according to the content of the symptoms, the behavior also changes; therefore, a good grasp of the patient symptomatology and behaviors is important.

Obsessions

The qualities of the obsessions become important when a biobehavioral approach is required. Intensity, frequency, and content are three major elements that will influence treatment outcome. For a behavioral or cognitive approach, the obsessional content is primordial. The following are some of the more common types of obsessional symptoms:

- aggressive (e.g., urge to stab, throw someone over a banister, push someone into the railroad or subway tracks)
- morbid (e.g., urge to harm oneself or others, feeling of impending doom, thoughts of death, disease, tragedies)
- religious (e.g., blasphemous thoughts against God, believing one is possessed by the devil, continuous fears of being punished in the afterlife)
- sexual (e.g., believing one is homosexual, staring at genitals, thoughts of having sex with animals or children)
- reviewing of conversations (e.g., trying to recall exactly what each party said in a discussion)
- need to know (e.g., pondering over questions that intrude into the mind and are of no relevance to the present functioning of the patient)
- somatic (e.g., being overly concerned with having an illness such as cancer or AIDS, listening to one's own breathing)
- right and wrong (a need to know when thoughts are right, and if they are wrong, the need to stop doing other activities until one gets the right thought)
- obsessionality with place (difficulty recogizing where one is, e.g., one may not know whether he is awake or asleep, whether his eyes are open or closed; he may have doubts whether the house he lives in is his or someone else's)
- obsessionality with light (a focusing of attention on luminous objects, typically chandeliers, electric bulbs, even the sun—we have seen two patients who spents hours watching the sun to the point of damaging their eyes. Whether this is atypical obsession or the manifestation of a secret magical thinking or a ritualistic mechanism has yet to be determined.

Karen delivered a beautiful baby who became the joy of her life and her reason to live. Nonetheless, six months after delivery she noticed a certain amount of detachment toward her baby. Gradually, she got the idea she could throw her baby out of a window in her fifth-floor apartment. Ideas of killing her baby on an impulse began to haunt her day and night. She disposed of every single knife or sharp object, and had a carpenter permanently lock all the windows.

Peter is obsessed with God and the saints. Now that he is 40 years old, he knows (without a solid explanation) that he will be unjustly condemned to hell. Therefore, he curses constantly at God and the saints. He has bizarre ideas that torture him further. He feels the need to rape the Virgin Mary, and he fantasizes with this imperative idea. Lately, he has begun to verbalize his curses at home, and now he is afraid he will do it in public, so he refuses to leave home.

Nick is a factory worker. He lives approximately five miles away from the Canadian border. His life is centered around the right moment, word, thought, or anything else, in order to adequately live. When he drives to work he heads toward the Canadian border, and two miles before the border he turns right, toward the factory address. To do this, he must have the right thought before turning—otherwise, he keeps going. He goes through customs and immigration and keeps driving, now in Canada, for as many hours as needed to get the right thought. The severity of his obsession is such that he carries an overnight bag, just in case he becomes stuck with the wrong thoughts in Canada. The intensity of his symptoms and his inability to resist them caused the loss of his job.

Compulsions

Compulsions are a major symptom of the OCD phenomenology and the most important symptom to be treated with behavior therapy. Compulsion and impulsion are two of the four moving forces existing in the human body, the others being pulsion and retropulsion. An impulsion is a sudden force that moves the body without logic or reasoning; a compulsion, on the other hand, is a thought-out act that cannot be resisted and is therefore carried out. A compulsion is never a fast act or a reaction; it gradually builds up. Furthermore, the compulsion often gives rise to anxiety, rather than anxiety giving rise to the compulsion. For the behaviorist, the presence or level of anxiety is a measure of the treatment's success. There are two types of compulsions: mental, or ideational, and motor.

Ideational Compulsions
Ideational compulsions are performed in the mind and are not physically observable. The following are some examples:

- counting (e.g., devising games in the mind in order for sentences, objects, or situations to end up in a certain number or some combination of a favored number)
- list making (e.g., making mental lists of activities, shopping items, trip itineraries, and continuously reviewing or revising them)

- praying (e.g., saying prayers mechanically and without conviction, engaging in the practice of litanies, or rosary praying, with the aim of accumulating a large quantity of daily prayers without religious finality)

Rose Marie, age 24, female, and single, worked in a canning factory. One of her major complaints was her urge to count every single can that moved down the conveyer. After eight hours of this compulsive activity, she would go home and compulsively count paper napkins. She was certainly aware of the purposelessness of her act, but she was unable to resist it.

Sometimes the compulsion is extremely bizarre and challenges the correctness of an OCD diagnosis. A case in point is Gabriel, a seclusive person who kept his feces in a leather suitcase he kept under his bed. Or the case of Toby, who could not dispose of the garbage, which she saved in black garbage bags; this same person would handwash compulsively for fear of germs! In cases like these, a differential diagnosis with schizophrenia must be considered.

Motor Compulsions
Motor compulsions are urges to perform a certain physical act. They are almost always accompanied by related obsessions. Some common compulsions are as follows:

- aggressive (verbal, as in coprolalia; physical, as in self-mutilation); an aggressive compulsion should not be mistaken for anger
- physiological (e.g., defecating, spitting, urinating, drinking, swallowing, eating, copulating, masturbating)
- movement (e.g., touching, squeezing, jumping, throat clearing, rocking, rubbing, echokinesis, exercising)
- cleaning/washing (e.g., excessive showering, handwashing, grooming, toilet routine, toothbrushing, cleaning of household items or other objects)
- checking (e.g., checking locks, stove, appliances, for accidents while driving, reviewing work to correct mistakes)
- repeating (e.g., rewriting, rereading, standing up several times until it "feels right")
- counting (e.g., similar to an ideational compulsion, but overtly counting and devising number configurations)
- ordering/arranging (e.g., wanting objects in a certain place and noticing if they are slightly altered, organizing clothes in closet according to color, shape, or size, labeling cupboards, having hangers facing a certain direction)

- hoarding/collecting (e.g., piling up newspapers, filing articles, keeping junk mail, magazines, saving shopping bags, garbage)
- need to ask, tell, or confess (e.g., urge to ask for information, providing information that others do not ask for, seeking reassurance, providing information in different ways to make sure that it is understood)
- retracing (e.g., exiting a room the same way one entered it, driving back home on the same streets as one took to get to work, getting into bed the same way as getting out of bed)
- somatic (e.g., taking one's pulse or blood pressure continuously, checking body for signs of illness, excessively performing breast examinations)

Alice is 30 years old and severely dysfunctional because of her compulsion to retrace all her steps backwards. She lives in Idaho and decided to consult with us at the Institute in New York. She couldn't travel by a plane, which would mean walking backwards in the airport, in the aisle of the plane, and so forth, so some friends drove her to the Institute, thus minimizing the public exposure of her symptoms.

Motor compulsions involve the brain motor regions in OCD. OCD motor activity may be increased (e.g., pacing the floor, restlessness), decreased, or suppressed (immobility, catatonia). The motor act can be normal or abnormal (e.g., twitches, repetitive or stereotyped movements). Motor pathology should be considered, and examined for, in the diagnosis of OCD.

Sal, a 14-year-old high-school student, must record every single movement of his body. This type of obsession to record and his compulsion to move in a nonautomatic manner led him to a visible motor slowness. Gradually, the only way he could control his symptoms was slowness or suppression of his movements by remaining still.

We have come across several cases of severe OCD with catatonia and psychotic or schizophrenic features. Three patients remained standing up for prolonged periods of time (10–20 hours); two developed serious leg ulcers, and the other, varicose veins with an incipient ulcer.

Ritualization
An OCD ritual is an activity performed to fulfill certain beliefs or convictions, needed to undo unacceptable thoughts or beliefs or to prevent harmful events from occurring. Rituals are also known as ceremonies, and they

can be observed in every world culture as a way to celebrate events or to honor authority.

Their origin is traced back to magic, religion, and superstition. Further, OCD rituals are associated with magical thinking: The patient may believe the performance of rituals will ward off the horrible consequences of his obsessional thoughts.

A ritual is considered a compulsion by many behaviorists. Actually, a ritual is an engaged behavior performed as part of a compulsive act. A compulsive hand washer may wash his hands 100 times per day; each time he washes, he uses the same sink, the same brand of soap, and always spends 15 minutes in the act of washing. The actions accompanying the washing are known as rituals.

> Anne was a 32-year-old single, female market analyst with an IQ of 148. At the age of 18, to avoid harmful thoughts and to prevent others from dying (e.g., close family members), she began to take hours-long showers. When this ritual did not satisfy her harmful obsessions, she added the task of splashing water on the bathroom walls. This entire ritual could take up to ten hours of her time.

> Thomas is a 30-year-old married businessman who engages in grooming rituals around bathing, hair combing, clothes selection, and dressing. All these rituals are conducted before going to work. Over time, the frequency and intensity of the rituals necessitated his wakening at 3:00 A.M. so that he could complete them before work. Unfortunately his rituals aggravated: What was a four-hour task became an eight-hour ordeal. Needless to say, he lost his job, became depressed, and had to be hospitalized.

Doubting

In 1875, Legrand du Saulle referred to OCD as the disease of the doubt (folie du doute). Doubting is a very important symptom because it may affect life quality by interfering with the decision-making processes. We are listing it here as another symptom, rather than merely as a form of obsession. Doubting refers to the patient's engaging in an exhausting internal dialogue in an attempt to arrive at certain decisions that are unnecessary or unimportant or to solve unsolvable problems, for example, "How many times did I have orange juice while on vacation?" Even if the patient arrives at an answer or a decision he or she may then start doubting again. Doubting refers to the internal dialogue process that takes place in order to arrive at a decision, whereas obsessing refers to an intrusive thought that one cannot repel from the mind.

Michelle is now 40 years old, but she began to seriously doubt at the age of 20. Because her doubting gradually worsened, it interfered with decision-making. Consequently, she became extremely dependent on others to make even the smallest decision. One day, at lunch hour she went to a music store to buy a compact disc. After five hours of browsing, a security guard called her in for questioning.

Although we have listed some of the most common obsessions and compulsions, it is not an exhaustive list. In chapter 2, a review will be provided of the psychological assessment tools that are most commonly used to diagnose OCD. For those who have little experience the questionnaires may be helpful.

Magical Thinking

Magical thinking is part of the thought process pathology. It is usually observed in psychotic disorders but can also be present in OCD. Magical thinking is a "divine" belief by which the mere act of thinking results in the realization of an event to prevent harm or wrongdoing, for instance, thinking of a good word or number every time a bad word or number enters the mind in order to prevent harm, crossing out in the mind a statement that one believes will lead to harm, or imagining a desired situation in lieu of a negative image or thought. Magical thinking often operates in conjunction with ritualization.

Epidemiology

According to the Epidemiological Catchment Area (ECA) survey (Karno, Goldin, Soreman, et al., 1988), OCD has a lifetime prevalence of 2.5% in the general population or a six-month prevalence of 1.6%. This means that approximately six million Americans will suffer from the disorder in their lifetime.

- Male-to-female ratio: forty years of epidemiological data indicate that the ratio is 1:1 (Neziroglu, Yaryura-Tobias, Lemli, et al., 1994).
- Marital status: There are significantly more single OCD males than single OCD females. Female OCD patients are married at the same frequency as females in the general population.
- Occupation: 15% to 65% of patients demonstrate occupational deterioration.

- Birth history: No significant differences are noted between OCD patients and the general population.
- Drug abuse: Less drug abuse is found in the OCD population than the general population
- Alcohol consumption: The OCD population shows a 7% prevalence of problem drinkers. Many patients report using alcohol and/or marijuana to reduce their symptoms. This is not an uncommon finding in patients with anxiety disorders. However, on the whole, the OCD population abstains from drinking significantly more often than the general population.
- Age of onset: Almost 80% of patients develop OCD before the age of 25. Elsewhere, we reported a bimodal distribution in which women with children reported having developed OCD during pregnancy, while childless women developed it during puberty (Neziroglu, Anemone, & Yaryura-Tobias, 1992).
- Family psychiatric history: One-third of patients' parents have some form of psychiatric illness.

Course

On the average, a patient does not seek treatment for OCD until he or she has had the disorder seven to ten years. Patients give several reasons to explain why they don't consult earlier. The illness waxes and wanes, so they are initially optimistic that the disorder will spontaneously disappear. Many patients report that during the first few years they believed they would get better. When asked why they thought their symptoms would disappear without any treatment, they cannot give a reasonable answer. Most often they say that there were periods when they did better and so it seemed during these times the symptoms were dissipating. Also, during the good periods they thought that with some effort they could *will* the illness away. There is also a group of patients whose very bizarre symptoms embarrass them. These patients hide their condition from others, including close family members. It may take years and overwhelming symptomatology that incapacitates the patient before he or she finally asks for help.

The course of the disorder is generally insidious and progressive, with periods of fluctuation. The good periods may last from a day to several months. In some cases the length of the recovery may be more than one year, although this is unusual.

After more than 25 years of researching and treating patients with OCD, we have met very few patients who have had "spontaneous" recovery without treatment. Those that did had the intuition to resist their urges, unknowingly engaging in behavior therapy. In other words, spontaneous recovery occurred because they prevented themselves from washing their hands or checking the stove, etc. They devised idiosyncratic methods of exposing themselves to their fears or preventing themselves from engaging in their compulsions.

At times, childhood OCD may disappear only to reappear in young adulthood. It is unclear whether the child did in fact unknowingly engage in behavior therapy or whether the disorder just vanished. In some cases, when childhood OCD is treated successfully the disorder never returns; but whether it will cannot be predicted. The practitioner can only treat the child and hope that the treatment will be successful. If symptoms do return it is usually when the patient is in his or her early twenties to early thirties. The average age when symptoms worsen is in the early to mid-thirties.

Typical and Atypical OCD

Much of the literature (e.g., Rachman & Hodgson, 1980), notably behavioral, discusses OCD as one type of disorder. This concept is partially supported by the presence of two major compulsions: "washers" and "checkers," which comprise the largest group for behavior treatment. In fact, for the behaviorist, the OCD classification is based on symptom content rather than on symptom context. Conversely, the phenomenologist chooses the context approach. One should not confuse content with symptom types or with classification, because each term has specific meanings that are not exchangeable.

There are several types of OCD classification based on phenomenology, etiology, or pathophysiology grouping, or OCD association with other major neuropsychiatric disorders. For therapeutic reasons, OCD is classified as typical, or primary, and atypical. This division is important in determining treatment, which will be discussed in chapter 6. For now, it is important to know how to group patients. *Typical OCD* refers to patients who exhibit obsessions and compulsions, as described previously, and who have good insight (discussed below) and no personality disorder. These patients are usually highly motivated for treatment and have demonstrated good social functioning prior to the onset of the disorder. The content of their symptoms is irrelevant as long as their insight is good.

Atypical OCD refers to patients who have poor insight into their illness, personality disorders, severe impairment in functioning, poor hygiene, or bizarre mannerisms, and may present with cerebral structural damage.

Factors that determine whether patients should be classified as typical or atypical are the following: thought pathology (insight, beliefs), comorbid axis I diagnoses, comorbid personality disorders, and psychotic features.

Thought Pathology

Insight is the ability to recognize if one is ill. Although in primary OCD insight is preserved, in OCD subtypes insight might be altered (as in atypical OCD). Because insight preservation partially depends on cognition, it is important to assess thought pathology and to verify whether a belief is true or false.

A *belief* is a state of mind by which trust is placed on a person, idea, or a thing. Beliefs may not require certainty but they do require acceptance. There are several forms of beliefs that can be observed in thought pathology. Beliefs may intertwine with OCD thought pathology, notably in association with OCD subtypes with psychotic features, body dysmorphic disorder, hypochondriasis, and eating disorders.

Thought pathology operates by several processes: stream of thought, thought content, judgment, and the ability to consider alternatives.

Judgment alterations will affect the acceptance or rejection of a given thought process. Abnormal thought processes include four major pathological ideas: delusional, fixed, obsessional, and overvalued.

1. A delusional idea is a primary experience that affects a person's life and changes his or her capacity to reason. These ideas, which are extremely difficult to change or challenge, are mostly seen in paranoid syndromes.
2. A fixed idea is similar to a delusional idea, but with one exception: The fixed idea does not alter everyday life. Fixed ideas are observed in an individual whose judgment is impaired in a single area without interfering with other aspects of life function.
3. An obsessional idea has already been described, but one should remember that the person attempts to resist it, although it cannot be rejected, and certainly challenges the belief.

4. An overvalued idea is a strong belief with an underlying affective component. It is an elaborated mental observation that is accepted in spite of being exaggerated and bizarre. An overvalued idea is extremely difficult to resist or suppress. Overvalued ideas occupy a grey area between obsessionality and delusions, because the belief may be challenged, as in an obsession, or it may be extremely hard to challenge and change, resembling a delusional quality or an unchangeable belief.

The above concepts are fundamental not only to establishing a correct diagnosis but also to grasping the notion of symptom dynamics necessary to implement therapy. This type of thought pathology occurs in three major disorders with which we are concerned: OCD, body dysmorphic disorder, and schizophrenic processes. These disorders may phenomeno-logically converge. The concept that more than one nosology may coexist in a parallel fashion, interfacing or shifting back and forth, is appealing and exciting. This idea opens the door to reviving the old theory that the brain houses one single illness manifested as a continuum (Griesinger, 1867/1965). Although we ascribe to this hypothesis, in this book we will use the term "comorbidity" for the sake of understanding.

Comorbidity is the presence of two or more nosologies coexisting in time and space. Comorbid processes may emerge together or follow an insertion model. When OCD shares pathology with other conditions, a new disorder is born, requiring good diagnostic and therapeutic skills; one of the problems of OCD and its comorbidity is the possibility of misdiag-nosis. Misdiagnosis is usually the result of diagnostic ignorance and/or a superficial and short psychiatric interview. Advance communication sys-tems for quickly gathering information and health care organizations' penchant for profit have undoubtedly added unduly to the suffering of the mentally ill, who do not receive a good examination under such circum-stances. We are rapidly moving into an era of time frenzy that seems to affect our way of handling patients and the time given to them; time is becoming a rare and precious commodity.

Comorbid Axis I Diagnoses

Patients who have comorbid schizophrenia are usually unable to socially and occupationally function at the same level as those with pure OCD. These patients tend to be more dependent and less able to take care of their day-to-day needs. More is said about OCD and schizophrenia comorbid-ity in chapter 8. There is an atypical form of OCD that is characterized by manic depressive symptoms, in which patients have a manic depressive onset preceding or following OCD. In addition, the administration of antidepressants for the treatment of OCD may precipitate an underlying manic depressive illness (bipolar illness), which should not be mistaken for a hypomanic reaction to an antiobsessive-compulsive agent. Once the manic depressive illness is treated, the OCD symptoms may reappear. Therefore, both conditions need to be treated simultaneously.

Comorbid Personality Disorders

Certain personality disorders are found to impede treatment. The patient may present him- or herself as atypical both in appearance and behavior. Consistently, patients with schizotypal personality disorder are characterized by isolation, inability to formulate positive interpersonal relations, bodily illusions, odd or eccentric behavior or appearance, excessive social anxiety, odd beliefs or magical thinking, and vague or metaphorical thinking and speech. This patient population is slow to respond to both behavioral and pharmacological treatment. Other personality disorders that are comorbid to OCD and difficult to treat are the dependent and narcissistic personality disorders.

Obsessive-Compulsive Psychotic Features

Patients with OCD showing psychotic features may have schizophrenia, schizotypal personality disorder, or schizoaffective disorder. It is unclear how these patients should be classified, since they do not readily fit into the comorbid axis I or axis II diagnosis category. They have been referred to in the literature as atypical OCD or OCD with psychotic features. These patients exhibit many of the negative symptoms of schizophrenia, such as blunted affect, impaired social functioning, and convoluted thinking, but do not exhibit the positive symptoms, such as hallucinations and delusions. One may wonder whether the perceptual distortions noted in OCD (e.g., images, visual misperceptions, sounds, or melodies) are similar to hallucinations, or are comparable to idyllic or reasoning hallucinations.

The OCD Spectrum and Associated Disorders

The OCD spectrum involves a number of clinical syndromes whose symptomatology is predominantly obsessive-compulsive. In addition, there is a group of syndromes clinically associated with OCD, whose characteristics share OCD features. These two groups, the OCD spectrum and the associated disorders, may benefit from OCD treatment. For the description and treatment of the OCD spectrum see chapter 8.

Conclusion

OCD seems to have an early onset in life, but it has also been observed in later years. These observations must be taken into account when formulating a diagnosis. OCD is a heterogenous complex syndrome further complicated by the common presence of comorbidity or associated conditions. These emergent nosologies interface with phenomenological and physiological variables, thus modifying course and treatment outcome. The complexity of the OCD clinical condition constitutes a challenge to good diagnosis and treatment.

OCD is found worldwide, and various cultural factors affect certain aspects of OCD. OCD rituals may be influenced by religious practices that include rites and ceremonial acts. This is observable in Catholic, Jewish, and Islamic ceremonies (Yaryura-Tobias & Neziroglu, 1997). Nonetheless, the OCD core remains unchanged in every culture; therefore, it is safe to assume that research findings and treatment modalities are applicable across geographic borders. It is important to note that OCD can be found in all economic strata; the concept that OCD affects only patients of high economic status is no longer viable.

Finally, the variability of the OCD course points toward unpredictability and challenges the practitioner. One pending question, to be addressed in later chapters, is: Can we determine treatment outcome? In the next chapter we start to look into the behavioral therapeutic approach to OCD.

2

Biobehavioral Assessment
of OCD Symptoms

THIRTY TO FIFTY PERCENT OF OCD cases are treatment refractory (Yaryura-Tobias & Neziroglu, 1997). This is a very high percentage, considering the great advances in the field of OCD therapy. Causes of treatment failure include early childhood onset, brain anatomical lesions, comorbidity, schizotypal personality disorder, borderline personality disorder, severe family psychiatric pathology, sabotage, wrong medication, poor medication management, and poor understanding or knowledge of behavior therapy.

We believe a number of patients are incorrectly treated because an integrated approach is missing. Using a biopsychosocial model will reduce the number of refractory treatment cases.

The biobehavioral management of OCD addresses the biopsychosocial issue; it is a two-track program designed to control symptoms and then to restore social, work, leisure, interpersonal, and academic activities. In order to achieve these goals, the patient must be evaluated thoroughly from both a medical and a psychological perspective. Although the initial presenting problem may appear to be OCD symptoms, it is necessary to determine if there is an organic basis, other comorbid conditions that are more of a priority in treatment (e.g., severe depression), factors unrelated to OCD that maintain the symptoms, other symptoms that the patient is embarrassed to report (e.g., self-mutilation), and other medical illnesses that may interfere with medication usage. In an attempt to assess all of this, the following procedures are utilized:

- psychiatric examination
- physical examination
- laboratory tests, including biochemical tests, biological challenges, electrophysiological tests, and neuroradiological tests
- psychological examination
- biopsychosocial history

This chapter will introduce our systematic pretreatment study of a patient.

Psychiatric Examination

The psychiatric examination should be performed by a psychiatrist who explores both the mind and the body, rejecting dichotomy. This comprehensive examination deviates from the customary routine psychiatric exam, in that it returns to the basics of psychiatric medicine. In other words, the psychiatrist needs to determine whether there is a physical or medical condition to account for the patient's symptoms, such as epileptic forms of OCD, Parkinson's disease, or Huntington's chorea. Currently, most psychiatrists feel more comfortable practicing the psychological model, that is, limiting themselves to an examination of the mind and excluding the neurological and nonpsychiatric symptomatology. When the psychiatrist suspects a physical problem, he or she usually refers the patient to a nonpsychiatric physician. With the advent of brain imaging, electrophysiological tests, and greater knowledge in the biochemical aspects of mental illness, an in-depth neuropsychiatric examination is possible, and, in our opinion, the role of the psychiatrist.

The first consultation records the reason for the visit, provides a diagnostic impression, determines the stage of the illness (e.g., acute, subacute, chronic), and begins the process of building rapport.

Asking about the reason for the consultation uncovers the patient's motivation for seeking treatment. The stated reason does not always point to the presence of symptoms, however. Some patients consult because they can no longer function as usual. Their impairment has begun to affect their daily routine. Their symptoms have become a priority. Other patients consult because of severe anxiety or depression, which masks the obsessive-compulsive symptomatology.

> Richard is a 60-year-old man who is married, retired, angry, and quite "mean." He consulted with us for depression following his retirement. "I have nothing to do," was the most elaborate discourse we could initially get from him. However, he became more at ease in subsequent interviews. Yes, he is depressed, and has lost 50 pounds. Why? Because he doesn't eat. Why? Because he won't use a knife. Why? Because he may hurt someone. He is obsessed with a fear of harm. If he ate before, it was because his wife cut up his food for him. Now, "she is fed up" with all "my nonsense, my anger, my fears." Had we stopped our examination with his symptoms of depression, we could have missed his hidden OCD symptomatology.

A diagnostic impression is not easy to reach. Many patients manifest a cohort of symptoms present in other disorders (e.g., body dysmorphic disorder), in which case the possibility of comorbidity should be considered.

Good rapport is necessary for good treatment. A personal touch when conversing with the patient is of utmost importance. The axiom that there are no diseases, only individual patients, is still valid. Each patient must be treated as an independent person. He or she needs support and empathy to develop trust toward the therapist. Mutual interest is conducive to a successful recovery, and time is required. In today's health care environment, time is a luxury. However, we feel that the provision of time is not only good medical practice, but also cost-effective in the long run. The biobehavioral management of the patient shortens treatment duration by reaching a team-based diagnosis, looking into the social and family milieu, and offering a comprehensive treatment modality. Consequently, what at treatment onset seems to be a large expenditure leads to an intensive and rapid approach. Patients soon improve and return to their daily activities.

During the first interview patients with OCD may be reluctant to narrate their whole story. They are distrustful, doubtful, and hesitant to convey what disturbs them. One way to ease tension is to move into the mental exam, postponing the completion of the psychiatric history. The mental status exam should check into the following:

- appearance and behavior
- speech
- time perception
- thought process
- perception (auditory, tactile, taste, smell, visual)
- mood
- insight
- judgment
- memory
- intelligence

Following the mental status exam, the family psychiatric and medical history should be obtained from the patient and/or a family member.

Before initiating treatment, the stage of the disorder should be determined and the laboratory or psychological studies completed. In severe cases, however, treatment is rapidly instituted without waiting for results of the studies.

A physical examination may be performed, if time permits, at the end of the consult, or it may be scheduled for another day. Below is a discussion of the benefits of a physical examination and an outline of the types of laboratory tests available.

In conclusion, a fruitful first consult is the result of the practitioner's use of intuition and clinical experience to make a diagnosis and to draw the first draft of the treatment program.

Physical Examination

The physical examination is an essential part of the biobehavioral treatment program. The exam helps to rule out any physical condition that may cause, precipitate, or aggravate OCD. Furthermore, it can result in the diagnosis of other conditions and/or identification of medication prescribed for them that may interfere with the OCD treatment.

However, a physical examination has not been part of routine psychiatric practice for many years. This has been caused by the strong influence of the Freudian school of thought, which produced a scientific dichotomy between mind and brain, and beheld psychiatry as a psychological specialty. Consequently, the medical aspect (e.g., a physical examination) of the specialty received little attention. However, the growth of biological psychiatry and progress made in brain pathophysiology are reversing this attitude. Biological psychiatry is the study of the medical aspects of psychiatric conditions and emphasizes the medical model over the psychological and social models of mental illness. It has strong connections with neurology as well as other medical specialties associated with psychosomatic medicine (e.g., dermatology, cardiology, gastroenterology, to name a few), and it relies on laboratory findings, EEGs, neuroimaging, and other medical procedures.

Psychiatrists are again thinking in "medical" terms. Biological components, including hereditary and genetic factors, biochemical imbalance, and cerebral anatomical lesions (e.g., brain atrophy), are being recognized as part of certain types of mental disorders. These components, within a pathological context, may determine the need for special management. Furthermore, they are expressed by the presence of subjective or objective symptoms, and are elicited by performing a physical examination and laboratory testing.

The following reasons underscore the necessity of performing a physical exam:

- to determine the presence of biological factors in mental disorders
- to establish the onset of medical illnesses with psychiatric symptoms
- to establish the onset of a psychiatric disorder with medical symptoms
- to rule out psychosomatic disorders
- to rule out somatopsychic disorders
- to administer and monitor psychotropic medication

Performing a baseline physical exam facilitates the management of psychiatric and nonpsychiatric symptoms and helps to safeguard the patient's health.

The presence of causative, concomitant, or precipitating conditions, or comorbidity, is often missed by psychiatric and nonpsychiatric physicians. One of the major reasons for treatment failure in both psychiatry and internal medicine is that most patients are not examined in an integrated manner. For example, a patient with a psychiatric disorder such as anxiety or depression may be suffering from a physical condition, such as lupus, pancreatic cancer, or an unrecognized drug abuse or alcoholic problem; an elderly person suffering from OCD may have an underlying cerebrovascular problem (see tables 2.1 and 2.2). A similar situation is seen in psychiatric disorders manifested with overt physical symptoms (e.g., vomiting in bulimia, obesity or anorexia in depression). Likewise, the onset of psychiatric illnesses usually is accompanied by a pattern indicating functional or organic pathology. OCD usually develops during childhood and adolescence; onset after the age of 40 signals the probability of a cerebral anatomical cause. This onset is also gradual, like the one seen in primary OCD. An acute onset of OCD or comorbid process indicates a toxic (e.g., drug-induced) or infectious etiology.

Who should perform the physical exam? We feel the psychiatrist should do the physical examination, as a way of further integrating the patient's medical information. If the psychiatrist feels uncomfortable performing the exam, he or she should refer the patient to a general practitioner or internist.

The physical examination includes all the major systems: skin, muscle-skeleton, ear, nose, and throat, cardiovascular, respiratory, gastrointestinal, neurological, and renal.

Breast, pelvis, and rectal examinations are excluded on the grounds that intimacy should not be shared with someone who delves into the emotional and sexual life of the patient. The patient's family physician or gynecologist may perform these examinations. Nonetheless, medical questions regarding the sexual organs should be asked (e.g., menstrual rhythm, sexual impotence).

A complete neurological examination requires more specific knowledge. However, a routine neurological examination is easy to perform, and it is of utmost importance. A mental disorder always affects the neurological system. For instance, anxiety is accompanied by tremors; schizophrenia, by grimacing; Tourette's, by twitching. In the brain, mental and motor activity are intertwined and therefore a central nervous system (CNS) illness will present both mental and neurological symptoms. A classic example is Parkinson's disease with its tremor, muscular rigidity, and depression.

Table 2.3 lists physical symptoms commonly observed in OCD and its spectrum.

TABLE 2.1 Psychiatric symptoms of medical conditions

anxiety

panic

depression

compulsions

obsessions

delusions

hallucinations

irritability

violent behavior

TABLE 2.2 Some medical causes of psychiatric conditions

cerebrovascular disorders

intracranial tumors or infections

head injury

AIDS

collagen diseases

nephritis

tumors

tuberculosis

nutritional disorders

myocardial infarction

hepatitis

rheumatoid arthritis

viral condition

TABLE 2.3 Physical symptoms related to OCD and its spectrum

- Fat: in eating disorders (obesity, cachexia)

- Skin: in anxiety, stress (eczema, psoriasis, neurodermatitis); self-harm (excoriations, cuts, scars, callouses, bruises); compulsive washing (contact dermatitis)

- Hair: in anxiety, trichotillomania, conversion hysteria, or alopecia factitious (hair pulling of scalp, eyebrows, eyelashes, body)

- Nails: in habits, compulsions (bitten nails, cuticles)

- Head: in head bangers (bruises, calluses caused by repetitive head banging, cuts, scars)

- Muscle skeleton: in severe anxiety or stress (neck or lower back pain, muscle soreness or stiffness, painful joints, temporo-mandibular joint syndrome)

- Cardiovascular system: in anxiety, mitral valve prolapse, panic, stress, phobias (blood pressure changes, tachycardia, extrasystoles)

- Respiratory system: in anxiety, aggression, panic, conversion hysteria, other somatoform disorders (dyspnea, hyperventilation, chest pain or oppression)

- Gastrointestinal system: in ulcerative colitis, spastic colon, gastritis, gastric or duodenal ulcers precipitated by severe OCD symptoms with a large anxious or aggressive component (belching, heart burn, pain, colic, diarrhea, constipation)

- Genitourinary system: in anxiety, stress, burnout syndrome, sexual aberrations, sexual traumas, sexual obsessions, borderline personality disorders, fears of contamination, infidelity (frequent urination, nocturia, premature ejaculation, anorgasmia soft penile erection, decreased vaginal humidity, vaginal pain during intercourse, loss of libido)

- Neurological system: in anxiety, tension, irritability, panic, phobias, Tourette's, hypochondriasis, organic OCD symptoms (headaches, dizziness, numbness, tingling, tremors, abnormal fine-motor coordination, involuntary movements, visual-spatial deficit)

- Interruption of daily habits: (eating, drinking, drug or alcohol abuse, tobacco use, sleep)

Laboratory Testing

Laboratory testing assesses the presence of dysfunctions in various organs that may contribute to psychiatric symptoms. Although there are no specific biological tests for OCD, research is being conducted to identify putative or associated biological markers, electrophysiological changes, and brain abnormalities. The idea is twofold: to investigate physiological parameters that may be correlated with OCD, and to apply those findings to establish medical tests to assist in diagnosing OCD.

Biochemical Tests

A routine laboratory profile that screens bodily functions includes complete blood count (CBC), electrolytes, calcium, magnesium, fasting glucose, urea, liver profile, lipid profile, renal function, thyroid profile with thyroid stimulating hormone, parathyroid hormone, and urinalysis. These tests may help pinpoint problems that are contributing to producing some of the patient's complaints. For example, if the thyroid is not functioning properly the patient may exhibit signs of depression unrelated to psychological causes. Lability in mood may be due to diabetes or other glucose metabolism malfunctions.

In our current social environment, tests for syphilis and AIDS should also be considered because these conditions have psychiatric symptomatology.

For heavy metal poisoning, urine and blood tests are examined. Metals such as lead, copper, and manganese may affect brain function and cause an array of psychiatric disorders, such as intellectual deficits in children, copper psychosis, and manganese parkinsonism. Industrialization has increased the risks of nickel poisoning in areas neighboring airports, as the result of fuel burning. If the patient has eaten seafood, poisoning from ocean mercury pollution may occur and affect the human brain. Aluminum used as an alkaline agent may, if ingested chronically, affect the brain anatomy. Aluminum is also considered one of the causes of Alzheimer's disease.

Drug and alcohol can be detected in urine, blood, or breath; screening is important because prescription drugs combined with alcohol or illicit drugs may be dangerous. In addition, they may offset the efficacy of anti-obsessive-compulsive agents. If drug abuse is confirmed, detoxification will precede any intervention to treat OCD. Many patients not reporting alcohol or drug abuse admit to their use once confronted with high liver enzymes or positive drug screening. Finally, the combination of OCD and alcohol or drug abuse is feasible. This combination is known as dual diagnosis, and requires expertise for proper treatment.

Biological Challenges

Biological challenges are tests designed to study possible correlations between OCD, neurotransmitter function, notably serotonin, and hormonal activity, with the ultimate purpose of validating a psychiatric diagnosis and studying its pathophysiology. Tests and neuroendocrine challenges for major depression have also been used for OCD (e.g., dexamethasone suppression test [DST], thyroid profile, 3-methoxy-4-hydroxyphenylglycol [MHPG], and 5-hour oral glucose tolerance test). The most consistent endocrine marker finding for OCD has been a blunted response to prolactin. In addition, abnormal levels of growth hormone and vasopressin have been found in patients with OCD.

Currently, the possibilities of a viral type of OCD and of a streptococcus infection related to a pharingitis are being considered. Briefly, the idea of infection as one cause of OCD is no longer far-fetched.

Electrophysiological Tests

An awake or sleep-deprived electroencephalogram (EEG), done with nasopharyngeal leads, may help to rule out cerebral pathology. Although there is no specific OCD pattern, as one may find in epilepsy, a moderate number of abnormal nonspecific EEGs tracings in patients with OCD have been reported. The unspecificity of these tracings shows that OCD does not have a valid correlation with an EEG tracing. Nonetheless, some EEG findings resemble seizure activity and they are recorded in the temporal regions. Of note is that seizure disorders may manifest obsessive-compulsive symptomatology (e.g., hypergraphia, hypermorality, retracing, anger). Epileptiform patterns warn the physician to carefully assess the use of drugs that lower the convulsive threshold (e.g., clomipramine) and to screen for the OCD epileptic subtype. This subtype is a comorbid condition characterized by the presence of OCD and seizure disorder.

Furthermore, quantified EEGs (a procedure that reads and measures EEG waves more accurately than human reading) may show specific abnormal frontal lobe bilateral activity in patients with OCD.

Neuroradiological Tests

OCD cerebral structure pathology can be diagnosed by computerized axial tomography (CAT) and magnetic resonance imagery (MRI). These tests help to detect tumors, atrophies, cysts, and cerebral-vascular pathology, notably arteriosclerosis and cerebral infarction. Single-photon emission computed tomography (SPEC) helps to study cerebral blood flow in OCD.

Positron emission tomography (PET) studies brain metabolism. Unfortunately, this test, due to its cost, remains a research tool. PET scans have been performed looking at glucose metabolism changes in patients with OCD. Results indicate glucose metabolism alterations in the frontal lobe, temporal lobe, and basal ganglia of patients with OCD. This cerebral loop, involving the frontal lobe, the temporal lobe, and the basal ganglia, has been associated with the pathology of OCD. These exciting findings are further enhanced by a few reports that have shown that cerebral glucose metabolism changes with medication or with behavior therapy. Although these studies used a small number of patients, they allow researchers to entertain the idea that behavior therapy may modify cerebral metabolic activity. This finding opens up a new avenue of research to explain the mechanism of action of behavior therapy in OCD. Similar findings were obtained by studying 3H imipramine binding and serotonin plasma levels in drug-free OCD patients undergoing BT.

Psychological Examination

A psychological examination is generally performed by psychologists and social workers, although it may also be performed by psychiatrists who conduct therapy in addition to medically managing the patient. A psychological examination explores the functioning of the mind, the cognition required to process external and internal stimuli, and the ensuing behaviors. In addition to a verbal interview, psychometric assessments are utilized. The administration and interpretation of psychological tests are the domain of psychologists. The psychological scales to measure OCD (see appendix) consist of both general scales to diagnose mental illness and to evaluate social and intellectual functioning and specific scales for OCD. The specific scales are diagnostic and evaluate intensity and frequency of symptoms. The following are standardized self-report measures and interview-based scales used in the assessment process of OCD.

Self-Report Measures

Behavior Measurement Chart: a chart prepared by the therapist to assess a patient's obsessions and compulsions throughout the day. The patient writes down his obsession or compulsion whenever it occurs, from the time he wakes up to the time he goes to sleep. The patient should be instructed to also write down anything he avoids. In addition, he must rate the intensity of his anxiety from 0 to 10 (known as the SUD, or subjective unit of discomfort, level) as well as the duration of time spent thinking or performing a compulsion. In the appendix is an example of a chart we give to our patients.

Beck Depression Inventory: a 21-item scale for assessing syndromal (e.g., feelings of helplessness, hopelessness, sadness, suicidal thoughts) and vegetative signs of depression (e.g., insomnia, appetite or sexual dysfunction); the total score indicates the patient's level of depression from mild to severe.

Beck Anxiety Inventory: a 21-item scale for assessing physical symptoms typically reported during anxiety episodes, yielding a total score.

Spielberger State-Trait Anxiety Scale: a questionnaire that yields two types of scores: the first assesses the patient's state anxiety, that is, the level of anxiety felt recently, usually within the last month; the second assesses the patient's trait anxiety, anxiety of longstanding duration.

Social Adjustment Self-Rating Scale for Obsessive-Compulsive Problems: a measure of the social functioning in many spheres of a patient's life. The patient is asked to rate how her obsessive-compulsive symptoms interfere with her functioning in several different areas, such as work, school, sex, leisure activity, interpersonal and family relationships, and home management. The scale consists of 9 points, from 0 to 8, ranging from not at all to slightly to definitely to markedly to severely.

Rational Emotive Behavior Therapy Homework Sheets: forms given to patients to practice challenging their faulty cognitions between therapy sessions. The forms can be designed in any fashion as long as they assess the four components of rational emotive behavior therapy: antecedent events, beliefs, consequences, and dispute. A patient fills out at least one of these forms between sessions and the therapist gives feedback during the next therapy session on the patient's ability to utilize cognitive therapy in dealing with excess negative emotions. Excess negative emotions are feelings that are not only distressing but also excessive and therefore usually inhibit one from taking action. Depression, anxiety, anger, inadequacy, and inferiority are considered to be excess negative emotions.

Interview-Based Measures

Yale Brown Obsessive-Compulsive Scale (YBOCS): the YBOCS measures symptom severity and assesses change with treatment without being influenced by the number and type of obsessions and compulsions (Goodman et al., 1989). It is a 16-item scale—10 items comprise the scale's core, 5 of which pertain to obsessions, 5 to compulsions. The sum of the 10 items is reported as the total score. The other 6 include insight (overvalued ideation), avoidance, indecisiveness, sense of responsibility, slowness, and pathological doubt. The first five items of each subscale assess time spent on obsessions or compulsions, interference, distress, resistance, and control. Each item is rated on a 0-to-4 scale, where 0 corresponds to no symptoms, 4 to extreme symptoms. An asset of this scale is that it relies not on symptom quantity, but quality.

Obsessive-Compulsive Symptom Checklist: Because the YBOCS does not describe OCD symptoms, the clinician administering the YBOCS must be familiar with the disorder to properly evaluate patients and to score items. This symptom checklist allows the clinician to review with patients their past and current symptoms, prior to evaluating the severity of their disorder on the YBOCS. At times the list of symptoms may not be sufficient for the clinician who is not familiar with OCD symptomology. Even with the list, the clinician often has to explain and elaborate on the symptoms for the patient.

Hamilton Anxiety Scale: a 14-item scale for assessing anxiety, particularly physiological experiences of anxiety.

Hamilton Depression Scale: a 14-item scale for assessing depression. While the Beck Depression Inventory assesses a more cognitive or syndromal form of depression, the Hamilton concentrates more on vegetative symptoms, such as loss of weight, sleep disturbance, diurnal variation in symptoms, loss of libido, etc.

Overvalued Ideas Scale (OVIS): a scale to evaluate the degree or strength with which patients with OCD, body dysmorphic disorder, and hypochondriasis hold onto their fears and/or beliefs. Patients report their three main obsessional beliefs (e.g., My nose is too big; I am contaminated by germs or AIDS; If I don't check the stove I will start a fire). They then rate themselves, on a 1-to-10 scale, on the following questions: How strong is your belief? How reasonable is your belief? In the last week what was the lowest rating for these beliefs? In the last week what was the highest rating for these beliefs? How inaccurate is your belief? How likely is it that others have the same beliefs about your situation? If other people do not have these beliefs, to what do you attribute this? What is the likelihood or probability of your compulsions/ritualistic behaviors being effective? Compared to others, how unusual is your belief? This is done for each of the three beliefs. A score for each and a total score for all beliefs are obtained.

Structured Clinical Interview for the DSM-III-R Diagnosis: Personality (SCID-P): a test that questions patients on various personality characteristics. Their responses determine whether they fit the criteria for a particular personality disorder as set forth in the *Diagnostic and Statistical Manual of Mental Disorders*.

Exposure Test

The exposure, or avoidance, test determines the patient's ability to be in contact with feared situations, objects, or people. The therapist exposes the patient to feared items, situations, or people and then evaluates the patient's anxiety levels on a 0-to-10 scale, 0 being no anxiety, 10 being extreme anxiety. For example, in the case of a feared item, levels may be obtained by varying exposure according to the distance in feet from the item, the amount of hand insulation prior to touching the item (e.g., the number of paper towels used), or the amount of time in direct contact with the feared item.

Neuropsychological Studies

Neuropsychology studies the relation between brain function and behavior. A neuropsychological examination tries to establish a correlation between changes in mental processes and specific brain locations. Thus, neuropsychology contributes to the understanding of the role of neuroanatomical regions in mental functions. The assessment of a brain lesion by neuropsychological tests has been partially replaced by cerebral imaging. However, neuropsychological testing also probes, with considerable certainty, the performance of the brain and measures cerebral deficits. Although the use of neuropsychological tests in OCD is limited, some research suggests that there are some differences between patients with OCD and normals.

Most of the research has concentrated on frontal lobe dysfunction and memory dysfunction. The frontal lobe is involved in the programming, regulating, controlling, and processing of voluntary goal-directed behavior. It also is involved in adapting to one's changing environment. Usually when there is frontal lobe dysfunction there is rigidity and inflexibility in behaviors. There is an absence of response inhibition, resulting in perseveration and stereotyped behaviors. Because patients with OCD engage in repetitive and stereotypic behavior, one may suspect that there is dysfunction of the frontal lobe. It has been suggested that checkers may have memory dysfunction or information processing problems. Doubting, a very common and prominent symptom of OCD, also resembles problems of memory or information processing. There have been some neuropsychological studies to investigate problems in these areas.

Flor-Henry (1983) hypothesized that there is a loss of inhibitory processes from the dominant frontal lobe. The loss of inhibition prohibits the termination of verbal processes and gives rise to obsessive thinking. Malloy (1987) suggested that the dorsolateral frontal zones may be involved in OCD patients' inability to terminate behaviors. The dorsolateral frontal zones are responsible for monitoring the environment and signaling the person to change his or her response. If there is a defect and the signal doesn't reach the limbic system, the person may continue to react with overarousal when there is no danger. When OCD patients were compared to controls via evoked potentials, the former had lower amplitudes in the orbitofrontal areas as compared to the latter. This dysfunction may reflect disruption of the dorsolateral-limbic pathways or orbitofrontal dysfunction. Further evidence for dysfunction of orbitofrontal zones is provided by increased glucose metabolism in OCD patients in the left orbitofrontal gyrus as well as bilaterally in the caudate nucleus.

Neuropsychological tests also provide evidence of frontal involvement in OCD. However, the tests are not sensitive enough to discriminate orbitomedial versus dorsolateral frontal lobe dysfunction. Most of the neuropsychological test results have noted that OCD patients have more problems with sequential learning and shifting tasks than controls.

Tests measuring memory have not found deficits in memory function within the OCD population, although patients report problems with memory, perception, and motor activities (Yaryura-Tobias & Neziroglu, 1997). Only one study (Sher et al., 1983) found that college students who tended to doublecheck their work tended to have poorer memory as assessed by the cognitive failures questionnaire (Broadbent et al., 1982). Despite the limited evidence for memory dysfunction, the relationship between frontal lobe dysfunction and specific memory dysfunction warrants further research. It may be that OCD patients' general memory is intact but their ability to recall incidental information is dysfunctional. In other words, patients may recall specific information but not the incidental information, such as when a task was performed and whether it was performed the way it should have been.

The presence of soft neurological signs in OCD patients has also been investigated. One such study (Hollander et al., 1990) compared medication-free OCD patients with normal controls and found that the patients had more problems with fine motor coordination, involuntary and mirror movements, and visuospatial functioning. Moreover, these problems were more apparent in patients who were more severely ill. An excess of abnormal findings on the left side of the body and abnormalities of cube drawings suggest right hemispheric dysfunction in an OCD subgroup.

In another study (Conde-López, de la Gandara Martin, & Blanco Lozano, 1990), OCD patients were compared to a group of phobics and a group of normal controls. The OCD patients showed a higher global incidence of soft neurological signs, especially more alterations in movement coordination for upper extremities and balance, with a tendency to show more anomalies in dominance-laterality.

There is growing interest in the connection between obsessive-compulsive behavior and specific areas of the brain that may be affected. In the paragraphs above we discussed some studies that suggest frontal lobe dysfunction. Many more studies are needed to correlate between neuropsychological test findings and specific areas of dysfunction in the brain.

Biopsychosocial History

The biopsychosocial history is an account of the most important biological, emotional, family, and social events in the life of the patient, including both positive and negative milestones. This history reveals significant biological and psychological factors present in mental disorders. The biopsychosocial history includes genetic and social components, and is molded by language development, learning processes, knowledge, and self-awareness.

The genetic aspects determine a great part of the fate of the individual by giving the anatomofunctional structure (our body) that will carry us during our lives. The development of the body and the brain, including its higher functions and intellectual capacity, depends on nutrition and environmental care and stimulation. Here the family, school, and community play a role.

One major psychological component of the history is the development of the "personal self," which is often overshadowed by the social self. The personal self is what we choose to be; the social self is what others choose for us to be. Another psychological component is fear. Fear is a normal and strong response to any external or internal stimulus that threatens human integrity. Fear has an anatomical seat in the brain, involving four regions—the prefrontal, limbic system, pons, and medulla—and is reflected in changes observed in the autonomic nervous system. Fear undoubtedly affects the life outcome of every human being, and therefore is an important part in the construction of the biopsychosocial life of the OCD patient. The introduction of fear as a pathological element is known as anxiety. Anxiety is the most common stage of fear; other stages are panic, phobia, and terror. Fear, as the pivotal determinant of personality traits, plays an important role in the genesis and maintenance of phobias that go hand in hand with OCD. Phobic patients must make extraordinary efforts to overcome their fears so that they can face their OCD symptoms.

The biopsychosocial history consists of questions geared to evaluate the impact of the mind on the surrounding milieu (family and society), and vice versa. The biopsychosocial history of any individual considers aspects applicable to the design of a therapeutic program. This history is subdivided into three histories: medical, psychological, and social.

The *medical* history may begin with birth: Was the delivery premature or overdue? Spontaneous or induced? Were forceps used? Was it a cesarean section? Was the pregnancy normal? Was the mother taking medications during pregnancy or abusing alcohol or drugs? One looks for factors that may injure the fetus or the newborn.

Although an abnormal birth is not implicated in the development of OCD, there are instances in which an abnormal birth can be linked to OCD-associated disorders (e.g., attention-deficit/hyperactivity disorder [ADHD] or encephalitis). It seems that 25% of patients with OCD have a history of ADHD. A history of clinical or subclinical encephalitis may precipitate, later in life, OCD or its spectrum. Childhood encephalitis may unfold into aggressive behavior, ADHD, or OCD in due time. Therefore, questioning the presence of ADHD or encephalitis at any age makes sense.

A patient's neurobiological developmental history can suggest correlations between OCD and existing conditions (e.g., stuttering, pervasive disorder, mental retardation, self-mutilation, hyperactivity, learning disabilities). Furthermore, these disorders may introduce symptoms and behaviors that blend with OCD core symptomatology and modify the clinical picture. Some of these symptoms are mind racing, aggressiveness, mood swings, intellectual deficits, and social handicaps.

Patients with OCD may present with psychosomatic disorders (notably bronchial asthma), gastrointestinal disturbances (e.g., irritable bowel syndrome), or allergic reactions to ecological or alimentary factors. These collateral factors need treatment since they may interfere with OCD evolution. The interference is caused by the presence of additional symptoms that increase the feeling of being ill. Moreover, the patient might be taking medication that may interact negatively with OCD medication.

The *psychological* history of the patient analyzes the patient's personality, an important modifier of treatment outcome. Patients with a borderline, histrionic, or dependent personality are poor candidates for treatment.

The *social* history includes a crucial consideration in treatment outcome—the patient's support system. The patient's family constitutes the basic support system. An understanding, empathic, and helpful family is crucial for a successful recovery.

The patient's educational background, social interaction, and occupation conform other aspects that, in the overall, influence treatment outcome.

Conclusion

In the current managed care climate we face the problem of how to offer a comprehensive exam. The nonsalubrious trend of cost-effective medicine is inexorably taking its toll on psychiatry. One way to increase cost-effectiveness is to reduce the time spent examining a patient. This time constriction affects the biobehavioral treatment of OCD.

The numerous probes being researched are not yet part of clinical practice. Most tests are still experimental and research presents two major problems: methodological flaws and small patient samples. Conversely, psychological assessments are quite helpful and most are reliable and valid. They cannot, however, replace the clinician's art in diagnosis and implementation of good medical and psychological practice.

Finally, the long-term goal of the biobehavioral approach is to integrate psychiatry and psychology. As they are known and practiced, these two specialties live across an intellectual and ideological gap that badly needs to be bridged. The time for change is now. These two disciplines can no longer be practiced as they have been in the past.

3

Treatment Choice

O CD TREATMENT CHOICE IS BASED on several factors. One factor is the practitioner's area of expertise. Another is the patient and his or her family; they may have a predetermined preference for treatment choice. For instance, the patient may prefer a psychological treatment over a drug program. This is a common choice, because patients fear adverse effects of medication. Another factor is the degree of illness severity. A fourth factor is that health care management companies may try to impose their treatment of choice. They usually prefer drugs over psychological treatment, believing that patients in need of hospitalization must be medicated. Furthermore, management companies limit the hospital stay to less than what we consider reasonable.

Treatment choice, determined by the practitioner and the patient, is indirectly supported by the theoretical OCD models, which are roughly divided into two groups: neurobiological and psychological.

Neurobiological Models

OCD is described as a neurobiological condition based on cerebral structural changes, electrophysiological disturbances, and biochemical alterations. The neurobiological models consist of both factual evidence and theoretical work, and include anatomical, biochemical, cybernetic, and unified models.

The *anatomical* model hypothesizes that OCD involves circuits reminiscent of Parkinson's disease, seizure disorders, and limbic pathogenesis. OCD symptoms seem to follow a neural pathway involving primarily the basal ganglia, the frontal, temporal, and parietal lobes, and the limbic system. This hypothesis has been partially tested by studying the correlation of OCD symptoms with diseases of the brain. Cerebral atrophies, brain tumors, and brain cysts, without a specific location in the brain, have been associated with OCD. Chorea, Parkinson's disease, and seizure disorders are some of the neurological disorders that present OCD symptoms.

Overall, these findings strongly suggest an anatomical participation in OCD pathogenesis. Further evidence is presented by studies done with cerebral positron emission tomography (PET) (Baxter et al., 1987), magnetic resonance imaging (MRI) (Garber et al., 1989), single-photon emission computed tomography (SPEC) (Hoehn-Saric & Benkelfat, 1994), and electroencephalogram (EEG) (Okasha & Raafat, 1990).

The *biochemical* models of OCD involve several mechanisms with neurotransmitters, hormones, minerals, and electrolytes. A disturbance in the neurotransmitter serotonin (5-HT) has been implicated as a major factor in OCD pathogenesis. The serotonergic model encompasses two factors: (1) lack of available brain serotonin, reflected by the presence of low whole blood serotonin levels, and (2) the successful response to treatment with anti-obsessive-compulsive drugs that make serotonin available in brain tissue. The serotonergic model stresses the decrease or deficit of available serotonin as the major culprit in OCD pathogenesis.

Reports indicate that 5-HT is stored in the raphe, located in the back of the brain, and from there 5-HT rides on the neural paths toward the prefrontal lobe. Therefore, nervous fibers and neurotransmitters putatively implicated in OCD follow an identical trajectory. To designate 5-HT as the culprit for OCD pathology is simplistic; it is feasible that more than one neurotransmitter is involved (e.g., norepinephrine). Moreover, hormones (e.g., vasopressin, melatonin) and electrolytes may be directly or indirectly involved in the pathogenesis of OCD. More research is required in order to build up a solid model.

The *cybernetic* model of OCD is based in the application of cybernetics, that is, the comparative study of the automatic control system formed by the brain and the nervous system, and an electromechanical device (e.g., a thermostat). The brain uses this mechanism to regulate, command, adjust, carry out, and evolve. These faculties are certainly disturbed in OCD.

The cybernetic model proposes a cerebral malfunction in the following steps: receiving, interpreting, and processing an external or internal input, and storing and retrieving information. The steps are performed by: (1) a motivator, (2) a receptor, (3) an operator, and (4) an effector. These steps are mandatory to elaborate logical thinking and motor processing (see figure 3.1). A failure in one or more of these steps may result in OCD. The inability to shift from one task to another, to interrupt one task, to delay decision making, to stop doubting or double-checking, and to reject a thought and acquire a new one are some of the altered cybernetic OCD functions. Motivator pathology is determined by pulsion functionality (pulsion, compulsion, impulsion, and retropulsion). Pulsion is the expression of a forward force against an obstacle (e.g., the human pulse and the arterial wall). An impulsion is a specific force directed without logic to a predetermined

Cybernetic Model

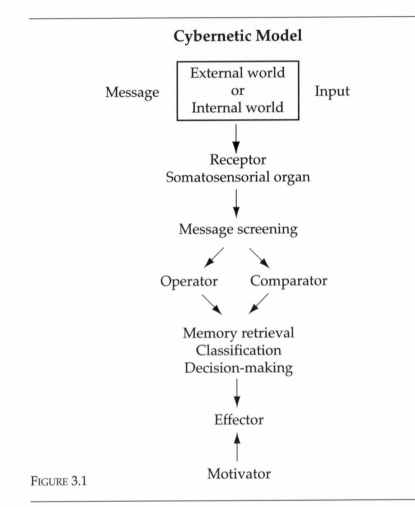

FIGURE 3.1

object (see chapter 1). A retropulsion is an impulsion in quantity but not in quality. Pulsion depends on available energy and intensity of the drive. For example, when a patient with OCD is bored, no desire for motivation is present. Receptor pathology is an excess or lack of information, manifested by somatosensorial deficits or their counterpart: a magnified reception and perceptual doubting. Operator pathology comprises switching ability (a task difficult to achieve in OCD), excitation-inhibition balance, vigilance, drive, and ability to compare. Effector pathology is the inability to respond to the incoming input with an appropiate answer. For example, this is reflected by the patient's inability to make decisions. Behavior therapy and cognitive therapy may utilize cybernetic concepts to remediate cerebral cybernetic impairment.

The *unified* theory of OCD suggests an OCD system operating on a pathological continuum. This continuum functions within a two-tier skeleton: Tier 1 is the primary OCD and tier 2 is a second condition. The primary OCD in tier 1 may couple to the condition emerging in tier 2 (e.g., self-mutilation, depression, movement disorder, anorexia, etc.), bonding both phenomenologies. In other words, the second condition is grafted onto the primary OCD symptomatology, a situation often called comorbidity. However, we use the term only when OCD and another condition have a simultaneous onset; if the condition appears after the onset of OCD, the condition is part of the continuum.

The unified theory can be explained in anatomical-biochemical terms. Let's assume an exogenous or endogenous noxa reaches the brain. The force of its impact in a given anatomical region will trigger a ripple effect, a response that will invade additional cerebral areas. If two targets are impacted, two ripple effects will produce waves in an overlapping manner, causing a series of symptoms that, in sequential order, will shape the OCD spectrum. The anatomical area affected by these impacts will subsequently affect the underlying histochemical region with its subcellular correlates. Therefore, a pathological substratum of cells, chemistries, and electrical responses starts the mechanism of action of OCD and its spectrum.

Psychological Models

There are three psychological models: (1) psychodynamic, (2) behavioral, and (3) cognitive.

The *psychodynamic* approach includes the analytical and phenomenological interpretations. The analytical theory proposed by Freud explains OCD as the result of childhood development arrested at the anal stage. Hence, anal-erotic and sado-masochistic impulses dominate the child's life, due to a sado-sadistic superego and a masochistic ego. The mechanisms of defense employed by the patient with OCD are: isolation, undoing, reaction formation, and identification with the doer. Undoing is the predominant mechanism, which is the compulsion performed that reduces anxiety.

Phenomenologists place anxiety at the focal point to explain OCD. They emphasize that anxiety results in or causes two major OCD aspects: blockage of self-realization and misperception of the world. While French phenomenologists tend to stress intellectual or obsessive aspects of OCD, the Germans more commonly emphasize the compulsive acting out. Patients with OCD view the future bleakly, and this forces them to move inward, adopting a passive attitude. This negative aspect of self-realization compels patients to a magic counter-world. These dynamic aspects of OCD are also observable in some patients with depression and in schizophrenic patients who exhibit obsessive-compulsive symptoms.

The *behavioral* model originates in Mowrer's (1960) two-factor theory. The first factor, classical conditioning, attempts to explain the acquisition of fear; the second represents the operant conditioning stage that explains the maintenance of fear. Mowrer's theory originally proposed to explain the development of fear, and later it was used to explain anxiety disorders. Because OCD is classified as an anxiety disorder, this theory has been adopted to explicate OCD.

There are too many unresolved questions about the anxiogenic theory of OCD for it to be readily accepted. For instance, anxiolytic medications have been found to be ineffective in OCD treatment. If OCD were solely anxiety-based, anxiolytics should be effective. And obsessions and compulsions are not the result of anxiety; conversely, they cause the anxiety.

The *cognitive* model sees OCD as an anxiety-mediated condition. The anxiety is viewed as originating with the appraisal of a threat and the individual's inability to cope with it. This anxiety component is modifiable by changing the patient's faulty beliefs. These beliefs stem from overestimating the probability of danger. Consequently, patients engage in obsessions and compulsions to reduce the intensity of their anxiety.

Three major factors constitute the core of OCD phenomenology: (1) anxiety as the foundation of the illness, (2) the world as a threatening place, and (3) the acquisition and maintenance of fear. These factors are common to the analytical, cognitive, behavioral, and phenomenological schools. The main underlying factors are fear, anxiety, and threat. Another important factor is the depression caused by the disruption in the patient's life.

As noted above, obsessions and compulsions produce anxiety rather than the reverse. Therefore, anxiety can be classified as a secondary symptom. An unperformed compulsion causes anxiety, the relief of which can occur only if the compulsion is later performed. The triad of obsessions, compulsions, and doubting needs to be targeted by the therapeutic regimen.

Comparison of Neurobiological and Psychological Models

There are two major differences between the neurobiological and psychological models. The first is the conceptualization of the disorder and the second is the treatment approach. As already stated, the neurobiological approach views the OCD spectrum as a neurobiological entity. The psychological model, specifically the behavioral or cognitive approach, views it from a social learning perspective. The former uses medication as the primary tool, emphasizing the use of selective 5-HT reuptake inhibitors. The latter primarily uses exposure and response prevention with cognitive therapy as an adjuvant tool. Cognitive therapy challenges the patient's belief system, trying to bring awareness of the psychological aspects of the condition. Although the cognitive approach is as effective as the medical approach, OCD pathogenesis appears biological. There is some evidence, which will be discussed later in this book, showing that cognitive therapy may actually modify biological parameters, including 5-HT levels.

Similarities also exist between these two models. For example, both models assess the patient's discomfort, frequency, and duration of symptoms, as well as his or her ability to control and resist symptoms. Based on the above theories, treatment options emerge. The preference of one treatment program over another is usually determined by the type of education the practitioner has received. A psychological model accepts a priori the use of psychotherapy to control the symptoms, while the neurobiological model approves a priori the use of medication. Both are geared to symptom control. At the current state of knowledge, a combination of both seems to be the route to follow.

Making the Right Choice:
Single or Combined Treatment

The right choice takes into account the logistics of the therapist or the team approach and the clinical decision. A psychologist's office will certainly offer what it knows best: a psychological treatment. Similarly, a medical office will offer what is known best: a pharmacological treatment. The ideal situation is to offer a combined treatment, or at least the ability to determine if both should be used.

The following are indications that pharmacotherapy should be considered:

1. The patient obsesses to the point that he or she is unable to discuss or engage in any fruitful attempt to treat OCD.
2. The obsessions are bordering on the realm of delusions or overvalued ideas.
3. The patient is extremely anxious and rejects behavioral therapy or demands immediate symptom reduction.

4. The patient is unable to comply with behavioral assignments.
5. The patient "cheats" with the homework.
6. The patient achieves secondary gains by sabotaging treatment.
7. The patient is afflicted by comorbidity.
8. The patient lacks sufficient time to follow intensive behavior therapy.
9. The patient refuses psychological treatment.
10. The patient has a poor response to behavioral treatment.

The following are indications that behavior therapy might be the appropriate choice:

1. The patient fears medication.
2. Drug therapy is ineffective.
3. The patient is a child.
4. The patient is pregnant.
5. The patient suffers from an illness incompatible with anti-obsessive-compulsive medications.
6. The patient is more compulsive than obsessive.

Factors suggesting a combined behavioral-pharmacological approach include:

1. It offers the best of both treatments.
2. The patient is severely ill.
3. The illness has a duration of at least seven years.
4. The illness is chronic and requires an aggressive approach.
5. The patient did not respond well to either single form of therapy.
6. Clinical experience indicates that it is the best approach for that type of patient.

What a Therapist Needs to Know

Anyone who is going to treat OCD or its spectrum should be familiar with the illness and feel comfortable treating it. The OCD spectrum is complex, demanding skills to make the right treatment choice and readiness to refer the case when necessary. The practitioner should be acquainted with appropriate treatments for various age groups, prognostic indicators, and comorbid conditions.

In our practice of 25 years we often come across treatment failures caused by inappropriate therapies applied by practitioners unfamiliar with OCD. Many times behavior therapy is misapplied or incorrectly conducted. Other times, the prescribed medication is improper, given in insufficient amounts, or administered for periods of time too short to exert sufficient therapeutic action.

When to Refer to a Psychiatrist or to a Psychologist

The primary care physician should refer the patient to a psychiatrist who is acquainted with OCD treatment. The recommended orientation is the biobehavioral treatment approach, which favors team intervention and integration. It is precisely the sum of knowledge of several disciplines, including medical and psychological (among others), that enhances a good prognosis. Whether a psychologist or a psychiatrist is the primary therapist, working together will positively potentiate therapeutic efficacy.

When a patient is seen by a psychologist, a referral to a psychiatrist should be made if:

1. The patient is unable to comply with exposure and response prevention or cognitive therapy.
2. The patient has high overvalued ideas.
3. There is suspicion of schizophrenia, manic depressive illness, severe depression, or atypical OCD form.
4. The patient is nonfunctional or homebound.

A psychiatrist should always refer to a psychologist who specializes in OCD for behavior therapy. Research indicates that patients who have undergone behavior therapy have fewer relapses when compared to those on medications alone (Marks, Stern, Mawson, Cobb, & McDonald, 1980). We try to remove medications within one year after starting treatment whenever possible. This policy permits the patient to utilize the behavioral techniques that might modulate any possibility of relapse. Discontinuation of medications for patients who have never received behavior therapy, however, leads to a 80% to 90% chance of relapse (Pato, Hill, & Murphy, 1990; Pato, Zohar-Kadouch, Zohar, et al., 1988).

Inpatient Versus Outpatient Treatment

Psychiatric hospitalization has a poor connotation, because it implies a worsening of the illness, a hopeless mental case, or "being dumped in a back ward." Nonetheless, hospitalization is one of the treatment options therapists and patients should consider as a reasonable alternative in the treatment of OCD.

Two main reasons to admit patients to hospitals are: low levels of functionality and the need to monitor treatment closely. Some patients are unable to function because symptoms are severe and cause incapacitation. In the case of a patient with severe fears of contamination, for example, the patient may impose a quarantine, even attempting to isolate family members from the outside. Those coming from the outside must remove their clothing immediately upon arrival and put their clothes in a designated hamper placed at the entrance of the house. Thereafter, they must wear fresh clothes to walk in the house. The house may have designated "free zones" where people move around at will. Other areas of the house are considered forbidden. The house may have a couple of pieces of designated furniture that only the patient can use. Finally, some patients force family members to perform rituals on their behalf. Because these patients function very poorly in their home environment, they often need to be removed from their homes temporarily in order to learn new habits. They can then gradually try out their newly learned habits in their homes.

When patients cannot resist their compulsions, external restraint needs to be used. In the hospital, response prevention may be implemented, enabling patients to resist their compulsions. For instance, for severe handwashers, the bathroom faucets are closed or removed altogether. A description of how to implement these techniques will be discussed in chapter 5.

In conclusion, many patients requiring close supervision may benefit from hospitalization. The following is a list of reasons to recommend admission:

1. to prevent patients from avoiding feared items and situations
2. to discourage patients from sabotaging treatment
3. to break the dependency existing between patients and family members living with them
4. to study patients' daily habits and behaviors
5. to have access to trained staff 24 hours per day
6. to monitor the administration of medication in patients whose conditions may be affected by serious untoward effects.

Conclusion

In this chapter we have examined OCD models and treatment choices. Models are patterns put forward to explain the mechanisms of OCD, how the disorder starts, and what its pathophysiology is, leading to symptom correction.

The anatomical model is relatively new but is being enriched with additional knowledge gradually acquired by utilizing MRI, PET, and SPEC findings. This model is the foundation of the biological basis for OCD.

The biochemical model interfaces with other biochemical models proposed for major psychiatric disorders. Probably the new findings and concepts of biochemical subreceptors will eventually assist to differentiate the biochemical basis of each mental disorder.

The cybernetic model, although far from being "trendy," presents a good deal of information about the mechanics of thought processing and motor activity. In time, the cybernetic model will determine the guidelines for OCD treatment. Unfortunately, this area requires more substantial research.

The unified model is an incipient model with a strong emphasis on psychopathology and symptomatology. This model helps us to understand the overlapping of other psychiatric disorders that present OCD symptomatology. The unified model aims to gather all major psychiatric disorders under one common organic substratum. Furthermore, it is an organizer of diagnostic procedures. It helps us to keep in mind the presence of other disorders that may share obsessive-compulsive pathology.

The psychological models are proposed in terms of anxiety as the pivotal factor from which OCD emerges. The psychodynamic models include the Freudian model, which relies on the arrest at the anal state with anxiety as a modifier, and the phenomenological model. The phenomenological model considers anxiety, obsessions, and compulsions as a set that determines a very vague future for the patient with OCD, consequently precipitating further anxiety. The behavioral model approaches OCD symptomatology by accepting that acquisition and maintenance of fear (anxiety) is the crux of therapy. Finally, those who adhere to cognitivism state that the false beliefs or intrusive (obsessional) thoughts are an anxiety-mediated condition.

Overall, the use of these models as theoretical and experiential background facilitate understanding, encourage research, and improve treatment.

How are we to treat and manage OCD and its spectrum? The combination of OCD and comorbid entities transforms OCD from a homogeneous to a heterogenous condition. Research advances suggest that OCD therapy must be redesigned to accept a novel direction. This goal is far from being achieved.

4

Principles of
Behavior and Cognitive Therapy

THE NEXT TWO CHAPTERS will examine behavior and cognitive therapy. Chapter 4 introduces the underlying principles of behavior and cognitive therapy, and chapter 5 provides specific illustrations and guidelines to conduct this treatment. Behavior therapy is an experimentally derived treatment modality that has its foundation in social learning, or conditioning, theory. In this way, it differs from most other forms of psychotherapy that have a theoretical basis but not an empirically validated foundation. Similar to behavior therapy, cognitive therapy also has its roots in scientific research, emphasizing the importance of information processing and development of cognitive schematas.

Behavior therapy is currently the most important aspect of OCD treatment. Although new research suggests that cognitive therapy alone may be as effective as behavior therapy, the research is too new and there is only one controlled study (van Oppen et al., 1995). In addition, the trend is now to call cognitive and/or behavior therapy "cognitive behavior therapy" rather than differentiating the two. For example, rational emotive therapy, a form of cognitive therapy proposed by Albert Ellis, is now called rational emotive behavior therapy. On the other hand, behavior therapy for anxiety disorders is now referred to as cognitive behavior therapy for anxiety disorders. We have purposely chosen not to do this, because the two modalities are separate and have their foundation in different theories. Because the distinction of behavior therapy from other forms of psychotherapy has been in its experimental foundation, we fear this will be lost if behavior and cognitive therapy are not studied as separate treatment modalities. Of course, this is not to imply that the effect of a combined approach should not be studied, but rather that they are not the same form of treatment. By lumping them together, their unique contribution as well as an understanding of the mechanisms by which they operate will be lost.

Behavior Therapy

Acquisition and Maintenance Theory

The social learning theory of the acquisition of compulsive behavior is based on Mowrer's (1960) two-factor learning theory, which explains the acquisition of fear and avoidance. This theory has been applied by Dollard and Miller (1950) to the acquisition of OCD. They suggested that the first stage of learning is *classical conditioning;* the second, *operant conditioning.* Classical conditioning refers to the process whereby a neutral stimulus is paired with an unconditioned stimulus and acquires the same properties as the unconditioned stimulus and thus elicits anxiety. The second stage of learning consists of a negative reinforcement paradigm that is based on operant conditioning, in which new responses are learned to decrease the anxiety in the presence of the conditioned (neutral) stimulus. These learned responses are termed avoidance or escape responses. They remove anxiety and therefore are negatively reinforcing.

How does this theory apply to obsessive-compulsive patients? For example, a conditioned stimulus may be a red mark on a doorknob that leads into a medical laboratory. The patient associates the red mark with death; therefore, the unconditioned stimulus is death. The unconditioned response is anxiety. Washing one's hands removes the anxiety that was elicited by the doorknob with the red mark, thus, hand washing becomes negatively reinforcing. It is this negative reinforcement that helps maintain the compulsive behavior.

Behaviorists do not have an eloquent explanation for the acquisition or maintenance of obsessions. Rimm and Masters (1974) offer two explanations: First, obsessing is in some way rewarding for the individual, because most obsessive-compulsive individuals have above-average intelligence and therefore enjoy thinking, especially thinking that is of a problem-solving nature; and second, obsessions have an anxiety-reducing component. This does not, however, explain obsessions that are anxiety-evoking. In fact, for most obsessive-compulsive patients obsessing is very aversive; rather than reducing anxiety, obsessiveness increases it. Neither of these explanations seems complete or plausible. Later on in this chapter we offer a biochemical hypothesis to explain the presence of obsessions and compulsions.

Exposure and Response Prevention

Until the late 1970s, behavioral treatment approaches to OCD consisted of the following: systematic desensitization, aversion therapy, paradoxical intention, and thought stopping.

Systematic desensitization is based on reciprocal inhibition principles and states that if a response inhibiting anxiety can be made to occur in the presence of anxiety-evoking stimuli, then the bond between these stimuli and the anxiety will weaken. In the treatment of OCD, it is implemented by teaching patients relaxation and then exposing them to situations or objects they fear, for example, a contaminated object. Although systematic desensitization appears to be effective in treating phobias, it is ineffective with OCD patients. Perhaps it is ineffective because relaxation counteracts the effects of exposure. In other words, it doesn't allow extinction or termination of the response.

Aversion therapy is based on operantly conditioning a strong aversive stimulus (e.g., shock, buzzers, rubber bands) to conditioned stimuli or feared objects (e.g., dirt, gas stoves, negative mental images). Patients are exposed to contaminated objects or fearful situations and then told to shock themselves. Much of the research (LeBoeuf, 1974; Solyom, 1969; Wolpe, 1973) in this area has been mainly case reports pointing to its inefficacy. There are two forms of aversive conditioning: anxiety-relief, which is based on avoidance training, and aversion-relief, which is based on escape training.

Avoidance training procedures are quite resistant to extinction. For example, in the case of an obsessive-compulsive patient who fears germs or dirt, avoiding certain objects results in positive feelings, whereas approaching the same objects leads to anxiety. Thus, the objects become conditioned to avoidant behavior. In order to decondition this avoidant behavior, Mowrer (1960) suggested that the "dirty" objects be repeatedly paired with the positive feelings of relief that accompany the termination of a strongly aversive stimulus.

The paradigm for escape training or aversion relief is one in which an occurring behavior is punished, and the punishing stimulus continues until the individual ceases the behavior and possibly performs an alternate behavior, at which time the aversive stimulus terminates. Unlike avoidance conditioning, punishment may not be avoided in escape training, but rapid execution of a behavior incompatible with the one punished will bring about termination of the punishment.

Aversion relief has been used in several single case studies. Rubin and Merbaum (1971), for example, applied electric shock upon emission of compulsions and terminated it upon contact with the contaminated object. This was not too successful in stopping the compulsions. On the other hand, Wolpe (1990) applied it successfully to a food obsession and overeating problem. Solyom (1969) shocked a patient every time she had an obsession and/or performed a compulsion. After 70 sessions the patient reported still having obsessions but no longer needing to perform her compulsions. Similar techniques have been used by others with equivocal results.

Paradoxical intention encourages patients to do the very things they fear, for example, to expose oneself to bacteria rather than avoid then. Paradoxical intention should not be confused with symptom prescription, a technique often used by the family systems therapists. In the latter, for example, a "washer" would be told to wash his hands for longer periods of time than he had prior to treatment and to do it at inconvenient times. Paradoxical intention is an integral part of logotherapy and has been found to be somewhat effective because of its similarity to the exposure component of exposure and response prevention.

Thought stopping refers to inhibiting an obsession by eliciting another thought. When an obsession occurs, the individual is instructed to shout, "STOP, STOP, STOP, etc.," until the obsession is transiently eliminated. There does not seem to be any sound basis for this treatment and its efficacy is questionable. We have not found it clinically helpful.

Around the same time as these treatment modalities were being used for OCD, Meyer (1966) introduced exposure and response prevention (ERP). Meyer exposed patients to anxiety-evoking stimuli, while constantly supervising them to prevent compulsions. These procedures were derived from animal experimental studies. Fixated or stereotyped behaviors in animals are considered analogous to repetitive or compulsive behaviors in humans. Maier (1949) found that the guidance technique could be effective in deterring a response: Rats were prevented from carrying out a fixed response by being guided manually toward the previously avoided situation. In a similar manner, Baum (1966) taught avoidance behaviors to rats and then prevented their response. The avoidance behavior was extinguished. This approach was utilized by Meyer (1966) for the treatment of OCD in humans.

Prior to this formal application of ERP, as early as 1903 Janet discussed the merits of having patients face their fears, what is now called exposure. Exposure and response prevention refers to exposing patients to their feared stimuli and then preventing them from engaging in compulsions. It has been demonstrated that exposure reduces anxiety and response prevention reduces the compulsive behavior. Thus, both components are necessary during treatment.

Another term often used for exposure is "flooding." For example, patients who obsess about AIDS may be asked to use public phones in medical buildings, visit hospitals, go to oncology departments, have blood drawn, and then be prevented from handwashing. Patients who obsess about running people over while driving may be asked to drive without retracing their route, without constantly checking the rear-view mirror, and without checking the newspaper for accidents. While having patients expose themselves to the above situations, the therapist may describe the feared consequences, thus engaging patients in imagining the worst possible outcome of the exposure. If a distinction is going to be made between flooding and exposure, perhaps it would be that the former may involve continued exposure in imagination throughout the day while the latter is actual confrontation of the situation, be it in vivo or in imagination, at a given time.

ERP is an effective treatment modality, although only 60–75% of patients are able to comply (Hiss, Foa, & Kozak, 1994). Although the success rate of 20 sessions of ERP treatment has been reported to range from 60% to 85% (Yaryura-Tobias & Neziroglu, 1983), most clinicians are unlikely to obtain that level of success. Those levels of improvement have been obtained by clinicians specializing in the treatment of OCD and with very compliant and "pure" OCD patients; in clinical practice, patients usually present with comorbid conditions and other pathologies.

Our clinical experience indicates that the best treatment outcome occurs when ERP is applied intensively with cognitive therapy. Treatment usually consists of 90-minute sessions for 5 days a week over 6 weeks, in which patients are exposed to their fears and then prevented from performing a compulsion. The consistency of the exposure is important for habituation or extinction to occur. For example, to overcome an AIDS contamination fear, a patient would be exposed to phobic stimuli and prevented from washing her hands, showering, or discarding shoes, clothes, and so on, constantly and consistently. A double-checker would be asked to practice walking out of the house without checking lights, stoves, and doors. Exposure in vivo combined with exposure in imagination is most efficacious since it allows patients to be exposed to all cues that elicit anxiety.

A more thorough exploration of ERP treatment will be presented in chapter 5.

How Does Exposure and Response Prevention Work?

The mechanism by which ERP operates is known as habituation. Habituation occurs when the continual bombardment of sensory neurons results in fatigue and thereby in extinction of anxiety. In other words, when patients are continuously exposed to their fears and experience high levels of anxiety, the anxiety response eventually becomes extinct. All exposure-based therapies operate on the process of extinction via habituation.

As habituation occurs, patients report that they no longer feel as anxious or have no anxiety at all. They can face situations they once feared. They sense they can cope with whatever comes their way, whereas before they would have either escaped from the situation or avoided it in the first place. Thus habituation is the extinction of the patient's fear.

Patients who are most successful in therapy are those who experience anxiety during exposure and whose reactions decrease within and between sessions. Unfortunately, there are some patients who exhibit within-session habituation but not between-session habituation. All patients who demonstrate between-session habituation also react the same way within sessions. Without between-session habituation the prognosis is poor. It appears that within- and between-session habituation is governed by two different mechanisms. It has been suggested that short-term habituation (i.e., within sessions) may involve the autonomic nervous system, whereas long-term habituation (i.e., between sessions) may involve cognitive processes (Groves & Lynch, 1972). Groves and Lynch also noted that habituation of cellular activity occurs in the area of the brain stem reticular formation, particularly in the mesencephalon.

Assessment of habituation has been obtained from self-reports as well as from physiological measurements (e.g., heart rate). Patients who react physiologically with high arousal habituate slower than those who demonstrate lower levels of arousal. Subjective reports of anxiety are not as reliable because most patients report high levels of anxiety. In addition, patients who are concomitantly depressed habituate more slowly than those who are not depressed and therefore their response to treatment is also poorer.

Neurochemical Changes

A few researchers have investigated neurochemical changes of ERP, specifically exposure in vivo and exposure in imagination. Cerebral blood flow has been found to increase during relaxation and exposure in imagination and decreased during exposure in vivo. This is in contrast to what one would expect. A plausible explanation is that during exposure in vivo, a highly anxiety-provoking state, blood may have been directed away from the cortical areas of the brain to other areas, such as the caudate nucleus or orbital gyri. Baxter et al. (1987, 1992) conducted PET blood flow, glucose, and oxygen extraction studies to further investigate neurochemical changes.

In their study of PET scan changes as a function of behavior therapy, Baxter et al. (1992) found that changes in metabolic rates in the caudate nucleus decreased significantly, compared with pretreatment values in response to behavior therapy and fluoxetine. Nonresponders and normal controls did not demonstrate metabolic changes in the caudate nucleus when compared to baseline. The percentage of change in OCD symptom ratings correlated significantly with the percent of caudate nucleus change with drug therapy and a trend was observed with behavior therapy.

Baxter et al. (1987) also found that following successful treatment, brain glucose consumption is decreased to the normal range. Further, it is these regions in the brain that have been correlated with OCD symptoms.

We (Neziroglu, Steel, Yaryura-Tobias, Hitri, & Diamond, 1990) studied serotonin activity change in eight patients: The results indicated that platelet-poor plasma serotonin (5-HT) decreased and imipramine binding (Bmax—a measurement of the number of serotonin receptor sites) and Kd affinity (the strength of the bond to the receptor site) increased after three weeks of intensive behavior therapy (90-minute sessions, 5 days a week). At follow-up 4 weeks later, plasma-poor platelet 5-HT values returned to baseline, while Bmax and Kd affinity remained the same as at posttreatment. These findings were quite encouraging, suggesting that behavior therapy alone without any medications may modify the biochemistry of patients with OCD.

Comparative Studies

To date, only a handful of studies have compared behavior therapy, medications, and the combination of both. Marks et al. (1980) examined the effects of clomipramine (CMI) with and without ERP. They concluded that the combined approach was more effective than either CMI or ERP alone and that this superiority could be attributed to an additive effect of two effective treatments. Similarly, Mavissakalian, Turner, and Michelson (1985) concluded that both pharmacological and behavioral intervention is the optimal treatment. However, 20% of patients who were treated with the combined approach failed to show improvement.

Solyom and Sookman (1977) compared 6 weeks of CMI treatment to 6 months of ERP, conducted twice weekly. They concluded that there were no differences between the two in reduction of depression and obsessive-compulsive symptoms. However, at a three-year follow-up, those patients who had behavior therapy continued to show improvement while those on drugs did not.

It has been suggested that CMI may reduce compulsions sufficiently enough for patients to engage in behavior therapy. In one study, CMI administered for 4 weeks yielded a 60% reduction in symptoms (Neziroglu, 1979). Thereafter, ERP treatment was commenced for 10 weekly sessions. A further reduction of 18.7% was noted. At six months' follow-up, gains were maintained, and at 1 year, 9 out of 10 patients were symptom-free (Neziroglu & Yaryura-Tobias, 1980).

A meta-analysis indicated that the effects of tricyclic medications, mainly CMI, and ERP did not significantly differ from each other. However, both were significantly superior to nonspecific treatment programs (Christensen et al., 1987).

Most comparative studies have investigated the efficacy of CMI. One study looked at the efficacy of fluvoxamine with anti-exposure instructions (F), fluvoxamine with exposure (Fe), or placebo with exposure (Pe) in 60 patients for 24 weeks (Cottraux et al., 1990). Most patients did not comply with anti-exposure instructions. All three groups improved with regard to rituals and depression, with a slight but nonsignificant superiority of the combined approach (Fe) at week 24.

Despite nearly 30 years of research in behavior therapy and more than 20 years in psychopharmacological outcome studies, little is known about the additive or interactive effects of these two approaches. Nor do we have data on whether medications should be used prior to behavioral treatment, as suggested by Foa and Steketee (1984), or whether tricyclic medication is itself a treatment worthy of a direct empirical comparison with behavior therapy (Christensen et al., 1987). Our experience of over 20 years using both medications and ERP has lead us to believe that for the majority of patients, the combined approach is most efficacious, cost effective, and shortens duration of treatment. These clinical observations are now being experimentally tested. Maybe the crucial questions are the following: Who responds to medications and to which ones? Who responds to behavior therapy? Who needs the combined approach, and for how long?

Long-Term Effects of Behavior Therapy

There are some follow-up data on behavior therapy's long-term efficacy (for a review see Baer & Minichiello, 1990; Neziroglu & Yaryura-Tobias, 1994; Yaryura-Tobias & Neziroglu, 1983). In one study, 34 patients with chronic OCD were followed up 6 years after receiving ERP, clomipramine, or placebo (O'Sullivan et al., 1991). The authors found that the group as a whole remained significantly improved on obsessive-compulsive symptoms, work or social adjustment, and depression at the end of 6 years; however, the group returned to pretreatment levels of general anxiety. The best predictor of long-term outcome was improvement at posttreatment. Also, those patients who had received 6 weeks instead of 3 weeks of behavior therapy were doing better. This finding has been confirmed in many other studies—the longer a patient initially receives behavior therapy the better the long-term outcome. In these days of managed care it seems that longer, more intense behavior therapy may be more cost-effective.

At present, the long-term effects of exposure in vivo have been well established, ranging from 2 years to 6 years. However, 20% to 30% of patients fail to maintain treatment gains at 1 year follow-up (Kirk, 1983; Steketee et al., 1982). Again, this may be due to the fact that the patients did not initially receive a sufficient length of behavior therapy treatment.

In our experience, patients who receive more intensive behavior therapy for longer periods of time do better than those who engage in short-term behavior therapy. We generally recommend, for the average patient, 6 weeks of intensive treatment (90-minute sessions, 3 to 6 times a week) and then weekly sessions for 6 months to 1 year. What constitutes an average patient? One who is either obsessing or engaging in compulsions 3 hours or more a day, is very distressed about his or her symptoms, and demonstrates dysfunctionality in at least one or more of the following areas: work, school, interpersonal relations, household responsibilities, leisure or social activities, and sex.

In addition to initially implementing effective and sufficient duration of treatment, maintenance programs are important. In a study conducted by Hiss, Foa, and Kozak (1994), it was found that those patients who received a relapse prevention program as short as four sessions did better than those who did not. We also looked at the efficacy of a maintenance program of 6 months' duration, during which patients had weekly 10- to 30-minute phone contacts with therapists to review their progress and set up behavioral goals. Six months after the maintenance phase the patients continued to maintain the gains they had made at the end of treatment, except for their depression, which returned to pretreatment levels. It is our experience that relapse prevention programs as well as booster sessions are usually necessary and beneficial.

Cognitive Therapy

Cognitive therapy has its roots in cognitive psychology, the study of how we process information. Specifically, emphasis is placed on deployment of attention, encoding, categorization, storage and retrieval of information, as well as the reconstructive process involved in memory. The area of cognitive psychology that is potentially most relevant to psychopathology is the research on factors affecting errors made in judgment about the world. Such judgments, about future probabilities, the past, explanations for events, for example, are rarely error-free even in normal individuals, since the information upon which they are based is incomplete. This means that for all of us reality may be distorted because we make inferences when remembering the past, perceiving the present, or generating expectancies about the future. These inferences may be faulty because they are often due to factors internal or external to us and of which we are not aware. For those suffering from anxiety or depression, the inferences may be even more biased and include many misconceptions. Thus, the cognitive therapy approach deals with the inferences made about ourselves and our environment and how these inferences determine our feelings and behaviors. As Epictetus, a Stoic philosopher from the first century A.D. stated, "Men are disturbed not by things, but by the view which they take of them."

Cognitive theory includes many different forms of cognitive therapy, all of which may be effective in dealing with anxiety and depression. The term "cognitive therapy" was coined by Beck, Rush, Shaw, and Emery (1979) and was primarily designed for the treatment of depression. Another contributor to the treatment of emotional disturbance via cognitive therapy is Albert Ellis (1962) who called his form of therapy *rational-emotive therapy* (now called *rational emotive behavior therapy*). It has been adapted to the treatment of anxiety disorders.

At the core of all the cognitive modalities used in the treatment of anxiety and depression is the assumption that individuals incorrectly infer information about themselves and the world. These inferences take the form of negative automatic thoughts, erroneous assumptions, and global and fixed internal attributions that are primarily negative in nature. The aim of cognitive therapy is to correct irrational or faulty cognitions.

When cognitive therapy is employed in OCD, its aim is to modify the anxiety component of the disorder. This is achieved by altering patients' faulty beliefs, which are rooted in their appraisal of threat and their ability to cope with it. Carr (1974) suggested that patients with OCD overestimate the probability of the occurrence of danger. Expanding upon this, McFall and Wollershein (1979) formulated a cognitive-behavioral model of OCD. They stated that after the "primary appraisal" of danger a "secondary appraisal" occurs, in which the individual believes he or she is unable to cope with the danger. Thus, anxiety results from these faulty appraisals and the individual engages in obsessive-compulsive behaviors to reduce or avoid anxiety.

Another useful application of cognitive therapy besides the anxiety component may be in modifying overvalued ideas. Overvalued ideas refer to the strength of the patients' belief in their fears and/or in their obsession, such as, "I will get AIDS if I don't wash" or "I am ugly." As human beings we have the ability to judge our own thoughts, to be the observer and the observed at the same time, and therefore we can evaluate the beliefs we formulate, and if necessary change them.

Within cognitive therapy, recognizing and challenging one's faulty or irrational thoughts is of utmost importance. The identification of these thoughts is not easy and if the wrong ones are challenged it is unlikely that the patient will experience any long-term reduction of anxiety and/or obsessional thoughts. In addition, if the patient holds onto the thoughts as if they are absolutely correct, then it is also difficult to get a reduction in symptoms. Below we discuss some of the faulty thoughts we have identified within this OCD population as well as the significance of overvalued ideas.

Faulty Cognitions

All of us have intrusive thoughts, but we do not give credence to them or believe they are likely to occur, or if they were to occur we usually believe we could cope with them. In other words, we appraise the thought and take action accordingly. We may avoid unpleasant thoughts by distracting ourselves. This requires the ability to divert attention from one thought to another. Thoughts that evoke fear may be handled by appraising the content of the thought as unrealistic and unlikely to occur.

Similarly, obsessive-compulsive patients may also appraise their intrusive thoughts as unrealistic, but as highly likely to occur. This seems like a contradiction. How can something be unrealistic and yet very likely to occur? It is the uncertainty of their appraisal that seems to lead to the confusion. They also believe they are unique and therefore things that may not happen to others are likely to happen to them. Patients with OCD also don't like to risk any possibility of harm, regardless of the probability.

In addition, they seem unable to inhibit one thought and replace it with another. Diversion of attention is a difficult task. Although unknown at this time, perhaps there is a problem in the area of the brain that involves response inhibition. Of course, this may be true not only in inhibiting one thought and moving on to another but also with compulsions. Patients often exhibit an inability to inhibit their washing, checking, or other compulsive behaviors.

Following are some faulty cognitions that we have identified and have found useful to challenge.

- I must have guarantees.
- I cannot stand the anxiety / discomfort.
- I must not make mistakes.
- I am responsible for causing harm.
- I am responsible for not preventing harm to others.
- I am responsible for others
- Thinking is the same as acting.
- It is awful, horrible, terrible to make the wrong decision.
- There is a right and a wrong in every situation.
- I must have complete control over everything at all times.
- I am in continuous danger.
- I must be perfect.
- Bad things are more likely to happen to me than to others.
- I must be noticed (in body dysmorphic disorder [BDD]).
- I must be outstanding (in BDD).
- My self-worth is dependent on my appearance (in BDD).
- I cannot cope with the risk.
- I should not take the risk.
- Always look for the safe solution.

A prominent characteristic of patients with OCD, BDD, and other OCD-related disorders is their overinflated sense of responsibility, fusing thoughts with action, giving tremendous importance to thoughts, need for control, and uneasiness with ambiguity / uncertainty. Patients' beliefs may be specific to OCD symptoms or core beliefs. OCD-specific beliefs are obsessive thoughts that are related to OCD symptoms, for example, "Germs are harmful and I am responsible for preventing their harm"; "If I think I will hurt myself or others then I will"; "If I think hard enough I will come up with the perfect solution." Core beliefs on the other hand are thoughts that are central to the individual but are not specific to symptoms, for example, "One should explore all angles of a situation before making a decision"; "I believe the world is a dangerous place"; "It is necessary to resolve ambiguity even in minor matters.

In challenging the intrusive thoughts of patients it may be necessary to dispute not only the OCD-specific beliefs but also the core beliefs. The above list of faulty cognitions may be used as a guideline in challenging the intrusive thoughts.

When patients' beliefs are very strong, we say they are overvalued and thus more likely to be resistant to change. It is often necessary to spend a lot of time challenging overvalued ideas. The patient's beliefs have to be tested, much as one would test a hypothesis.

Overvalued Ideas

When is a thought an obsession, an overvalued idea, or a delusion? It is not within the scope of this book to discuss this very difficult area. Readers who are interested in this topic may consult the literature on overvalued ideas (Kozak & Foa, 1994; Neziroglu, McKay, Yayura-Tobias, Stevens, & Todaro, 1996; Wernicke, 1900). However, in discoursing about cognitive therapy it is important to mention that cognitive therapy may be a very useful tool in challenging overvalued ideas. Therefore, from that perspective alone it is important to recognize them.

Overvalued ideas refer to the strength of the belief in the obsession. They are fixed ideas that do not fluctuate from day to day. In chapter 5 we will present ways to assess the presence or absence of overvalued ideas. For now it is sufficient to say that they are present in many spectrum disorders and that their presence makes behavior therapy very difficult. For that reason, we suggest that overvalued ideas be treated first via cognitive therapy and/or medications before proceeding to behavior therapy.

Cognitive Therapy Research in OCD

Although far less researched than ERP, cognitive therapy for OCD has also been studied. Two forms of cognitive therapy have been used: rational emotive behavior therapy, developed by Ellis (1962) and the cognitive therapy described by Salkovskis (1985) and further explained by van Oppen and Arntz (1994), which challenges OCD patients' overinflated sense of responsibility and the fusion of thoughts and actions. In both of these cognitive therapies it is essential to challenge patients' underlying beliefs rather than their obsessional thoughts per se.

It has been theorized that cognitive appraisal of intrusive or obsessional thoughts is a factor in the development and persistence of OCD (Freeston, Ladouceur, Gagnon, & Thibodeau, 1993). The first attempt to use cognitive therapy on OCD was by Emmelkamp et al. (1980) and the first to put forth a cognitive-behavioral formulation of obsessions was Salkovskis (1985).

The cognitive-behavioral formulation states that obsessions are cognitive intrusions, the content of which patients interpret or appraise as harm to themselves or others and which it is their responsibility to prevent from occurring (Salkovskis, 1985; Salkovskis & Warwick, 1985). In order to diminish the possibility of harm and their sense of responsibility, patients neutralize their thoughts, images, or impulses (Salkovskis & Westbrook, 1989). By neutralizing their thoughts via covert rituals or reassurance seeking, they prevent reappraisal of the true risks and amplify preexisting beliefs about responsibility. Cognitive therapy is focused on (1) preventing neutralization and thus increasing exposure to the obsessions, (2) modifying attitudes toward responsibility, (3) modifying the appraisal of intrusive thought, and (4) increasing exposure to responsibility by exposure in vivo and stopping reassurance seeking.

Research comparing rational emotive therapy (RET), thought stopping, and exposure in imagination to pure obsessions indicates that RET is equally effective as exposure (Neziroglu & Neuman, 1990). However, thought stopping was completely ineffective. Although cognitive and exposure therapy both seemed to reduce obsessions, there were only six patients in the study and therefore more research is needed to confirm these results. Clinical experience indicates that obsessions that respond to behavior and cognitive therapy are those that have a theme, disastrous consequences, or magical thinking. Obsessions that do not respond well to behavior and cognitive therapy are repetitious numbers that do not have any significance or a single meaningless sentence or word.

Emmelkamp (Emmelkamp & Beens, 1991; Emmelkamp, Visser, & Hoekstra, 1988) found that modification of cognitions via self-instructional training does not enhance the effectiveness of exposure in vivo but that rational emotive therapy is as effective as exposure in vivo. However, both studies suggest that cognitive therapy does not add anything to exposure in vivo. A controlled study directly comparing cognitive therapy with ERP found that cognitive therapy following Salkovskis's model equaled and in some respects even exceeded the efficacy of ERP (van Oppen et al., 1995). On the other hand, a recent review of cognitive therapy research by James and Blackburn (1995) highlighted that there are still very few controlled studies of cognitive psychotherapy and OCD. Much more research is needed before conclusive evidence can be reached.

5

Conducting
Behavior and Cognitive Therapy

THIS CHAPTER OFFERS A STEP-BY-STEP treatment protocol for OCD. Of course, there are always patients whose pathology may not be completely suited for the treatment suggestions made here but the guidelines given in the next few pages can always be modified. Although there is more and more research evidence supporting the efficacy of behavior and cognitive therapy, few clinicians implement the treatment. Some may try a few "techniques" here and there, but without consistent application the results will not be encouraging. Contrary to popular belief, behavior and cognitive therapy is not a set of "techniques" that one can learn and apply occasionally to the "real" treatment. Unfortunately, often clinicians resort to a bag full of "behavioral tricks" when all else fails, or they talk to the patient, give advice, and believe they are doing cognitive therapy.

Before embarking an a treatment program it is preferable to have an understanding of behavioral theory (see Wolpe, 1990). A good behaviorist would also do a thorough behavior analysis of the patient, including assessment of behaviors and cognitions. Suggestions will be given on how to achieve this and how to set up an appropriate behavioral program. Below is a session-by-session program to conduct behavior and cognitive therapy.

Consultation Visit

As indicated in chapter 2, a consultation visit may be conducted by a psychiatrist or psychologist. The types of questions each will ask are different because each needs different information in order to treat. For example, the psychiatrist may be more interested in the patient's medical history in order to ascertain whether the medication he or she may prescribe will be contradindicated. The psychologist who is behaviorally and cognitively oriented is interested in knowing what maintains the patient's maladaptive behaviors and the cognitions that lead her* to feel anxious or depressed.

In the psychological consult visit, be sure you direct the questions. A common mistake is to allow the patient to tell her life story during the first visit, which leads to information that is not very valuable in making a diagnosis and/or planning treatment. Detailed information should be obtained during later sessions. It is preferable to include a family member in the consult; often family members and/or friends provide further, or different, information. In addition, because the patient may be anxious, an accompanying individual will help her remember the comments and suggestions you make at the end of the consultation.

Begin with the following two questions:

- *What is the reason for this visit?*
- *What are your current complaints/problems?*

Make a list of the major categories of symptoms. Do not ask for specifics and try to cut the patient off if she gives too much detail. If the patient is slow to respond or unclear, ask specifically about the major obsessive and/or compulsive areas (aggressive, sexual, number obsessions, magical thinking, washing, cleaning, hoarding, checking, symmetry, organization/arrangement compulsions, etc.). In eliciting major symptoms, give the patient examples because she may be reluctant to report embarrassing or shameful symptoms (e.g., images of having sex with children or animals, being possessed by the devil, being tortured, stabbing others, checking her feces for blood). In addition to the list of obsessions and compulsions, it is important to inquire about situations, objects, or people that the patient may avoid. She may not realize she has a problem until she begins to think about her avoidant behaviors. For example, a patient may avoid sitting next to anyone other than her spouse because of a fear of stabbing others. Another patient may not purchase fresh produce because it is dirty and can never be washed thoroughly.

Following are other questions to ask during the consultation visit:

When was the onset of your OCD?
If you did not perform your compulsions, what are you afraid would happen?
What are the disastrous consequences of not engaging in compulsions?

---

*For the sake of clarity and simplification, we have used the female gender to depict symptoms or to illustrate treatment protocol. Although there are an equal number of males and females who have OCD, females are more likely to develop some of the spectrum disorders.

How strongly do you believe these consequences would occur? On a 1 to 10 scale, how reasonable is your fear/belief? Here you are trying to assess for overvalued ideation.

Do you or did you ever obsess about any physical aspect of your body? Did you ever think you were unattractive or look in the mirror for long periods of time? If the answer is yes, what parts was/is she obsessed with? You are trying to assess if the patient has or had body dysmorphic disorder (BDD). Find out the time of onset.

Do you or did you ever obsess or feel anxious about your health? Did you ever become so concerned with your health that you went to emergency rooms or called your doctor a lot or asked reassurance from your family that you were well? If the answer is yes, what was/is she obsessed with? You are trying to assess for hypochondriasis (HC). Find out the time of onset.

Do you or did you ever pull your hair? If the answer is yes, did/does she pull her eyebrows, eyelashes, pubic hair, etc? You are assessing for trichotillomania. Find out the onset. If a patient's only complaint is trichotillomania, then the initial consult would proceed along a different line (see chapter 8). Although BDD and HC are usually comorbid to OCD, often a patient has only trichotillomania without any other OCD symptoms.

Do you or did you ever have an eating disorder such as anorexia and/or bulimia? If the answer is yes, what type of eating disorder? Find out the onset. If the patient is a female, did she stop menstruating? If she did, upon the restoration of menstruation did she engage in self-mutilation? You are trying to assess for compulsive orectic mutilative syndrome (COMS). Women who suffer from COMS have a long history of OCD with an eating disorder, developed usually during puberty, during which menstruation often ceases; after the restoration of menstruation they begin to compulsively self-mutilate.

Do you or did you ever suffer with any other anxiety disorder such as panic, social phobia, posttraumatic stress disorder?

How depressed are you—mild, moderate, or severe? Depending on the answer, inquire whether she is suicidal. In order to differentiate primary from secondary depression, question whether the total elimination of her OCD symptoms would alleviate her depression. Secondary depression is present when the depression is due to the fact that the patient cannot function as desired. There is no reason to be concerned about secondary depression because it will lift as treatment of the OCD progresses. If the patient is suicidal, regardless of whether it is due to primary or secondary depression, then consider hospitalization.

How do you handle your anger? Do you yell, scream, throw things, punch, slam doors, break objects? For those who engage in aggressive behavior, order an electroencephalogram. Some patients have abnormal EEGs as well as glucose dysfunction that trigger their aggression. Of course, this does not mean that every OCD patient who is unable to control her anger suffers from these other comorbid conditions. Often patients become very angry and violent when their rituals are interrupted.

Are you currently on medications? What medications have you tried? For how long and at what dosage level? Find out the positive and negative effects.

Have you ever been hospitalized? How many times?

Have you ever been in therapy? What type? What did you do? Was it effective? Even if a patient tells you that she received behavior therapy, inquire what she actually did in the sessions. She may not have received exposure and response prevention. Many patients who report having been in behavior therapy have received systematic desensitization, thought stopping, or relaxation treatment, which are not effective for OCD. If the patient received exposure and response prevention, ask specifically what that entailed. For example, often exposure and response prevention fails if it is not conducted outside of the office setting where problems are more likely to occur. Also ask how frequently she went for therapy. For many patients with severe obsessions and compulsions, intensive treatment is more effective.

Let's discuss family psychiatric history. Do you know of any family members, aunts, uncles, cousins, grandparents, etc., who might have had phobias, OCD, panic disorder, depression, manic depressive illness, schizophrenia, alcoholism, drug abuse, or anything else?

Is there anything else you want to tell me that I have not already asked you?

After concluding your line of questioning, you will be ready to make a diagnosis and develop a treatment plan. You will have to make a decision about which symptom to treat first, at what frequency, where, and whether behavior therapy needs to be combined with medication.

If the patient has complained of many symptoms, you may be overwhelmed with the number of symptomatic areas that you will need to treat. Determining where to start is important and can set the tone for treatment compliance. If the patient feels you know what you are doing and begins to feel some relief of the problem, she is more likely to follow your suggestions.

I (FN) will never forget how I felt at the end of my consultation with Mary Ellen. As when I asked her how I could be of help to her, she began to tell me she cut her hair off because she could no longer tolerate fussing with it. I inquired whether she felt unattractive or thought her hair would come in fuller if she cut it off (assessing for BDD). She replied "No, I'm not a knockout, but I'm happy with my appearance."

"Do you want your hair to come in perfectly and evenly?" (assessing for OCD)

"Yes, I think that's it."

However, in addition, she pulled her hair (trichotillomania) and then played around with it and at times would swallow it. She also told me she was a very anxious person, always fidgeting, couldn't sit still, and had difficulty with concentration (attention deficit disorder). Her anxiety sometimes manifested itself by fears of driving. "Ahh," I said to myself, "she may have double-checking problems and need to know if she ran someone over while driving." I thought of double-checking because of her compulsion to have her hair grow in evenly and her constant checking to see if it was coming in perfectly or not.

But she said, "No, I just get scared. My heart starts to pound and I get a queasy feeling in my stomach."

I thought of panic disorder with or without agoraphobia, and began to inquire about fears of going through tunnels, over bridges, taking public transportation, etc. She responded affirmatively to all of these questions. I was afraid to go on. She was depressed but not suicidal. Here I had a patient with OCD (she had other symptoms besides perfectionism), trichotillomania, panic disorder with agoraphobia, and secondary depression (secondary because she was depressed over her inability to function with the symptoms). All I needed to hear was that she had an insurance plan that allowed her to be treated within 10 sessions!

I quickly informed her that I could not perform miracles and suggested we start treatment with the symptom that was most disturbing to her. In my mind, her hair cutting and panic disorder with agoraphobia inhibited her from working and socializing. The principal form of treatment is the same for both: exposure to one's fears at a rate one is able to tolerate the anxiety. Mary Ellen agreed that she needed to work on these two areas first.

During the interim between this consult and the next session I asked Mary Ellen to try to refrain from swallowing her hair even if she couldn't resist pulling it. I explained how dangerous it was to eat one's hair and that the hair might need to be removed surgically. To help resist her urges I suggested she have a psychiatric consult and consider taking some medication. She agreed and started on medication and began behavior therapy.

The guidelines we use in determining whether to use medications are the following:

- Patients who have demonstrated some efficacy of medication should probably continue with their medications and begin behavior therapy. The goal would be to discontinue the medications after approximately one year.

- For patients who have never tried medication and whose symptoms consume more than three hours per day and/or whose functioning levels are severely restricted, recommend both a trial of medication and behavior therapy.
- All patients should be strongly urged to undergo behavior therapy because research has shown that treatment gains are better maintained in patients who have had behavior therapy compared to those who have not (see Yaryura-Tobias & Neziroglu, 1983, 1997). However, in many cases the combined approach yields quicker and better results. Patients who are opposed to medications should be told that behavior therapy will be attempted, but if they are unable to comply medication will be strongly recommended. Of course, fears about drugs should be discussed and any misconceptions should be dispelled.

Following are some guidelines for determining the frequency of the sessions:

- For patients who are totally dysfunctional in all spheres, including work, school, interpersonal, dating, sexual, leisure activities, etc., we usually recommend 90-minute sessions six days a week. For these patients, their compulsions usually consume practically the whole day.
- For patients whose compulsions consume at least three hours a day and whose functioning is impaired in several areas, we recommend 90-minute sessions three times a week.
- Patients who are functioning but experience a lot of anxiety may benefit from 90-minute sessions once a week.

Intensive treatment (several times a week) may last from four to eight weeks, with an average duration of six weeks. The total duration of behavior therapy is approximately one year. Of course, there are exceptions to this and some patients may need chronic care in order to function.

At times, hospitalization needs to be recommended. Consult chapter 3 for reasons for hospitalization. If hospitalization is necessary, the patient should be referred to a facility specializing in OCD. Usually the expected time of stay in the hospital is four weeks.

At the end of the consult the patient should leave the office with a diagnosis, or diagnoses, and a recommendation for specific treatment. We often give patients a packet of self-report measures to fill out. The assessment packet consists of the YBOCS symptom checklist (not the YBOCS itself, which is clinician-administered), the Beck Depression and Beck Anxiety Inventories, Spielberger's State-Trait Anxiety Scale, a self-monitoring-of-rituals scale, and the Structured Clinical Interview for the DSM-III-R Diagnosis questionnaire for personality disorders (SCID-P). Patients should be told to fill out the questionnaires slowly and to have them finished by the next session.

Sessions 1–4: Behavior Analysis

The next four sessions are devoted to information gathering, which consists of doing a thorough behavior analysis. The patient should be told that information regarding every aspect of her life will be gathered during the next four sessions and that treatment will not begin until the behavior analysis is completed. Explain that you need a thorough behavior analysis so as not to miss information that would be crucial for developing a personal, specific, successful treatment program. If you describe exactly what to expect, the patient will not feel you are wasting time with questions while she is suffering. Although she may have had the illness for a long time prior to treatment, she wants relief within a few sessions. Be specific about what to expect. Try to schedule the sessions as closely as possible. This may mean setting up four 90-minute sessions in one week in order for the patient to start treatment as soon as possible.

Session 1: Target Symptom Assessment

The first session is devoted to identifying target symptoms. Collect from the patient the packet of self-report questionnaires that were given at the end of the consult visit and tell her you will review them for the next session. Administer the YBOCS and the OVI scales.

The target symptoms may be derived from one or many different diagnoses. In other words, you may begin assessing the patient's washing compulsions (OCD) and her frequent checking of her nose in the mirror (BDD). It is sometimes impossible to keep symptoms separate. However, you may have to address one set of compulsions before you can proceed to another.

Once the target symptoms are identified, cues that trigger them need to be assessed. Determine under what circumstances the patient engages in compulsions. Understand the environmental context under which obsessions and compulsions are evoked. Determine what maintains obsessions and compulsions besides simple anxiety reduction. For example, are there secondary gains, fears of responsibility, or family expectations that the patient may not be able to fulfill? Try to think like the patient and understand the intricacies of the obsessions.

It is very important that you comprehend the obsessions and compulsions, and the reasoning behind them, in order to devise good in vivo exposure exercises. For example, if a patient states that she has to walk past a particular person three times in one day, find out would happen if she did it only two times. What would happen if, by accident, it was more than three times? How does she manage to locate the person three times? How does she choose the person? Is there a pattern to walking around the person, in front of the person, left or right side, etc.? Most of session 1 will be taken up by discussing the target symptoms in detail, including disastrous consequences and overvalued ideas.

Session 2: Childhood Background, School, and Work Assessment

If the assessment of target symptoms was not completed in session 1 then continue with that in session 2. Proceed to obtaining childhood background. Did the patient have any problems during childhood or adolescence? If so, what kind of problems? Is there a history of sexual or physical abuse? Alcohol or drug usage? How does she react to adversity? This type of information will be helpful to understanding the coping style of the patient. Furthermore, it is indicative of previous adjustment levels.

Go on to school and work history. Start with the first day of school. How did the patient adjust to school? Did she experience separation anxiety? Did she have friends, playmates? What kind of grades did she get? How did she get along with authority figures? Go through the entire school and work history. Assess the patient's previous level of functioning. Did she give up when things got tough or did she plow along? Was she dependent on others or on herself? What was her frustration tolerance?

Session 3: Interpersonal, Sexual, and Medical History

How does the patient relate to others? What is her interaction style? Ask about her dating history. This is important because many OCD patients have no dating experience because in the past their symptoms interfered with their ability to date and later in life they are embarrassed about being perceived as inexperienced. Consequently, they may even hold on to enough OCD symptoms so they do not have to date. If the patient does date, what, if any, problems does she then encounter? Assess whether the problems are related to OCD. For example, does she go out on one or two dates and shortly thereafter end the relationship? If this is the case, is it because she becomes frightened of the person due to contamination reasons, or is she simply not able to make commitments?

Often patients who get better are fearful of sex. This may seem unusual for someone in adulthood, but if they never went through the milestones of adolescence then it is understandable. Socially, as well as in many other ways, developmental lags may be observed. Sexually the individual may be functioning at a much lower age. If the patient is married, does her spouse have to undergo elaborate cleaning rituals before or after sex? What is the nature of the patient's interpersonal relations with friends, neighbors, and family? Does she socialize? How do people usually respond to her? If there are marital conflicts, ask the couple to wait until the OCD is properly treated before considering divorce. Although the couple may actually be incompatible, it's possible that the OCD symptoms have completely altered the nature of the relationship. It is hard to determine what the marriage would be like without the OCD. Inquire as to whether the OCD interferes with the patient's relationship with her children. At times, OCD patients cannot touch their own children or allow them to have friends over to the house.

When the symptoms begin to greatly affect the children and/or other household members, then intensive therapy is advisable. It is necessary to immediately reverse the situation because the patient will suffer not only from the symptoms of the illness but also from guilt and anger. Patients feel guilty over not properly parenting their child, not assuming their household responsibilities, and not being a good spouse, and/or anger at significant others for not understanding them. Therefore, in addition to anxiety they then develop secondary negative emotions such as guilt, anger, and depression. It is important to understand the patient's feelings, as well as interaction and coping styles. A thorough medical history should also be taken. Are there significant events in the patient's life that may affect her appraisal of illness? What is her attitude toward illness? Critical life events, the family's attitude toward physical illness, and personal experience with illness are very important factors in evaluating development of hypochondriasis. Of course, when considering medication as part of the treatment, the medical history is of utmost importance to ensure that the prescribed medications are not contraindicated.

Session 4: Psychoeducation and Development of Anxiety

Most patients will ask what caused their OCD. This may be during this session or before. Usually we tell the patients the following:

No one is certain what causes OCD. However, it is most likely that certain individuals have a biological propensity to develop it, and under the right environmental conditions it manifests itself. In the early 1970s we compared platelet serotonin levels of OCD patients to normals and found that serotonin, a neurotransmitter (a particular substance in our bodies), was lower in the OCD population. Other researchers further investigated this in the blood and in cerebrospinal fluid and found serotonin levels to be altered in OCD patients. Later on we investigated serotonin levels in patients who did not take any medication but underwent a three-week intensive behavioral program. What we found is that the serotonin levels were altered with behavior therapy alone, without any medications. It seems that behavior therapy may have the same action as medications. Also, Baxter, another researcher, has looked at glucose absorption levels before and after behavior therapy. He and his research team found that behavior therapy can modify glucose absorption levels. All this seems to imply that behavior therapy may be working similarly to medications.

Despite all this, we must remember that our environment and learning play a significant role in shaping our behaviors. There have been studies showing that 90% of the general population has intrusive thoughts similar to yours. The difference between your thoughts and theirs is that they are able to easily dismiss them. They are not as easily upset by them and they do not do anything to reduce their uncomfortableness. Unlike non-OCD individuals, you learned to interpret your environment as dangerous, you don't trust your ability to cope with adversity, you learned it is best to avoid risks, and perhaps you found that compulsions allow you to avoid or escape from anxiety-provoking situations. How you learned these things I am not sure. [At this point you may want to offer the patient a hypothesis based on your behavior analysis.]

Allow the patient to express her concerns and offer her own hypotheses. Due to extensive media coverage, most patients ask repeatedly how behavior therapy is going to help them with a neurobiological disorder. Citing our research on serotonin levels and Dr. Baxter's work on glucose absorption changes after behavior therapy is often reassuring.

After explaining possible reasons for having OCD, discuss treatment outcome studies. For more information on this, consult chapter 4. We tell patients that most studies indicate that 75% are able to achieve tremendous symptom reduction after behavior therapy and that these results are maintained years later.

Next, inform patients what to actually expect during behavior therapy and why—something along the lines of the following:

During each session we will expose you to the various situations that you are currently afraid of. We will do it slowly and in a manner that is comfortable for you. We will never force you to do anything you do not want to do. We may try to convince you that it is not dangerous, and that it is in your best interest to approach rather than avoid a particular situation, but we will never force you. Also, you will be informed about everything we do, so that nothing will come as a surprise. We will obtain your permission before we proceed to the next step. Although most patients think they are going to experience a tremendous amount of anxiety, our experience has been that the anticipation is worse than the reality. Most patients are surprised at how easily behavior therapy comes to them.

In addition to exposing you to various situations, we are going to ask you not to engage in your compulsions or to avoid other situations. It should be very clear to you that washing [for example] is the same as not touching a contaminated object. There is no difference. Often patients think they are doing well because they are not engaging in the compulsion but they are merely avoiding what frightens them and thereby they don't need to do the compulsion. We will come up with ways that will help you with response prevention. Of course, most of the effort comes from your own efforts at refraining from the compulsion and tolerating the anxiety. However, if you flood yourself in imagination, as we will teach you to do, whenever you are confronted with anxiety-provoking situations, your anxiety will eventually go down.

As we expose you to your fears, your anxiety will initially go up, but it will come down. This process looks like what we call a bell curve. In other words, your anxiety goes up and then comes down [illustrate with your hand]. Your anxiety may come back up again within a few minutes or within a few hours, but each time it will go up less and less. What is happening is that you are habituating or getting used to the anxiety until it no longer bothers you.

We are going to ask you to rate your anxiety from 1 to 10 (or 0 to 100) with 1 being no anxiety and 10 being a panic state. These ratings are called "subjective units of discomfort" or SUDs because you are subjectively telling us how anxious you feel. We will just say to you, "What is your SUD level right now?" and you will give us a number. That will help us gauge how you are feeling. Besides your treatment sessions with us, you will be given homework assignments. You are to practice everything we have done in the session and to continue to do the very things you were taught in previous sessions. You may avoid those situations that we have not worked on. However, if accidently you are confronted with something we have not worked on, try not to give into your compulsion. Flood yourself to it and call me if you need to.

The self-monitoring sheets on which the patient has recorded the intensity, frequency, and duration of her obsessions and compulsions may be used to set up the anxiety hierarchy. On these sheets the patient has noted the situations where she experiences anxiety. Also, by going through a typical day for the patient in detail, you can gather a lot of information about the areas of discomfort.

The difficulty lies not in determining events that trigger compulsions, but in grading the level of discomfort. Most patients report that their SUD levels are 10 in almost every situation. It is often up to the therapist to break it down into smaller gradients. A patient who is afraid of using telephones due to an AIDS phobia may experience a SUD of 3 if asked to use a public phone in an office building but a 7 in a hospital and a 9 in a blood-drawing laboratory. Among hoarders, throwing out some items may be less anxiety-provoking than others. Those with aggressive obsessions may have less anxiety holding a knife in the presence of adults as compared to children. Some sample anxiety hierarchies are provided in tables 5.1, 5.2, 5.3, and 5.4.

TABLE 5.1 Sample anxiety hierarchy for AIDS

Situation	SUD*
red spot in a book	60
using a public telephone	25
using a phone in a building with a lab	35
being touched by someone who went to visit a friend or family member in the hospital	40
paying a "sickly" cashier	50
walking close by a "homeless" person	55
giving money to a "homeless" person	60
walking in Greenwich Village	70
eating in Greenwich Village	80
going to a homosexual district	90
having blood drawn in a regular lab	100

* subjective unit of discomfort

TABLE 5.2 Sample anxiety hierarchy for double-checking

Situation	SUD
house door	20
car door	25
stove	30
electrical appliances	50
paperwork at home	55
paperwork at work	65
checkbook	70
stock computations	85
certificates of deposit	90
stock certificates	100

TABLE 5.3 Sample anxiety hierarchy for magical thinking

Situation	SUD
out of bed / left foot	20
enter / exit room / left foot	25
sitting in blue chair	30
sitting at head of table	40
leaving TV off on channel 4	50
seeing a handicapped person	60
hearing of illness—linking to family	70
using certain words, e.g., nothing, six, Elaine	95
hearing certain words, e.g., devil, dammit	100

TABLE 5.4 Sample anxiety hierarchy for scrupulosity

Situation	SUD
forgets to return a borrowed pen	20
returning lecture notes to a classmate	30
receiving a gift worth over $10,000	40
lost check is found	55
telling a white lie	65
possibly hurting someone's feelings	75
not reporting income earned	90
being on payroll of father's business, but working minimally	100

Sessions 5–29: Treatment

Treatment usually consists of 90-minute sessions of exposure in vivo, accompanied by the therapist verbalizing the patient's feared disastrous consequences. The therapist may model appropriate behavior for the patient. Cognitive therapy is utilized under specific circumstances, which are listed in table 5.5. If cognitive therapy is to be used, it may be included within the behavior therapy session or administered for 12 to 20 sessions before commencing behavior therapy. If the former style is applied, the 90-minute session may be divided into 30 minutes of cognitive therapy and 60 minutes of exposure and response prevention. If the latter style is chosen, the therapist may set up 45-minute sessions ranging from 12 to 20 sessions and after that begin with behavior therapy. We typically include cognitive therapy within the 90-minute sessions. The few occasions when cognitive therapy may be utilized initially are if the patient is severely depressed and/or anxious and unable to proceed with behavior therapy. Later in this chapter we will illustrate the application of cognitive therapy.

Exposure and Response Prevention Application

Working through the Anxiety Hierarchy
At the beginning of each session, review the hierarchy and what is planned for that session. It is likely that as you work on one item of the

TABLE 5.5 Circumstances when cognitive therapy is utilized

high overvalued ideas
doubting
indecisiveness
severe depression
axis II diagnosis problems
family problems
interpersonal problems resulting from OCD
patient is too anxious to engage in behavior therapy
body dysmorphic disorder
hypochondriasis
religious beliefs prevent engagement in behavior therapy

hierarchy the patient may add new items. Incorporate new items as they appear. Most often, several items of similar difficulty can be worked on in any given session; try to group items of equal difficulty and in proximity to one another. For example, at the grocery store you may need to work on picking up contaminated produce as well as purchasing dented cans that are in the front rather than way in the back of the shelves. During another session you may repeat the same exercise and add another fear, such as paying a sickly-looking cashier.

Before you start the session agree with the patient what you will work on at the designated location. Once you get there your plans may change if the patient encounters more anxiety than anticipated and/or a new fear occurs. For example, one patient saw an exterminator truck parked in front of the grocery store and then refused to go in, fearing the store was recently sprayed.

Conducting Therapy outside of the Office
Because you are conducting therapy outside of your office it is best to decide how you will be introduced to others if the occasion arises. For example, if we work with a patient in her office or school, we may go in as a friend or someone interested in learning about the job. You have to be clever in devising means of approaching fearful situations without drawing attention to yourself or to the patient. If you go into a store and want the patient to be exposed to certain items, you might have to engage the

salesperson in conversation while the patient holds the item. Also, you may rub a tissue over the object and then have the patient carry the tissue and then perhaps later ask her to rub her bed with it. This is done for further exposure at home, as a homework assignment.

Larry was a patient who had religious obsessions. Every time he went into church he had an urge to curse at God and every time he thought of or saw a priest, he had sacrilegious thoughts. During his behavioral program we went to different churches and left little curse notes on the benches. We then spent long periods of time in a religious store touching various items of clothing, jewelry, and religious paraphernalia. I asked the patient to try on a cassock. Because it was a small store and sold very specific items the store owner inquired whether the patient was a priest. We had decided beforehand that if he was questioned he would reply that he was thinking about it and trying to get used to the idea. I was a friend who was just accompanying him. The store owner's religious interest triggered more obsessions for the patient and therefore proved to be another source of exposure.

Managing Anxiety

Humor Exposure in vivo can be made into fun for the patient. The use of humor is very important. However, humor does not imply sarcasm; rather, the exercise should be done in a fun and entertaining manner. Although our experience is that most patients respond well to humor, it is a clinical judgment when and with whom to use it. The humor should be incorporated into the exposure exercise, for example:

I can't believe you actually took an appointment card from the receptionist after touching the dirty floor! I bet you she will be sick on account of you. She will get all of us sick and the whole clinic will be shut down next week. Perhaps the department of health will have to investigate because so many people got sick after your visit. This is all because you touched that dirty floor!

Audiotapes While exposure in vivo is being conducted, it is helpful to verbalize to the patient the feared disastrous consequences. This helps expose her to all the cues of the feared objects. Very often we make tapes of the exposure exercises for patients to listen to at home. The content of the tapes is similar to what has been done during the sessions. Of course, tapes can also be utilized when dealing with situations that you may not have direct access to. We have found tapes to be very useful when dealing with pure obsessions. Often we will make a couple of tapes ourselves and then have the patient bring in tapes that she has done. This allows us to give feedback on how well she is flooding herself outside of the sessions. It usually takes about five to ten tapes before the patient is actually flooding her-self properly. Initially the flooding tapes simulate obsessing and/or recounting her thoughts when anxious. Below are two examples of expo-sure in imagination via an audiotape:

For a washer: You are at the supermarket and you notice a disheveled, sickly looking man in the same aisle as you. You go past him with your cart, which accidently touches him. You notice he is returning the can of tomatoes to the same shelf from which you just picked up yours. It makes you realize that he must have touched your can while he had selected his own. You study him and notice his rashes and you are con-vinced he has something seriously wrong with him, possibly AIDS. You want to run out of the store and go home to shower, but you don't. Your body begins to feel hot. You are dizzy, perspiring, and you feel exhausted. You want to avoid the spot where he touched your cart but you accidently touch it while trying to make a decision whether you should leave or stay. Suppose he had blood on him and somehow it got on you. You go through the cashier, hoping it is not the one he went through. You had succeeded in not following him and thus avoiding the aisles, cashiers, and people he had contact with. However, he returns to your cashier to get his receipt, which he forgot. You feel more contami-nated than ever. You want to throw away all the groceries you just bought but you don't. Think about that.

Here is an optional ending:

He has touched you and your groceries have been contaminated by him. You don't shower and a few months or years later you get sick. After many examinations, the doctor tells you that you are HIV positive. When people eventually find out they start to avoid you. You end up alone and isolated. You are dying and no one is around except for a few family members. Everyone deserts you.

For a double-checker: You decide to stop checking the stove, toaster, food processor, and all the other electrical appliances in the kitchen when you leave home. You have decided you are sick and tired of having to wake up and devote one hour each morning to checking over the kitchen before leaving. You know you are the last person to leave the house and therefore the one responsible if anything goes wrong. You have had it. You are pleased when one or two weeks go by and nothing happens.

One day while at work you get a phone call from your neighbor. Your nightmare comes true. You drive home and see fire trucks parked in front of your house. You inquire about what happened and the chief fireman says, "Some jerk left the oven and stove on in his house. We never understand how people can be so irresponsible." Of course, he doesn't realize it is your house and you are the "jerk" he is talking about. They put out the fire eventually but there is a lot of damage. Your spouse and children believe you acted irresponsibly. They lose trust in you and their respect for you never returns.

Paradoxical Intention   Paradoxical intention refers to exposing patients to their fears and increasing their anxiety by exaggerating the disastrous consequences. Obviously this method can only be used when consequences exist. Humor is often used during paradoxical intention. Paradoxical intention was used in the example above when the whole clinic got sick because a patient picked up an appointment card from the receptionist. However, the paradoxical intention can also be administered in a cut-and-dry style. An example of paradoxical intention using a cut-and-dry style with magical thinking symptoms would be the following:

> Because you didn't think of a good word when you picked up the phone at the office, you will lose your job, and when your family finds that out they will be angry at you for losing your job and kick you out of the house. You will have no job and no money. You have to be very careful to control your thoughts. Think about losing your job, angering your family, and having no money because you picked up the phone with a bad thought in your mind. You should never have a bad thought when you pick up the phone or that one mistake will cost your life.

Modeling   Modeling sometimes enables patients to reduce their anxiety; seeing others do things they perceive as risky allows them to reappraise the situation. Instruct patients to call you when they are unable to resist a compulsion. Your reassurance, as well as indications that you would not hesitate to do what they fear, will enable them to approach rather than avoid situations. You can also encourage patients while on the phone to do the things that they are afraid of. Family members and friends can also help by modeling and encouraging patients to resist the compulsion.

Necessity for Close Monitoring During Sessions
In conducting behavior therapy it is important to closely observe the patient. OCD patients gain their confidence in the therapist by knowing that the therapist is thoroughly familiar with their disorder and the tricks of the trade, so to speak.

Some of the common methods by which washers and double-checkers try to circumvent their anxiety during or after an exposure exercise include the following:

- partly touch feared objects
- use only one hand while touching it
- touch only with fingertips
- subtly wipe their hands after touching it
- use handiwipes or other cleansing objects not specifically mentioned
- after the session wash or dry clean clothes, throw out items
- wear different clothes even though you told her to wear the same clothes as the previous session (they may look very similar and she hopes you will not notice)
- compartmentalize by putting contaminated objects in different places
- avoid without seeming to, e.g., walk around a contaminated object
- make an excuse and go back to check
- while walking away and when you are not looking, quickly turn around to check
- quickly check side or rearview mirror while driving
- engage you in unrelated conversations

This is obviously a partial list. It is your responsibility to observe and at all times to be alert to these types of behaviors. It is not that patients are being resistant, in the psychoanalytic sense, or purposefully deceitful, or that they are unmotivated for treatment, but rather the anxiety is sometimes unbearable and they have found that these types of behaviors are effective in reducing anxiety. Actually, the more aware you are of these behaviors, the more confident the patient is in you and the greater the chances of compliance.

Cognitive Therapy

More will be said on cognitive therapy at the end of this chapter. However, patients who have learned cognitive therapy may be able to utilize it in reducing their anxiety. They can challenge their beliefs and generate new and less anxiety-provoking thoughts.

Implementation of Cognitive Therapy

As mentioned above, cognitive therapy may be included in the sessions in addition to behavior therapy or it may be used alone. New research indicates that cognitive therapy may be effective in treating OCD. As was mentioned in chapter 4, cognitive therapy has been directly compared to behavior therapy and found to be equally effective and, in fact, in some cases exceeded the efficacy of exposure and response prevention (van Oppen et al., 1995). The specific cognitions that are challenged are the overinflated sense of responsibility and thought action fusion (patients' belief that thinking is the same as taking action). However, research is still in progress and currently there is not sufficient evidence to recommend cognitive therapy alone. It is certainly useful to combine it with behavior therapy.

As discussed in chapter 4, cognitive therapy may take many forms, ranging from self-instructional training to Beckian interventions, in which evidence is sought for specific cognitive distortions, and Albert Ellis's rational emotive behavioral psychotherapy (REBT). Which type is utilized is a matter of preference. It is important to be familiar with the common cognitive distortions of OCD patients, as mentioned in the previous chapter. Cognitive distortions are derived by continuously questioning the patient via the Socratic method. Below is an illustration of cognitive therapy with a checker.

Patient: For over one hour every night, before going to bed, I check the kitchen appliances and that the house is locked It doesn't matter if we get home at three in the morning, I can't go to bed before checking.

Therapist: What do you check and what are the disastrous consequences if you don't check?

Patient: I check the toaster, the faucets, the coffee machine, the stove. After I am done in the kitchen, which may take me one hour, then I go to the front door and check that it is locked. Often I will get into bed and then get up and check the front door again.

Therapist: What are you afraid of? What do you think would happen if you didn't check?

Patient: I am always afraid that we will have a fire or flood in the house and that someone will break in.

Therapist: Has that ever happened?

Patient: No, but it could if I didn't check.

Therapist: Is your husband also concerned with having a fire or burglar?

Patient: Not really because he doesn't check and gets angry at me for checking.

Therapist: Do you have a fire or burglar alarm?

Patient: No we don't, but we used to in our other house. I don't think it matters because I used to worry that it wouldn't work.

Therapist: What are the chances that you will start a fire or a flood by not checking?

Patient: It is possible. Why take a chance? Besides, if anything bad is going to happen it will happen to me.

Therapist: What is the evidence that bad things happen to you more often than to others? And can you live without taking risks?

Patient: There may not be evidence that bad things happen to me more often, but it sure seems that way. My father has fibrillation and the doctor says given his heart condition it may be dangerous. My mother is sick, my husband may be losing his job, and I have OCD. Now tell me how many people have so many problems.

Therapist: There is no question you have many problems to cope with but I am not sure that it is more than the share of many other people. Can you tell me how many people are sick, getting divorced, have sick parents, etc.? What is the likelihood that only one bad thing happens at a time?

Patient: You do have a point. Many of our friends have lost their jobs. In fact, three of them had to sell their homes and move to apartments. Yes, they also have illnesses to contend with but it always seems worse when it happens to me.

Therapist: You see, once you challenge your thoughts you realize that they may not be correct. But let's assume that more bad or unpleasant things happen to you than to others; does that mean that you should be cautious to the point of not taking any chances in life? Do you think that even if you spent all day trying to be cautious that you would not make any mistakes and nothing bad would happen to you? Can you control your environment entirely?

Patient: Okay, I get the point. I know you can't sit around all day and try to devise ways to prevent harm. I know I can't control everything, but shouldn't I try to control those things I can? For example, if I can prevent a fire or flood why shouldn't I?

Therapist: Well, you certainly can do anything you want to do. However, I thought you didn't want to spend one hour every night checking your kitchen.

Patient: I don't. I can't help it. I am afraid not to check.

Therapist: We are back where we started. What would happen if you didn't check and a fire or flood did start?

Patient: I would feel horrible.

Therapist: What would you feel horrible about?

Patient: Well, my whole house might catch on fire and it would be my responsibility.

Therapist: Do you think you are responsible for everything that happens in the house? What about your husband?

Patient: I always think it is my responsibility. (Patient then gives a hypothesis as to why she has a strong sense of responsibility.)

Therapist: Although it is good to have a sense of responsibility, do you think it is possible for you to be responsible for everything all the time?

Patient: I guess not.

After challenging the patient's thoughts you would give her a homework assignment based on what you worked on. For example, after terminating the above dialogue you might tell the patient to go to bed without checking the kitchen. In the next session you would review her experience. The following session might be a repetition of the last session. You could also incorporate exposure in imagination and tape it for the patient to listen to at home, especially if she begins to obsess.

Cognitive therapy for other spectrum disorders is discussed in chapter 8.

6

Biological Therapy

BIOLOGICAL APPROACHES TO THE TREATMENT of OCD and its spectrum involve drugs, electroshock, neurosurgery, and other proven exogenous modifiers of the internal milieu, such as nutrition, exercise, and meditation.

Overall, drugs have been the main therapeutic tool for OCD, although, as discussed in previous chapters, cognitive-behavior therapy is favored by many therapists. Current drugs for OCD include: (1) anti-obsessive-compulsive agents (AOCAs), (2) anxiolytics, (3) anticonvulsants, (4) monoamine-oxidase inhibitors (MAOIs), (5) antidepressants, (6) psychostimulants, (7) lithium, (8) tryptophan, and (9) antipsychotics.

To facilitate the understanding of the role of medication in OCD treatment, we begin this chapter with a brief review of brain anatomy, its physiology, and the chemical substances operating brain electrochemical mechanisms. The practitioner then will be able to more successfully outline a therapeutic regimen.

The Brain

Anatomy

The brain is divided into the right and left hemispheres and embodies cortical (surface) and subcortical regions. The external surface, or cortex, includes four lobes: the frontal (in the front), temporal (near the temples), parietal (above the ears), and occipital (the rear). These lobes, formed by gyri, or convolutions, are traversed by sulci, or grooves, that limit the boundaries of these regions. The medial surfaces consist of the corpus callosum, the fornix, the cingulate, and two deep sulci, the upper parieto-occipital sulcus and the calcarine sulcus. The inferior surface is divided into the orbital and tentorial surface.

Deep in the cerebral hemispheres and in the upper brain stem is the basal ganglia, formed by the lentiform nucleus, the caudate nucleus (which together are referred to as the corpus striatum), and the amygdala.

The oldest region of the brain includes the rhinencephalon and the limbic system, which contains the olfactory pathway, the piriform area, and the hippocampal formation. The brain has other regions, such as the thalamus and the cerebellum. The brain stem is comprised of the midbrain, pons, and medulla oblongata.

The brain is protected by membranes, or meninges. The cerebrospinal fluid runs within the meninges and through the four communicating cavities, called the right, left, third, and fourth ventricles. This fluid carries nutrients and is the main communicator with the hematological system.

A different view of the brain divides it according to function, which helps us to understand normal and abnormal cerebral mechanisms. The lobes control the motor and somatosensorial activity: Higher cortical functions, such as thinking, are controlled by the frontal lobe, a region related to OCD; the temporal lobe is the seat for temporal epilepsy and behavioral seizures, which can be associated to OCD subsets or variants. The basal ganglia regulate motor activity; abnormalities in this mechanism are evident in Parkinson's disease, Tourette's syndrome, and hyperactive syndromes. Moreover, the basal ganglia also seem to be associated with OCD, as evidenced by a physiological study done with positron emission tomography (Baxter et al., 1987). The limbic system or emotional brain appears intimately related to OCD pathogenesis.

Neurons

Three to 10 billion nerve cells, or neurons, form a complex, highly sophisticated communication system that actively engages in the brain's biochemical processes. Each neuron connects with 10,000 to 20,000 other neurons, relaying messages and participating in chemical reactions. Chemical reactions take place both inside and outside the neuron in the synapse, or junction, between the cells and are mediated by receptors. Receptors are part of the neuron membrane and have the capacity to recognize a neurotransmitter or a hormone.

Once an order or response is chosen, a biochemical reaction takes place to transmit the impulse that carries the order. This order travels through the axon and dendrites, which propagate electrical impulses that are carried by neurotransmitters to the synapse. It is at this junction between two neurons where chemical reactions take place.

Physiology

Brain physiology is regulated by neurotransmitters and neurohormones, with active participation by amino acids, vitamins, coenzymes, minerals, and electrolytes. Amino acids and coenzymes are required for the formation of neurotransmitters. Neurotransmiters are chemical substances that carry stimuli through the synapse. Neurohormones are substances produced and secreted by the body that regulate cerebral and bodily functions.

Neurotransmitters or drugs interacting with a receptor (a process called affinity) are known as agonists and cause an identifiable response. Conversely, those that do not interact are called antagonists.

Psychotropic medications, including OCD agents, seem to act in the neuron synapse, affecting neurotransmitters' metabolism and transport, uptake and reuptake mechanism (which modulates the presence of neurotransmitters in the synapsis), as well the neuron's receptors.

The Autonomous Nervous System

The autonomous nervous system (ANS) plays a preponderant role in OCD mechanisms via its sympathetic, parasympathetic, and cholinergic pathways. These three pathways enable the brain to communicate with the rest of the body or periphery. The ANS modulates the activity of involuntary bodily systems (e.g., breathing, heart beat, urination, menstruation). Some of these systems may be altered in OCD and be reflected in such symptoms as tachycardia, hyperventilation, tremor, or dysmenorrhea. A medical history may reveal ANS dystonia related to OCD and to secondary anxiety. This ANS dystonia may be aggravated by the administration of anti-obsessive-compulsive drugs; therefore, it is important to diagnose ANS dystonia in patients with OCD.

Pharmacotherapy

Historically, attempts to treat OCD have utilized any imaginable drug. These drugs have included a wide range of compounds: barbiturates, amphetamines, cocaine, insulin shock, carbon dioxide, phenytoin, and stilbestrol. Results were disappointing.

The introduction of neuroleptics for the treatment of psychosis, of benzodiazepines for anxiety, and of monoamine oxidase inhibitors (MAOI), tricyclic antidepressants (TCA), and serotonin selective reuptake inhibitors (SSRIs) for depression, opened a new therapeutic avenue.

Currently, more specific anti-obsessive-compulsive agents and coadjuvant drugs have increased treatment choices. These choices permit the use of polypharmacy, that is, the combination of two or more drugs. As expected, these drugs present a variety of untoward effects that may disrupt treatment of OCD.

Special groups with OCD (e.g., children, the elderly, and pregnant women) require special attention when outlining a therapeutic program (see chapter 7).

Symptom heterogeneity and OCD comorbidity pose a therapeutic challenge. Conclusions about treatment outcome vary. The number of treatment refractory patients is rather substantial, duration of maintenance dose is disputable, and relapses after drug discontinuation are frustrating.

What to Ask Before Starting Drug Therapy

After examining the patient and determining a diagnosis, it is time to consider medication. In order to select the appropriate medication, it is important to know (1) the patient's medication profile, (2) that the medication will not interact with other medications the patient may be taking, and (3) any medical conditions the patient has as well as conditions that can be harmed by the medication introduced.

You should also find out how the patient responds to medication in general and to psychiatric medication in particular. Does the patient have a tolerance to drugs or a response to small doses? Are side effects a common complaint? Is the patient afraid to take medication? Is she a "pill popper"?

If the patient is female, is she pregnant or trying to become pregnant? Also ask the patient if he or she suffers from the following:

- allergies, including allergies to medications
- migraines or tension headaches
- visual defects
- narrow angle glaucoma
- dyspnea
- holding her breath
- difficulty swallowing
- digestive problems
- a thyroid condition
- inability to regulate body temperature
- tics or twitches
- seizures
- episodes of fainting
- accident proneness

- loss of balance
- urinary hesitancy
- prostate condition
- erectile dysfunction
- anorgasmia
- dysmenorrhea
- premenstrual syndrome
- alcoholism
- drug abuse

Anti-Obsessive-Compulsive Agents

Anti-obsessive-compulsive agents (AOCAs) or, as the name implies, drugs of choice for the treatment of OCD, are partial and selective serotonin (5-HT) inhibitors. Serotonin is one of the major neurotransmitters, and its presence seems to facilitate the electrical impulses regulating the frequency and intensity of OCD symptoms.

Clomipramine is a partial 5-HT inhibitor, and fluoxetine, fluvoxamine, paroxetine, and sertraline are selective 5-HT inhibitors. All these drugs make 5-HT available at the neural synapsis by preventing its reabsorption into the neuron. Their clinical efficacy is associated to a putative faulty 5-HT metabolism.

Side Effects

AOCAs present a side effect profile related to their chemical structure, their interactions with aminergic and cholinergic systems, and the action on cellular receptors and subreceptors. Side effects of AOCAs sometimes occur with the use of other psychotropic medications.

Side effects include bodily responses to the patient's individual biological profile, dosage prescribed, frequency of administration, bodily concentration, ability to clear the drug, and interaction with other drugs. The administration of drugs can affect any system in different degrees; the most affected systems are the gastrointestinal, cardiovascular, urogenital, and central and autonomous nervous systems.

Drug Selection

Selection of an AOCA depends on the drug's clinical efficacy and side effect profile. A drug history of the patient may be helpful in choosing the drug. Patients should also be asked the following questions before starting therapy:

- What drugs have you taken for OCD?
- What was the dose?
- For how long did you take it?
- Did you experience side effects?
- Was the drug efficacious?
- Do you have any other illness?
- Are you taking any medication?

Drug Administration

AOCAs are dispensed in oral form (see table 6.1), although clomipramine may also be administered intravenously. Drugs are given in divided doses, or as a single night dose. Although night dosing is more convenient for the patient, it lowers clomipramine blood levels, which may affect therapeutic response.

TABLE 6.1   AOCAs: Partial-selective reuptake blockers

Generic Name	Dosage Range
clomipramine	250 mg/po/day
fluoxetine	80 mg/po/day
fluvoxamine	200 mg/po/day
paroxetine	50 mg/po/day
sertraline	200 mg/po/day

Children and the elderly should be prescribed one-third of the regular dose. From that baseline, if patients are unresponsive, gradual increments might be considered. Long-term studies in children and geriatric populations are lacking. Pharmacotherapy for special groups is discussed in chapter 7.

Clomipramine

Clomipramine (CMI), a TCA, was the first drug to be used as an AOCA and is the most researched AOCA. The first double blind placebo controlled study was done at our laboratories in 1973 (Yaryura-Tobias, Neziroglu, & Bergman, 1976). CMI is a potent 5-HT inhibitor with less potent blocking activity on norepinephrine (NE). The therapeutic dose range has been established between 75 to 250 mg/po/day, with a 200 mg average. This dose seems to satisfy most therapeutic requirements, although some patients may need 300 mg or more per day. However, CMI's property to lower the convulsive threshold may dissuade the practitioner from using higher doses. A therapeutic schedule may consist of 25 mg for the first three days, 50 mg for the next four days, and 50 mg increases on a weekly basis until reaching the desirable dose. CMI should be given after meals to prevent nausea.

Intravenous administration may be used for refractory cases. Intravenous CMI is injected in a slow-dripping saline solution to a maximum of 250 mg/day dose after a gradual daily increase. The initial infusion consists of 25 mg of CMI in 500 ml injected about one hour. Thereafter, CMI is increased in 25 to 50 mg increments for a total of 14 infusions, with a maximum administration of 250 mg. Side effects of intravenous administration should be considered: myoclonus, seizures, orthostatic hypotension, and tissue necrosis around the injection site. Diazepam may be given for the neuromuscular side effects, and the use of a catheter for the infusion will prevent damage to the surrounding tissue from slippage. Some patients who respond to this approach may be able to continue with oral CMI.

- *Side effects* Clomipramine side effects are those seen in TCA therapy, including: dry mouth, perspiration, constipation, delayed urination, weight gain, tremor, orthostatic hypotension, anorgasmia, and delayed ejaculation. The combination of CMI and alcohol may trigger aggressive behavior.
- *Therapeutic efficacy* Improvement may be observed after four weeks, but substantial improvement requires at least 8 to 12 weeks. After six months, continue with a maintenance dose of about 75 mg. If the patient does not improve after three months of treatment, discontinuation of CMI or the addition of coadjuvant drugs should be considered (see table 6.2). Relapses may follow drug discontinuation in 10 to 99% of the cases (Pato et al., 1988). This broad range shows lack of uniformity in symptom control, indicating the role of patient individuality in treatment response. However, more studies are necessary to arrive at better conclusions about relapse.

Fluoxetine

Fluoxetine is a bicyclic SSRI given in doses ranging from 20 to 80 mg/po/day. Therapeutic levels should be gradually reached from a starting dose of 5 mg/po/day. Fluoxetine is available in capsule or liquid form.

TABLE 6.2   OCD and its spectrum: coadjuvant drugs

Generic Name	Dosage Range
alprazolam	1–4 mg/po/day
buspirone	15–60 mg/po/day
carbamazepine	200–800 mg/po/day
clonazepam	1–4 mg/po/day
lithium	300–900 mg/po/day
pimozide	1–6 mg/po/day

- *Side effects*   Fluoxetine has few anticholinergic and cardiovascular side effects. Conversely, TCAs present anticholinergic (dry mouth, constipation, urinary hesitance) and cardiovascular (e.g., hypotension, electrocardiographic changes) side effects. This contrast between TCA and fluoxetine establishes a different untoward side effect profile. Furthermore, rather than producing weight gain like CMI, it may cause weight loss in doses higher than 80 mg/day.

  Main side effects are nausea, intestinal cramps, headaches, nervousness, anxiety, tremors, and insomnia. Skin allergies may be present. Tardive dyskinesia has been reported. Bleeding, although rare, has been reported in older people or in those suffering from vascular pathology or platelet disturbances.
- *Therapeutic efficacy*   It takes at least 8 to 12 weeks to show improvement. Overall, 50% of cases show improvement.

Fluvoxamine

This monocyclic drug is an SSRI that has been recently introduced to the American market. The therapeutic dose is 50 to 300 mg/po/day in divided doses.

- *Side effects*   Fluvoxamine side effects are those observed with other SSRIs, including dry mouth, nausea, vomiting, diarrhea, somnolence, insomnia, asthenia, nervousness, and abnormal ejaculation.
- *Therapeutic efficacy*   Efficacy should be noticed within 10 weeks of treatment, with approximately 50% of the cases showing improvement. The therapeutic action of fluvoxamine in children and adolescents is still unavailable.

Paroxetine

This is a very potent SSRI. There is not much experience in the treatment of OCD with paroxetine. The therapeutic dose is 20 to 50 mg/po/day. Night administration may cause insomnia.

- *Side effects* The main adverse experiences are nausea, dry mouth, constipation, diarrhea, headaches, sweating, dizziness, tremor, fatigue, and abnormal ejaculation.
- *Therapeutic efficacy* Overall, efficacy is observed at the 50 mg/day dose. However, more studies are needed to establish the efficacy dose range. So far, as with the other SSRIs, efficacy is obtained in 50% of the cases.

Sertraline

Sertraline is another SSRI, administered in doses of 100 to 200 mg/po/day. At least four to eight weeks are required to observe therapeutic changes.

- *Side effects* The most common side effects are dry mouth, nausea, diarrhea, constipation, dyspepsia, headaches, fatigue, insomnia, somnolence, male sexual dysfunction, agitation, and abnormal vision.
- *Therapeutic efficacy* Sertraline offers an efficacy spectrum of 50%. Improvement can be observed in four weeks or more.

A Comment on SSRIs

SSRIs are very powerful substances that might exert adverse effects in the central nervous system. Psychiatric side effects include: nervousness, irritability, depression, anxiety, and hallucinations. Neurological side effects, although rare, may include tremors and oral dyskinesia.

SSRIs may cause a 5-HT syndrome as a consequence of 5-HT increase in blood. This syndrome is caused by an increase of 5-HT in the body, and it is characterized by a number of symptoms that may be confused with other side effects commonly seen with drugs inhibiting 5-HT (see table 6.3).

Overall, SSRIs and strong 5-HT inhibitors such as clomipramine are potent drugs that require a prescriber's therapeutic skill. Therefore, these drugs should only be prescribed by psychiatrists, who are acquainted with the use of psychopharmacological agents and specifically trained to prescribe them. In contrast, primary care physicians are limited to general medicine and may lack the knowledge required to handle psychotropics to treat the mentally ill. Perhaps the adverse publicity conveyed by the

TABLE 6.3   Serotonin syndrome symptoms

diaphoresis
nausea / diarrhea
abdominal cramps
hyperflexia
myoclonus
insomnia
psychosis
bleeding
flushing

media is the result of poor medical psychiatric management, considering that primary care physicians prescribe about 50% of all psychotropics.

A closely monitored therapeutic program should pose no serious problems in the hand of the experts.

Other Drugs Used for the Treatment of OCD and Its Spectrum

A coadjuvant drug for the treatment of OCD and its spectrum fulfills several needs: (1) potentiates the action of the primary drug, (2) has anti-obsessive-compulsive action, and (3) works on the OCD subset. Table 6.2 lists common coadjuvant drugs and the usual dose recommended for OCD.

Anxiolytic Agents

Anxiolytic agents have been widely used for the treatment of OCD. Since OCD is considered a clinical form of anxiety, the use of anxiolytic agents was never questioned. Nonetheless, the action of anxiolytics, notably diazepam, on OCD core symptoms is almost nil. Perhaps this is the most important evidence for classifying OCD as an independent disorder.

On the other hand, anxiolytics can be given to control the anxiety caused by compulsions. However, two adverse effects must be kept in mind: (1) diazepam's addictive properties and (2) the onset of aggression after anxiety or "fear" suppression. Further, behavior therapists avoid the use of anxiolytics because they need to work with a certain amount of anxiety to measure expected progress following exposure and response prevention.

The side effects of anxiolytics are abundant and should be considered before placing a patient on medication (see table 6.4)

Anxiolytics to be studied are the benzodiazepines and buspirone.

Benzodiazepines

Benzodiazepines (see table 6.5) mediate the action of GABA, a cerebral inhibitory neurotransmitter, and the participation of the chloride pump in the GABA inhibitory mechanism. One important pharmacokinetic property of the benzodiazepines is their half-life. The half-life indicates how long it takes the drug to be metabolized, and this assists in regulating the duration of drug activity. A long half-life reduces daytime functioning; conversely, a short half-life causes anxiety rebound phenomena between doses and anterograde amnesia. These effects should be considered when selecting a benzodiazepine. Short-acting, high-potency benzodiazepines (e.g., alprazolam) cause interdose rebound and dependency. Conversely, long-acting low-potency benzodiazepines (e.g., diazepam) are preferred for general anxiety.

- *Diazepam* is the most prescribed and most popular benzodiazepine. Structurally related to chlordiazepoxide, it has the advantage of producing direct muscle relaxation. Excessive muscle relaxation may be an unwanted effect in older patients because it may cause weakness of the legs, resulting in falls and injury. Diazepam is prescribed for anxiety in divided doses of 5 to 40 mg/po/day. However, for the treatment of OCD it has been given in doses up to 100 mg/po/day. Nevertheless, diazepam is not an AOCA. Long-term administration may cause aggressive behavior or anger by suppressing fear. Diazepam, a lipophilic (affinity with adipose or fat tissue) substance, gives fast and short relief of anxiety by moving rapidly into fat tissues; less lipophilic drugs (e.g., lorazepam) are slower to act but the action stays longer. Diazepam's half-life is 40 hours.
- *Chlordiazepoxide* is an old anxiolytic of the benzodiazepine family. It is prescribed in doses of 15 to 40 mg/day. Its half-life is 20 hours.
- *Alprazolam* is a high-potency benzodiazepine with a high receptor affinity that together with its short half-life causes many withdrawal side effects. Alprazolam is one of the treatments of choice for controlling panic disorder in OCD. We conducted a comparative study between alprazolam and imipramine, a TCA, in treatment of OCD. Alprazolam was prescribed in divided doses of 0.25 to 4 mg/po/day. Unfortunately, both drugs were equally ineffective. Like any other benzodiazepine, alprazolam may be habit forming and therefore discontinuation should be gradual. Alprazolam's half-life is 14 hours.

TABLE 6.4   Antianxiety agents: common side effects

Antianxiety Agent	Cardio-vascular Effects	Gastro-intestinal Effects	Renal Effects	Sexual Effects	Central and Peripheral Nervous Systems
Benzo-diazepines	dizziness	nausea, urinary retention, decreased appetite, dry mouth	urinary retention, nocturia	decreased sex drive, impotence	blurred vision, diplopia, vertigo, ataxia, nystagmus, dysarthria, sedation, fatigue (daytime), amnesia
buspirone	dizziness	distress			paresthesia, headache, restlessness

TABLE 6.5   Benzodizepines: specific compounds and dosages

Generic Name	Dosage Range (mg/day)	Half-life (hours)
alprazolam	1–4	14
chlordiazepoxide	15–40	20
clonazepam	1–4	18–50
clorazepate	15–60	60
diazepam	5–40	40
halazepam	60–160	60
lorazepam	1–6	1
oxazepam	45–120	9
prazepam	20–60	60

- *Clonazepam* is a benzodiazepine with anticonvulsant and antianxiety activity. It also has a serotonergic effect that makes it distinct from other benzodiazepines. It can be used as the treatment of choice for OCD. In a double-blind study compared to a control group it was effective in reducing OCD symptoms, independently of its anxiolytic action (Hewlett, Vinogradov, & Agras, 1990). Clonazepam is administered in divided doses of 1 to 4 mg/po/day. Clonazepam's half-life is 18 to 50 hours.

- *Clorazepate* is another benzodiazepine of rapid action. We have successfully used it to control OCD anxiety at a dose of 15 to 60 mg/po/day. Clorazapate's half-life is 60 hours.

- *Lorazepam* is another benzodiazepine that has been used to treat OCD. It is available in plasma after two hours of ingestion. Lorazepam exerts a sedative action on the central nervous system without affecting the respiratory and cardiovascular systems. Lorazepam's half-life is 14 hours.

- *Halazepam, oxazepam, and prazepam* are not frequently used in the treatment of OCD in the United States.

Buspirone

Buspirone is a non-benzodiazepine anxiolytic with special properties: It does not cause sedation or motor incoordination, it is compatible with alcohol intake, and the patient does not develop tolerance to it.

The administration of buspirone needs one to two weeks to show therapeutic effect. Dose ranges from 5 to 60 mg/po/day. Although some reports have indicated buspirone as an effective medication for OCD, these reports have not been confirmed yet. Some observations have found buspirone to have no direct action on OCD core symptoms. Its nonaddictive quality makes buspirone a possible alternative to benzodiazepine.

Anticonvulsants

There has been a renewed interest in the use of anticonvulsant medication in psychiatry. These drugs seem to promote mood stabilization and are therefore administered for manic-depressive illness, depression, panic, aggression, and OCD associated with seizures.

It is claimed that OCD is associated with temporal lobe pathology. For instance, temporal-limbic seizure disorder may present itself not only with motor symptoms but also with behavioral symptoms ranging from anxiety to hallucinatory experiences, including hypergraphia, scrupulosity, and some automatic behaviors. Certain types of OCD with seizure components may then respond to a combination of AOCA and anticonvulsants.

Two major anticonvulsants are currently prescribed: clonazepam, already described above, and carbamazepine.

• Carbamazepine is prescribed in divided doses of 200 to 800 mg/po/day. Acceptable serum levels are reached by the first week. High levels of carbamazepine cause diplopia, altered coordination, and sedation. A major concern with the use of carbamazepine is the danger of developing agranulocytosis or aplastic anemia. Periodic monitoring of plasma levels is a must.

Monoamine Oxidase Inhibitors

Monoamine oxidase inhibitors (MAOIs) inhibit enzymes that participate in amine metabolic pathways (see table 6.6). There are two major amine pathways: indolaminergic (serotoninergic) and catecholaminergic (dopamine and norepinephrine). Therefore MAOIs modulate the availability of serotonin and norepinephrine to perform their electrochemical activity (neural impulses).

MAOIs are classified into hydrazines (e.g., isocarboxazid, phenelzine), which irreversibly inhibit MAOIs, and nonhydrazines (e.g., selegiline, tranylcypromine), which reversibly inhibit MAOIs. In the latter, the drug effects begin sooner and end faster. The most important MAOI action is antidepressant. It works in major depression and mostly in atypical depression. Other indications are eating disorders and panic. MAOIs are efficacious in patients with OCD combined with borderline personality or with histrionic traits.

TABLE 6.6   MAOIs: specific compounds and dosages

Generic Name	Usual Therapeutic Dosage (mg/day)
isocarboxazid	30–50
phenelzine	45–90
selegiline	20–50
tranylcypromine	30–50

Reports of using MAOIs as the treatment of choice for OCD are anecdotal and results are equivocal. We have done open studies with tranylcypromine with negative results.

The usual dose for isocarboxazid is 30 to 50 mg/po/day; for phenelzine, 45 to 90 mg/po/day; for selegiline, 20 to 50 mg/po/day; and for tranylcypromine, 30 to 50 mg/po/day. Treatment should start with one 10- or 15-mg tablet a day, increased by slow increments of one tablet daily, until reaching the desired dose. The last tablet should be given before 6 P.M. to prevent insomnia.

MAOIs are potentiated by lithium or tryptophan. Note that in the United States, tryptophan is banned. MAOIs should not be given with other antidepressants or AOCAs, and patients on an MAOI regimen should follow a tyramine-free diet to prevent an arterial hypertensive crisis caused by tyramine augmentation. Foods to avoid are aged cheeses, sausages, fava beans, sauerkraut, red wine, pickled herrings, Chinese and Japanese food, and yeast.

Side effects are numerous (see table 6.7). One major side effect is orthostatic hypotension, which should be taken into account when treating the elderly.

TABLE 6.7　MAOIs: common or troublesome side effects

orthostatic hypertension
hypertensive crises (interactions with foodstuffs or medications)
hyperpyrexic reactions
anorgasmia or sexual impotence
sedation (particularly daytime and due to insomnia during the night)
insomnia during the night
stimulation during the day
muscle cramps and myositis-like reactions
urinary hesitancy
constipation
dry mouth
weight gain
myoclonic twitches

Antidepressants

Classic antidepressants include the tricyclic antidepressants (TCAs) and related tetracyclics, and the monoamine oxidase inhibitors (see above). These drugs are amitriptyline, clomipramine, desipramine, doxepine, imipramine, protriptyline, and trimipramine. The tretracyclics are amoxapine and maproptiline. These antidepressants work by blocking the effects of serotonin and norepinephrine, two major neurotransmitters.

New chemical structures include SSRIs (already discussed in this chapter), trazodone, bupropion, and venlafaxine. These medications might be

TABLE 6.8   TCAs: common side effects

Mechanism of Action	Side Effects
antimuscarinic	blurred vision, dry mouth, tachycardia, constipation, urinary retention or hesitancy
antihistaminic	sedation
antiadrenergic	orthostatic hypotension
reuptake inhibition	serotonergic/ catecholinergic
quinidine-like action	sinus tachycardia, supraventricular tachyarrhythmias, ventricular tachycardia, prolongation of PR, QRS, and QT intervals, bundle branch block, first-, second-, and third-degree heart block, ST and T wave changes

effective in certain cases of OCD and its spectrum, but they cannot replace the action of the AOCAs. Imipramine, a TCA used for the treatment of OCD, is significantly less effective than clomipramine. Because of their action on the histaminic, cholinergic, and monoamine systems, TCA side effects are very common and many times troublesome (see table 6.8)

Stimulants

Three major drugs show evidence as stimulants of the central nervous system: d-amphetamine, methylphenidate, and magnesium pemoline. In the 1930s, amphetamines were used for OCD with negligible effects. These trials tested the association between OCD and attention-deficit/hyperactivity disorder (ADHD) in a group of patients with OCD and ADHD history and/or symptoms. Magnesium pemoline has also been tried with OCD-ADHD disorder without conclusive benefits.

One other stimulant that has gained some attention and that has been reported to improve OCD is fenfluramine, a serotonergic agent with appetite suppressant qualities.

Lithium

Lithium, a drug usually prescribed for bipolar disorder and aggressive behavior, seems to potentiate AOCA action. The dose prescribed is about 300 mg/po/day in combination with an AOCA.

Lithium is also effective in the OCD manic-depressive subset. In these patients a cyclic obsession-mania rhythm ensues. This syndrome is difficult to control and sometimes hides behind a "mind racing" facade, which is usually ignored by the patient unless elicited during the exam. The major clinical characteristic is that obsessions are replaced by a hypomanic or manic phase. The treatment of this syndrome with only an AOCA is prone to failure. The ideal treatment requires additional lithium to control the manic phase. The combination of both an AOCA and lithium results in less dosage.

Tryptophan

Tryptophan (TRY) is an essential amino acid precursor of serotonin. After ingestion, TRY follows two main metabolic routes: the kynurenic pathway to become niacin (60 to 75%) or the indolaminergic pathway to become serotonin (5%).

In the early 1970s, we introduced TRY, following an open uncontrolled study, for the treatment of OCD. This was the first time an amino acid had been utilized for OCD treatment. The results were satisfactory in about 30% of the patients. Combining TRY and clomipramine permitted a decrease in the dosage of clomipramine and, therefore, fewer side effects. Concomitantly, TRY began to be used for insomnia and major depression.

Side effects are: nausea, drowsiness, headaches, sleepiness, aggressive behavior, paranoid symptoms, and the potentially fatal eosinophilia myalgia syndrome (EMS). In 1990, the United States banned the use of TRY after it caused EMS; it should be clarified, however, that the syndrome was the result of a contaminated batch of TRY sold by the manufacturer.

TRY should not be given in combination with SSRIs because it may cause hyperreflexia, myoclonic jerks, tremors, and confusion, suggestive of a serotonergic syndrome.

The dose of TRY ranges from 3 to 9 gm/po/day. It should be administered away from other proteins to permit an easier absorption. Since glucose facilitates TRY cerebral penetration, orange juice might be helpful for TRY absorption.

Antipsychotics

The antipsychotics are drugs with well-defined action in thought disorders accompanied by dysperception, altered judgment, and loss of insight. In the 1950s, antipsychotics were defined as neuroleptics (a definition still in use). A neuroleptic definition is based in five criteria: (1) depressant activity, (2) inhibitory action on psychomotor ecxitation, (3) therapeutic action on psychosis, (4) inductor of extrapyramidal effects, and (5) dominance over subcortical centers.

These drugs are chemically classified as: phenothiazines, thioxanthenes, dibenzazepines, butyrophenones, and indoles. The main characteristic of these agents is to control delusional thoughts and hallucinations. These clinical effects are related to their dopamine-2 blocking activity.

All of the antipsychotics, with the exception of clozapine and risperidone, act in the nigrostriatal system, lowering the levels of dopamine. The nigrostriatal system modulates motor activity, thus, dopamine blockage will cause drug-induced parkinsonism. A putative anatomical loop linking fronto-temporal-basal ganglia regions suggests antipsychotics may exert a therapeutic action in a segment of OCD phenomenology. For example, pimozide has been proved effective in the treatment of Gilles de la Tourette Syndrome, body dysmorphic disorder, and delusional hypochondriasis.

Untoward effects cause sedation, autonomous nervous system disturbances, endocrine effects, skin reactions, ocular complications, hematological changes, and neurological disorders (see table 6.9).

TABLE 6.9   Antipsychotics: common side effects

sedation
fatigue
dry mouth
constipation
photosensitivity
galactorrhea
dystonia
pseudo parkinsonism
akathisia

Before AOCAs became available, antipsychotics were used for OCD treatment. Studies were uncontrolled, lacking documentation about reliability and diagnostic guidelines consensus. Therefore, their therapeutic use in OCD was inconclusive.

In Tourette's syndrome, an OCD-associated disorder, haloperidol and pimozide have shown efficacy. Recently, it has been reported that clozapine and risperidone may be helpful in the treatment of OCD with schizotypal, paranoid, or schizophrenic symptomatology.

Anticholinergics

Anticholinergic agents (ACAs) are used to counteract the side effects of neuroleptics. They include, for example, biperiden (Akineton), trihexyphenidyl (Artane), and benztropine (Cogentin).

Hypnotics

Although insomnia is uncommon in OCD, in OCD with comorbidity (e.g., with major depression), it may not be. Many patients complain of difficulty falling asleep or remaining asleep. However, careful inquiry may show that patients sleep most of the time. A relative or friend should be asked to stay with the patient and witness the sleep pattern.

Several types of hypnotics are used: hypnotic benzodiazepines, barbiturates, nonbarbiturate hypnotics, sedative antihistamines, l-tryptophan, and melatonin.

The most prescribed hypnotics are the hypnotic benzodiazepines, while the least used are the barbiturates. Hypnotics should be prescribed for brief periods of time because they become addictive.

Treatment Algorithms

Although we believe each patient is an individual, with distinctive characteristics and an exclusive biochemical profile, the concept of treatment algorithms should discussed.

A treatment algorithm is a mathematical model designed to medicate the patient on a trial and error basis, and in a progressive manner. An algorithm is a revolutionary way to treat the mentally ill, by considering many variables that can be computerized, singled out, and treated. Algorithm

TABLE 6.10

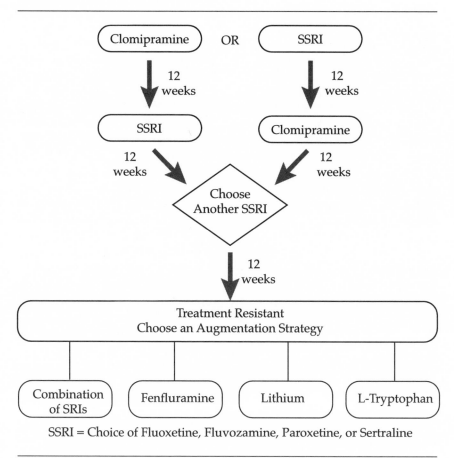

SSRI = Choice of Fluoxetine, Fluvozamine, Paroxetine, or Sertraline

treatment ignores the patient as an individual and puts him or her in an amorphous category; it bypasses biopsychosocial individuality to treat the patient as a consumer. Certainly, this treatment approach deserves analysis before its acceptance or rejection. Treatment algorithms provoke a certain degree of emotional and rational conflict by compartmentalizing the patient's illness to strict pharmacological and behavioral parameters, dichotomizing the patient from a biopsychosocial approach, which tends to integrate rather than separate. Table 6.10 is an example of an algorithm designed using a pharmacobehavioral approach.

Side Effects

Medication side effects (MSE) cause various degrees of discomfort and concern. The onset of side effects brings into focus a new cluster of symptoms or, if you will, a "new disease." Therefore, in addition to OCD symptoms, MSE control should also be addressed and may, in fact, require other medication (see table 6.11). Adverse effects are one of the major causes of noncompliance. However, patients with OCD tolerate, rather stoically, MSE as long as they notice improvement. On the other hand, patients with OCD with phobic components, panic, borderline traits, hypochondriasis, body dysmorphic disorder, or severe anxiety components are very frightened of being harmed by medication and either will refuse to take medication or stop treatment as soon as they feel any minor unusual physical sign departing from the norm.

It is important to discuss with patients and relatives forming the supportive network the possibilities of developing MSE. There are three medical side effects about which patients feel very strongly: weight gain, sexual dysfunction, and the feeling of being drugged. There is a group of neuropsychiatric MSE to be kept in mind by practitioners: anxiety, tremors, insomnia, akathisia, psychosis, and OCD worsening.

Avoiding MSE is an important therapeutic issue. Each patient has a unique biochemical profile that will distinctly interact with the drug, which makes it difficult to predict with certainty what side effects she may develop. However, knowing the biopsychosocial constitution of the patient and the major biochemical actions of the medicines in the bodily system may help. Keep in mind, too, that patients who have personality disorders, those who suffer from autonomous nervous system imbalance, or anyone presenting any other major medical illness may react to the given drug in a different fashion. This illustrates the need for a complete mental and physical exam.

TABLE 6.11   Medications for the side effects of antipsychotics

Generic Name	Brand Name	Formulations	Dosage Range (mg/day)
Primarily anticholinergic			
benztropine	Cogentin	tablet: 1, 2 mg parenteral: 1 mg/ml (2-ml ampule)	2–6
biperiden	Akineton	tablet: 2 mg parenteral: 5 mg/ml (1-ml ampule)	2–8
diphenhydramine	Benadryl	capsule: 25, 50 mg elixir: 12.5 mg, 5 ml (4-oz/16-oz bottle) parenteral: 10 mg/ml (10-ml/30-ml vial, 1-ml ampule)	50–300
ethopropazine	Parsidol	tablet: 10, 50 mg	100–400
procyclidine	Kemadrin	tablet: 5 mg	10–20
trihexyphenidyl	Artane	tablet: 2, 5 mg sequels: 5-mg capsule	4–15
Dopaminergic			
amantadine	Symmetrel	capsule: 100 mg syrup: 50 mg, 5 ml	100–300

Biochemical Actions

MSE are the consequence of the interaction between neurotransmitters affected by the medication and their receptor site. The main neurotransmitters affected are norepinephrine, 5-HT, dopamine, histamine, and acetylcholine. AOCAs have different kinds of affinity for neurotransmitter receptors. This affinity is determined by the drug potency.

Presynaptic (see table 6.12) or postsynaptic (see table 6.13) receptor blockade produces sequels, that is objective and subjective physical signs or symptoms manifested as MSE.

By knowing the interaction between drugs, neurotransmitters, receptors, and the site of action, the practitioner will be able to prescribe a priori and with some degree of accuracy the medicine that will cause less MSE to a given patient.

Most side effects occur at the beginning of treatment and slowly abate as the body adjusts to the substance. One way to bypass MSE is to administer the medication in small doses with gradual increments and with the largest dose given at bedtime. By giving the larger dose at night, higher drug levels will be reached while the patient is asleep. In this manner, if side effects occur, their intensity may go unnoticed or be more tolerable. When medicating, the physician should take into account that the circadian rhythm might be altered in certain pathologies, including OCD. For example, many patients with OCD report an increase in obsessionality toward evening, when the blood contains the lowest tryptophan levels; therefore, a larger nighttime dose seems justifiable. Nonetheless, as previously stated, we still favor a t.i.d dose.

Side Effects

The following is a detailed list of the most common side effects of AOCAs.

Drowsiness

Drowsiness is a very common MSE observed at the beginning of treatment. It takes a few days for the body to adjust to the AOCA; at that point drowsiness will disappear. An increase of the dose may also cause drowsiness, in which case the dose must be decreased.

Dry Mouth

Dry mouth is a very uncomfortable side effect; if severe, it may affect the normal speech flow. Patients who use speaking as part of their trade resent this MSE. Dry mouth represents a reduction of water in the tissues. Similar conditions are seen in dry skin and in constipation, a result of anticholinergic activity.

Relief can be found in taking small, frequent sips of water and chewing gum. In severe cases artificial saliva or urocholine can be prescribed.

Nausea

Nausea can be prevented by taking the medication after a meal.

TABLE 6.12   Sequelae of presynaptic neurotransmitter reuptake blockade

Neurotransmitter	Effects of Blockade
norepinephrine	• tachycardia • tremors
serotonin	• GI disturbance • sexual dysfunction
dopamine	• psychomotor activation • aggravation of psychosis

TABLE 6.13   Sequelae of postsynaptic neurotransmitter receptor blockade

Receptor	Effects of Blockade
histaminergic (H_1)	• sedation • weight gain
muscarinic	• dry mouth • constipation • memory impairment
adrenergic (a_1)	• orthostatic hypotension
adrenergic (a_2)	• blockade of antihypertensive effects: clonidine, guanabenz, a-methyldopa, guanfacine • priapism
dopaminergic (D_2)	• extrapyramidal effects • galactorrhea
serotonergic (5-HT_2)	• ejaculatory dysfunction • hypotension • alleviation of migraines

Abdominal Disturbances

Three major symptoms dominate gastroenterological MSE: epigastralgia, intestinal colics, and generalized abdominal discomfort. Patients may complain of diarrhea or constipation. Irritable bowel syndrome has been reported; AOCAs may precipitate, aggravate, or cause this condition.

Medications that will relieve abdominal disturbances include antispasmodics with an atropine base, phenobarbital, librax, and stool softeners. Appropriate diets should also be suggested: for diarrhea, a diet based on boiled rice, cheese, toast, bananas, apple sauce, and tea may suffice; for constipation, high amounts of fiber, fruits, and yogurt may restore intestinal motility and increase water concentration—overall, the best diet for constipation is vegetarian.

Blurred Vision

Blurred vision is caused by the loss of the lens's ability to focus, a direct consequence of oculomotor impairment. This MSE is caused by anticholinergic medications (e.g., Cogentin), which are given to counteract parkinsonian side effects. It is advisable for patients on psychotropics to let their ophthalmologist know what medication they are taking.

Glaucoma

Some antidepressants may aggravate narrow angle glaucoma.

Delayed Urination

Some patients complain of voiding difficulties. If the symptom is severe, urine retention may cause urinary infections. Patients may need catheterization. Incomplete emptying of the bladder forces the patient to go to the bathroom many times during the day, and it may also interrupt what otherwise would be a restful sleep. Delayed urination seen in patients with prostate pathology may worsen during the administration of an AOCA.

Menstrual Changes

The menstrual cycle is usually unaffected by AOCAs. In OCD treated with neuroleptic medication, dysmenorrhea or amenorrhea may be reported. Patients with OCD and concomitant severe anxiety or panic may complain of menstrual dysfunction as a secondary symptom. Discontinuing the medication restores the menstrual cycle.

Lactation

Prolactin augmentation, which causes lactation, is a rare side effect of AOCAs. Prolactin blockage is a function of neuroleptic medication and, to a lesser degree, of TCAs. This neurohormonal MSE may cause gyneco-mastia in males.

Weight Changes

One of the most unacceptable MSEs for female patients is weight gain. AOCAs, neuroleptics, and lithium can all cause it. Patients usually gain about three to four pounds. This increase can be controlled by food volume reduction and cardiovascular exercise, such as low-impact aerobics. Anorexigenic medications (e.g., amphetamine, dextrofenfluramine, penthermine) should be avoided, since they may also cause anxiety, irritability, anger, increased motor activity, and dysperception.

Patients voice three major complaints: "I gain weight without eating," "I'm always hungry," and "I have developed a craving for sweets." Several hypothetical mechanisms have been proposed to explain weight gain: (1) slow metabolism, (2) a decrease of depressive symptoms followed by appetite increase, (3) a dysregulation of the glucose hypothalamic center, requiring extra glucose, and (4) an increase of glucose consumption as the result of a faster tryptophan turnover into 5-HT.

The phenomenologies of OCD, anxiety, and depression intertwine with eating behaviors. Compulsive eating, loss of appetite (e.g., depression), appetite increase (anxiety), and a compulsion not to eat (e.g., primary anorexia nervosa) reflect the precipitating factors for some eating disorders. An indirect factor that prevents patients from eating properly is fear of food contamination, fear of handling food, fear of chewing or swallowing, fear of handling knives, and fear of eating in front of others at home or in public places.

Clomipramine seems to be the drug causing most of the weight gain observed, while SSRIs in larger doses may have an anorectic function.

Cardiovascular Changes

The most common side effect is blood pressure changes, either hypotension (e.g., with TCAs, neuroleptics) or hypertension (e.g., with venlafaxine, MAOIs). Postural hypotension may be minimized by avoiding fast postural changes. Patients on MAOIs may suffer from hypertensive crises, sometimes produced by the patient's failure to follow a low monoamine diet.

Antidepressants may cause tachycardia, extrasystoles, and conduction disturbances. TCAs may also deposit in the myocardium, causing conduction disturbances. Pimozide (Orap), a potent neuroleptic, may produce an increase of the Q-T segment in the electrocardiogram that if prolonged enough may cause cardiac arrest. Thioridazine, another neuro-leptic, causes cardiac dysrhythmia. Periodic electrocardiograms (EKGs) and vital signs recording help to monitor cardiac events.

Allergic Reactions

Most psychotropic allergic reactions are skin-related and thus easily detectable. Rashes and itching are two common complaints. Occasionally, allergies produce skin or gastrointestinal hives. Complaints of diarrhea may be a sign of intestinal allergic hives.

Treatment may need to be discontinued if symptoms are intense; over-all medication-lowering is ineffective. Antiallergic medication has only a relief effect.

Sexual Dysfunction

A variety of sexual disturbances may appear during psychotropic therapy. Anxiolytics and sedative neuroleptics may decrease sexual libido or inhibit female and male orgasm. One neuroleptic in particular, thiori-dazine, may cause delayed ejaculation. TCAs may cause loss of sexual desire, anorgasmia, delayed or inhibited ejaculation, and retrograde ejac-ulation. Similar MSEs are caused by SSRIs. A rare MSE is priapism, which can be caused by trazodone. Priapism is a continuous and painful erection that may require surgery.

Because sexual dysfunction may be present as part of OCD's cohort of symptoms, sexual side effects should be discussed with the patient before therapy initiation.

Sleep Disorders

Disorders of the sleep, either insomnia or hypersomnia, may be produced by AOCAs, SSRIs, sedative antipsychotics (e.g., chlorpromazine), or anxi-olytics.

Sleep disorders are uncommon to OCD symptomatology, but the possi-bilities of concomitant sleep pathology should be ruled out.

Sleep disturbances, particularly insomnia, are very annoying to the patient. Before making a diagnosis of insomnia, the practitioner should rule out "inability to sleep due to severe obsessionality" and the "no need to sleep" manifested in the manic state. AOCAs may produce insomnia or hypersomnia.

Insomnia appears in different forms: as the inability to fall asleep, fre-quent awakening interruptions, and the inability to fall asleep again after early awakening.

Sleeping medications are effective for about ten days, then seem to lose efficacy. Sudden discontinuation of hypnotics is inadvisable because of withdrawal side effects. Hypnotic substitutes are hypnotic-sedatives (e.g., diazepam), tryptophan in a 1- to 2-gm dose; trazodone, 75 to 150 mg/po at bedtime; diphenhydramine, 25 to 50 mg/po at bedtime; and phenergan 12.5 mg/po at bedtime.

Sleep pattern disorders are not necessarily a MSE. They can be part of the OCD spectrum pathology. For instance, hypersomnia may also be reported by patients with OCD and a strong depressive component. Some AOCAs, neuroleptics, and large amounts of anxiolytics may induce hypersomnia as well.

Some patients with OCD present a reversal sleep pattern. These patients sleep only during daytime. To correct this circadian rhythm alteration seems difficult. We are currently using melatonin 3 mg/po at bedtime, but results are anecdotal.

Loss of Balance

High doses of antidepressants (imipramine 300 mg/day), diazepam in the elderly, phenytoin (900 mg/day), and drugs causing hypotension may cause loss of balance. Loss of balance might be manifested not only by falls, but also by the inability to hold a steady gait, by being accident prone, or by bumping into objects. These masked manifestations of loss of balance are quite important and they should be noticed by an inquisitive observer.

Psychiatric Side Effects

Ironically, medications designed to improve mental disorders may cause psychiatric side effects. It is important to remember this if patients suffer from an aggravation of symptoms without apparent reason.

Nervousness, jitteriness, jumpiness, and restlessness indicate cortical hyperexcitability or CNS overstimulation. For OCD treatment, both excitatory and inhibitory medications are used. AOCAs, stimulants, and MAOIs have stimulant effects, mainly those acting on the catecholaminergic system, that is, the dopamine pathway. In fact, overstimulation may cause racing of the mind, hypomania, and in some instances precipitate a dormant OCD bipolar disorder subset. The addition of a benzodiazepine may bring the situation under control.

Anxiety has also been reported as a side effect. Because anxiety is a major secondary symptom of OCD, anxiety as an MSE may aggravate the condition. Clomipramine has been reported to cause paradoxical anxiety.

Anxiety can also be aggravated by exposure and prevention techniques. This anxiety is desirable when training the patient to handle the fearful stimulus. Anxiety control includes the use of benzodiazepines or buspirone.

Conversely, some drugs, such as benzodiazepines, sedative neuroleptics, and trazodone, may sedate in excess. Trazodone, although rather ineffective for OCD, has a great calming property that in high doses prevents its use during daytime. L-tryptophan has sedative properties that may interfere with daily activities if it is taken in large doses and without medical supervision.

Anger may be caused by the administration of benzodiazepines, MAOIs, and psychostimulants. Benzodiazepines, by removing or increasing the fear threshold, may release objective anger or aggressive behavior. Overall, substances that increase the brain's 5-HT concentration have a sedative action, while substances acting on norepinephrine may produce anger.

Neurological Symptoms

Neurological MSEs are common features of psychotropic medication. Major untoward effects are tremors, akathisia, oral dyskinesia, muscle rigidity, and loss of balance. These MSEs can be placed under the umbrella of drug-induced extrapyramidal syndrome (EPS). These MSEs are caused by a loss of equilibrium in the dopamine-acetylcholine ratio. Neuroleptics, in particular, cause EPS. AOCAs do not cause EPS, but they may cause tremor, akathisia, and oral dyskinesia. Tremor, with different degrees of intensity and frequency, is caused by all AOCAs. SSRIs have been reported to produce akathisia.

Serotinin Syndrome

The serotonin (5-HT) syndrome is the response to an increased level of 5-HT that exceeds the therapeutic needs. These side effects cause symptoms that affect different organs with varying results (see table 6.3, p. 107).

The Cytochrome P450 System

The cytochrome P450 system (CP450) is a family of more than 30 related enzymes that participate in the oxidative metabolism of different types of drugs, including psychotropics. The CP450 is mostly located in the hepatocite, the functional cell of the liver. CP450 activity may affect drug interaction by metabolizing most psychotropic substances. Conversely, some psychotropics may inhibit some of the enzymes of the CP450. As a result the prescriber has to be aware that combining two or more medications may cause undesirable high levels of the drug in plasma. Higher plasma concentration may produce MSEs or toxicity. Therefore, it is advisable to be aware of drug interactions and of the presence of CP450.

Electroshock

The use of electroshock therapy (ECT) for OCD was common before the introduction of AOCAs. Positive results were anecdotal and based on a paucity of data. ECT is primarily effective in agitated depression and may be indicated in refractory cases of OCD with agitated depression. Nonetheless, ECT efficacy is transient. Our personal experience with over 2,000 cases of OCD indicates that patients treated with ECT do not show improvement.

Neurosurgery

Neurosurgical intervention for psychiatric disorders is applied in refractory cases. There are several guidelines to help determine the eligibility of the patient for neurosurgery. These include failure to respond to pharmacotherapy or intensive behavior therapy, intense and severe symptomatology, and serious disability.

Surgical techniques include: anterior cingulotomy, subcaudate tractotomy, limbic leukotomy, anterior capsulotomy, thermocapsulotomy, and gamma capsulotomy. Overall, neurosurgery works on putative neuroanatomical pathways associated OCD pathological mechanisms. These circuits connect the orbitofrontal areas, the cingulum, the basal ganglia, and the limbic system.

During the 1970s and 1980s a surge of neurosurgery for OCD took place. However, the lack of adequately controlled studies to monitor diagnostic uniformity and follow-up procedures weakens the results reported. A high incidence of side effects, namely seizures and personality changes, and the great number of relapses made these procedures unfavorable. Moreover, ethical issues and societal pressure against neurosurgery slowed the interest in the use of this technique for OCD treatment (Yaryura-Tobias & Neziroglu, 1983).

Currently, new interest in neurosurgery is developing (Chiocca & Martuza, 1990). One major problem of neurosurgery for OCD is the lack of long-term improvement and the presence of subsequent depression, due either to a postsurgical syndrome or the frustration with unsatisfactory results.

Conclusion

Pharmacotherapy plays a prevalent role in the treatment of OCD. This role has been expanded by the addition of comorbid and associated conditions that also seem to respond to some form of drug therapy. The mixture of symptoms of different conditions in a single patient demands good therapeutic, diagnostic, and prescriptive skills. Two major issues are of high in priority when treating a patient: the choice of the right medication and the avoidance of side effects. Practical knowledge of brain anatomy, physiology, and fuctioning, as well as the ways in which drugs interact with the brain, will help you choose the right medication. Novel AOCAs (e.g., citalopram) and the SSRIs have added options to the traditional treatment armamentarium. Because SSRIs do not act the same way in all patients, the patient's biochemical profile must be considered. It may take several months to find the right treatment combination.

Pharmacotherapy is enhanced by the addition of vitamins as coenzymes and as radical scavengers (e.g., ascorbic acid, vitamin E). The patient should also adhere to a balanced diet and keep excessive body fat to a minimum to discourage certain medicines from being stored in fatty tissue, instead of working at the brain sites. An individual with good liver and kidney function will be able to metabolize and distribute the medication properly, favoring the therapeutic response. Finally, a careful explanation of drug therapy to the potential patient will go a long way toward preventing noncompliance.

7

Pharmacotherapy for Special Groups

INVESTIGATIONAL DRUG TRIALS are geared to four basic groups: adults, elderly, children, and adolescents. Most of the research is performed on adults, because they constitute less of a risk. The knowledge accumulated in these trials is applied when suitable to children and adolescents, elderly, pregnant women, patients with seizure disorders, and the mentally retarded. These special groups may present clinical characteristics constituting medical risks or ethical problems that often exclude them from experimental trials. As a result, patients with brain injury or mental retardation and pregnant patients in need of drug therapy may suffer from the lack of information needed to resolve therapeutic issues.

Children and Adolescents

Psychopharmacological treatment of children and adolescents requires special attention to physical and physiological development from birth to adulthood. The body, including the brain, grows mostly before the age of 20. There is also a gradual maturation of the physiological system as a consequence of hormonal growth and the development of the biochemical profile. Therefore, children and adolescents can be conceptualized as distinct clinical entities with a specific biopsychosocial pattern that is dynamic—in constant flux.

Diagnostic accuracy is difficult with this group because the mental pathology emerges during the neurodevelopmental process. During this process the personality of the child develops, and the child must also learn to adjust to the external environment. This is followed by adolescence, which brings further emotional changes toward maturation. The adolescent male or female must also react to and establish a balance with the external world. These changes are part of the growth process. In addition, comorbidity may pose further complications and hinder the determination of a proper diagnosis.

Children and adolescents are usually brought for diagnosis and treatment against their will. Parents and teachers are the ones who make the decision, often based on an unmanageable behavioral problem, which may reflect an underlying major psychiatric disorder frequently seen in childhood and adolescent OCD. This regrettable circumstance, in which the child has no say, creates an environment of subtle rejection toward the examiner. Examination and treatment refusal is a fundamental issue to address with the child. In-depth discussions with the patient and parents about the illness and the treatment, as well as giving them psychoeducational material to read, will foster cooperation and adherence to treatment.

Treatment Response

The main concern in child psychopharmacotherapy is the paucity of information about long-term monitoring of brain activity, sexual development, physical growth, behavior, or physical health in general. Fortunately, children tolerate drugs well, because their livers are able to efficiently metabolize those agents. The kidney also metabolizes medications, but to a lesser degree, as well as lithium.

Pharmacokinetics, that is, the passage of a drug through the human system, does not greatly differ between adults and children and adolescents; the same five basic functions regulate drug mechanisms: (1) absorption, (2) distribution, (3) metabolism, (4) storage, and (5) excretion. The normal performance of these functions is important for treatment response.

Treatment response may be jeopardized by a drug paradoxical response, that is, a drug reaction that is opposite to that anticipated for a specific disorder. Classic examples of a paradoxical response in children are barbiturates causing agitation, and stimulants (e.g., methylphenidate) causing sedation. Partial or selective 5-HT inhibitors rarely cause a paradoxical response, but physicians should be aware of the possibility.

Parents naturally resist authorizing the use of psychotropics in their children. In addition, FDA approval for drug use in children is not easy to obtain, since studies in adults cannot substitute for direct studies in children. These factors slow medication research in children and adolescents, making few drugs available for treatment. Consequently, before administering drugs to a child, other options should be considered, including behavior therapy.

Drug Doses

Under ideal circumstances, dosages of medications for children should be extracted from trials performed in children, rather than extrapolating adult data. Nonetheless, as in adults, treatment should be started with small doses, adjusted for weight. Once puberty is reached, drug metabolism is similar to that seen in young adults.

Psychotropic medications are highly lipophilic; therefore, fat content modifies drug deposit. At age 1, children have a high fat content, which gradually decreases until the prepuberal stage, when it increases. Liver functioning is also extremely influential in drug metabolism. Hepatic enzyme activity is fully developed by age 1. Furthermore, children's livers are proportionately larger than adults', causing drugs to clear faster. Table 7.1 lists suggested drug dosages of selected medications for children.

Because children metabolize and excrete medications quickly, medication must be given at regular intervals to maintain appropriate drug plasma levels so that withdrawal side effects do not occur. Common side effects are nausea, headaches, irritability, hyperactivity, and myalgia. The physician should determine how fast, after the last dose, those symptoms are experienced. Ideally, the dosage should be distributed throughout the day, rather than one single dose at nighttime. In children and adolescents, the occurrence of OCD with comorbid conditions, such as major depression, Tourette's syndrome, anxiety disorder, attention deficit disorder with or without hyperactivity, bipolar disorder, self-mutilation, body dysmorphic disorder, or eating disorders, requires further strategies to outline a therapeutic program. This medication program may include more than

Table 7.1   Suggested dosages of selected medications for children

Generic Name	Dosage Range*
clomipramine	up to 3 mg/kg/day
diazepam	1–6 mg/day
fluvoxamine	50–200 mg/day
haloperidol	0.5–3 mg/day
imipramine	0.3–2.5 mg/kg/day
pimozide	2–10 mg/day
phenytoin	5 mg/kg/day

* Medication should be administered in divided doses.

one drug, and therefore the possibilities of a negative drug interaction and side effects should be appraised.

Anti-Obsessive-Compulsive Agents

OCD in children has been treated with clomipramine (CMI) and SSRIs. Controlled studies have been done with CMI, fluoxetine, sertraline, and fluvoxamine. Several double blind placebo controlled studies with CMI confirmed its efficacy in doses averaging 140 mg/po/day, or 3 mg/kgm/body weight/day (Clomipramine Collaborative Study Group, 1991; Yaryura-Tobias, Neziruglu, & Bergman, 1976). Double blind, crossover trials of fluoxetine and placebo yield efficacy with a fixed dose of 20 mg/po/day (Grady et al., 1993). A study by Mallya and others (1992) indicates that fluvoxamine in doses averaging 200 mg/po/day relieve OCD symptomatology. The doses given to children are different from adults; doses given to adolescents are closer to the adult doses. However, we recommend starting with a very small dose for children and adolescents alike.

Treatment of OCD and Comorbid Disorders

Anxiety Disorders

Anxiety, separation anxiety, school phobia, and panic with agoraphobia are common disorders that may emerge in childhood OCD. The treatment of choice is cognitive-behavior therapy, with family participation, followed by AOCAs and, if needed, anxiolytics or antihistamines. Diazepam, which is useful in anxiety, has a 10- to 17-hour half-life in children, not as long as in adults. Diphenhydramine and hydroxyzine at 5 mg/kg/day are useful for anxiety and insomnia. Alprazolam is good for panic in divided doses not to exceed 2 mg/day. Imipramine has also been widely used to treat panic, in doses of 50 to 150 mg/po/day. Other TCAs and SSRIs have also been used with apparently good results.

TCAs may affect cardiac conduction, and children should have a baseline EKG before starting therapy. There are reports of imipramine-induced arterial hypertension. Finally, it has been reported in animal experimentation that TCAs may deposit in the cardiac muscle. The practitioner should think twice before giving TCAs to children for a long period of time. Periodic electrocardiograms are a good safety measure.

Affective Disorders

OCD may present collateral manifestations of depression. Depression in OCD may be a response to the inability to function or to biochemical changes. In depressed children, major depression and dysthymic disorder are more common than bipolar disorder, which may develop in early adolescence, sometimes with OCD comorbidity. In both cases, depression must be addressed and treated accordingly. Since AOCAs are used as antidepressants as well, the treatment may be easy to follow. TCAs and SSRIs are the treatment for major depression. For bipolar disorder in children age 6 to 12 years old, lithium 900 mg/day or carbamazepine 100 mg b.i.d. with gradual increments up to 800 mg in divided doses is the treatment of choice. Valproic acid, although effective in bipolar disorder, in children has a risk factor for hepatoxicity.

Attention-Deficit/Hyperactivity Disorder

Twenty-five percent of children with OCD present a history of attention-deficit disorder with or without hyperactivity. Evaluation of past medical history may elicit clinical or subclinical encephalitis. Clinical encephalitis is an inflammation of the brain caused by bacteria or a virus. Sometimes the symptoms of encephalitis are atypical and can imitate flu symptoms. Other times the encephalitis is accompanied by intense fever, vomiting, asthenia, headaches, and general malaise of a few days' duration. Other types of encephalitis are subclinical. Childhood encephalitis can be followed, early in life, by behavioral changes, hyperactivity, aggression, and obsessive-compulsive symptoms. Later in life, it may evolve into Parkinson's syndrome. Comorbid conditions of ADHD are Tourette's syndrome and partial seizure disorder. These elements should be considered when contemplating treatment choice. The most widely used medication for ADHD is methylphenidate, but amphetamines and magnesium pemoline are also prescribed. There have been reports indicating that vitamins (e.g., pyridoxine, B-complex) and a diet low in psychostimulant foods are helpful. Psychostimulant foods include coffee, chocolates, industrialized sugars (e.g., candies, cakes, ice creams, etc.), and foods rich in tyramine content (see diet for MAOIs in chapter 6).

Psychosis

Psychosis has not been reported in children suffering from OCD. However, schizophrenic-like symptomatology can be observed in adolescents with OCD. This symptomatology may be expressed as paranoid or catatonic features, which suggest the need to consider adding antipsychotics in the regimen. The combination of Tourette's syndrome and OCD may require the use of haloperidol or pimozide. Both are antipsychotic and are reported to be effective. Haloperidol may affect growth and cause cognitive impairment. Pimozide may cause tardive dyskinesia and cardiac conduction disorder.

Geriatric Population

The elderly undergo a process of biological changes with the passing of the years. We establish age 40 as marking the onset of senescence. However, the biological clock is modified by variables (e.g., lifestyle) that make individuals age at different rates. With aging, certain life parameters become prominent: fear, sadness, and the loss of hope. People fear illness, the proximity to death, the loss of loved ones, and most importantly, social rejection. Dreams no longer reachable push the individual to a state of final waiting: the end of the life cycle. "Normal" cognitive impairment adds insult to the psychological injury. Although not everyone shares such fears, beliefs, and attitudes, they ought to be considered when a mental disorder appears. In addition, the body's regulatory mechanisms undergo changes, affecting its physiology and subsequently drug intake. Finally, the prevalence of medical conditions at this age interacts with the administration of psychiatric drugs via the pathology of the illness (e.g., heart failure) and the specific medication for that illness (e.g., digitalis). The aging process also affects certain organs and related functions utilized to metabolize medicines.

The prescriber needs to be aware of the changes in the geriatric patient's physiology:

- reduction in liver metabolism
- reduction in kidney metabolism
- changes in the cardiovascular system (circulation, oxygenation)
- decreased serum proteins (increases free drug concentration)
- decreased dopaminic receptors
- decreased muscarinic receptors
- general decrease of cerebral monoamine activity
- decreased consumption of cerebral oxygen and glucose
- neuronal loss and decrease in brain volume
- decreased intestinal motility
- decreased gastric pH

These factors cause an increase of drug levels in the system, affecting its metabolism and producing toxicity. Adverse drug effects also increase with age in about 30% of the population. Therefore, the prescriber needs to judge with caution whether the patient must take medication, and if so, provide close supervision.

OCD usually develops during childhood and younger years (before age 24), yet a latent form of OCD has been observed in the older groups. There are two types of this form of OCD: the classical clinical syndrome and the organic type, based in anatomical structural changes.

The classical OCD form is medicated, applying the adult outline. Nonetheless, a few facts regarding dosage must be considered. For instance, the older the patient the smaller the medication dose. Clomipramine may be considered a second choice due to its cardiovascular side effects (electrocardiographic changes, hypotension) and its anticholinergic activity. Conversely, SSRIs are free from those side effects, but the possibility of neurological or mental side effects calls for close monitoring—patients may complain of tremors, akathisia, confusion, and even psychosis.

OCD with structural organic changes needs a more complicated program. Patients' symptoms resemble the mental, emotional, and behavioral symptoms observed in the organic brain syndrome. These patients present with an indifference to both the treatment and the illness, lack of anxiety, concrete thinking, agitation or irritability, and mildly or moderately impaired judgment.

Two important points to consider: Is the patient self-medicating? Is the patient abusing drugs and/or alcohol? Do not assume that patients do not use illegal drugs or alcohol. People raised in a wine or hard liquor culture measure alcohol intake quantity with a different yardstick than the physician.

Before prescribing for geriatric patients (or patients of any age), keep the following in mind:

- adherence to treatment
- exclusion criteria for psychotropics
- medical iatrogenesis
- drug interactions
- concomitant illnesses
- dosage
- onset of response to treatment
- duration of treatment
- adverse effects
- close supervision
- family/nurse awareness of the treatment program

Anti-Obsessive-Compulsive Agents

MAOIs are not used because their efficacy is questionable; besides, in the elderly serious cardiovascular risks, notably either hypotension or hypertensive crisis, make use of these drugs inadvisable.

In the elderly, polypharmacy (the combination of two drugs or more) increases the risk factor. For instance, the administration of antidepressants with antihypertensive drugs should be avoided. Hypertensive drugs may present MSE manifested by headaches, depression, loss of interest, loss of balance, irritability, sedation, somnolence, and blurred vision. These side effects may mimic or mask major depression.

The therapeutic strategy revolves around minimizing symptom intensity and frequency. For this purpose, AOCAs are administered with a small amount of anxiolytics or neuroleptics for agitation or irritability control. The family plays an important role in monitoring treatment at home.

Anxiolytics

As stated earlier, anxiety is an important component in the life of the elderly. Anxiety can be caused by psychological, medical, or pharmacological factors (see table 7.2). Anxiolytics prescribed are benzodiazepines, azapirones, antidepressants, neuroleptics, beta blockers, and imidazopiridines.

Benzodiazepines

Extreme caution should be exercised when administering benzodiazepines to patients older than 50 years of age. These substances (e.g., diazepam, alprazolam, lorazepam, clonazepam) may cause addiction, disinhibition resulting in aggressive behavior, dyspnea, depression, loss of

TABLE 7.2   Anxiogenic factors in the elderly

generalized anxiety
psychomotor excitation
delusional syndromes
organic brain syndromes
drug-induced anxiety
alcoholism
metabolic disorders
brain tumors
vascular disorders
endocrinopathies
collagen illnesses
anemia
nutritional deficiencies

memory, confusion, impaired cognition, ataxia, and loss of balance. It is best to give benzodiazepines that have a low half-life and a fast elimination rate. In a young person, diazepam's half-life is 20 hours; it increases 90% in an elderly person. Alprazolam's half-life of 11 hours almost doubles in the older individual. Administering the drug at small doses at regular frequencies maintains low drug levels with efficacious results and minimizes the risk of side effects.

Keep in mind the following drug interactions: benzodiazepines inhibit antimicotic absorption, antacids inhibit benzodiazepine absorption, and benzodiazepines produce depressant action with other depressants, block levodopa action, increase digitalis blood levels, and potentiate alcohol. Withdrawal of benzodiazephines can result in withdrawal syndrome, which is characterized by:

- bradypnea
- bradycardia
- sweating
- hot spells
- nausea
- irritability
- anxiety
- insomnia
- psychomotor excitation
- seizures
- hyperthermia
- hallucinations
- confusion

To avoid withdrawal symptoms, gradually decrease the dose in fifths every three days, and replace the benzodiazepine with an azapirone.

Azapirones

These substances have a short period of action (two to three hours). They are nonaddictive and produce less cognitive impairment. Buspirone is the only azapirone available on the market. The dose range is 5 to 60 mg/po/day. However, it takes about two weeks for the medication to act, a factor patients dislike, and physicians are not very pleased with their efficacy.

Antidepressants

TCAs and SSRIs are also used in small amounts to control anxiety combined with OCD, panic, agoraphobia, and simple phobias. Nortriptyline is the treatment of choice for patients over 65, because it has a mild hypotensive effect, a hypnotic action, and relatively fewer anticholinergic effects. In patients with OCD who experience depression and insomnia, trazodone has antidepressant action and a satisfactory hypnotic quality. Check for orthostatic hypotension, which can be bypassed by taking the medication at bedtime.

Neuroleptics

Small amounts of neuroleptics may help control severe anxiety symptoms. Thioridazine works well, but it may cause cardiac conduction problems or decrease intestinal motility.

Beta-Blockers

Beta-blockers, such as propanolol, have peripheral anxiolytic activity and help to control aggression as well in patients with organic OCD.

Pregnancy

The possibility of pregnancy in the present or immediate future presents complexities for the patient, the fetus, and the physician. Pregnancy modifies the physiology of the woman, because the body must be ready to lodge the fetus. Excessive weight increase, increased blood pressure, and transient hyperglycemia are some of the parameters to check during pregnancy. The concomitant presence of disorders such as epilepsy or an emotional condition requires close monitoring of the patient's condition. For example, a woman with epilepsy requires continuous medication for seizure control. A woman with a predisposition to certain types of mental disorders may develop that disorder during pregnancy (e.g., OCD) or after pregnancy (e.g., postpartum psychosis). Nursing mothers may pass their medication to their children via milk. A woman with alcoholism or a heroin addiction may give birth to an "addicted" child. The administration of psychotropics during pregnancy may also affect the fetus. Sometimes genetic questions are raised, and genetic counseling may then be indicated. Finally, the emotional status of the patient may not allow the mother to raise the child properly.

Questions to consider:

- Is the patient involved in a stable relationship?
- Is the patient medically suitable for pregnancy?

- Does the patient have any other children?
- How old is the patient?
- Any other concomitant illness (diabetes, seizures)?
- Is the patient a drug or alcoholic addict?
- Does the mental disorder permit drug discontinuation during pregnancy?
- In the case of OCD, will behavior therapy suffice?
- Is the patient emotionally suitable to be a mother?
- How were previous pregnancies handled?

It is very difficult to predict how pregnancy will affect OCD; it may ameliorate, aggravate, or initiate it. Our experience with OCD, bipolar disorder depression, and schizophrenia shows that these disorders follow an unpredictable course during pregnancy. In depression, even if the pregnancy evolves uneventfully, postpartum depression may set in.

Six major risks occur during pregnancy:

- anatomical teratogenesis
- behavioral teratogenesis
- toxic effects on the fetus
- complicated labor and delivery
- drugs in the mother's milk
- fetal withdrawal symptoms

Anatomical teratogenesis includes any minor or major bodily dismorphology. Drug-induced teratogenesis is difficult to prove in many instances, yet it should be kept in mind when investigating for a causative noxa.

Behavioral teratogenesis affects higher cortical function, with neurotransmitter and/or receptor activity. As a result, cerebral function in general might be affected and maladaptive behaviors might be observed as the body changes.

Toxic effects on the fetus are caused by opiates, notably heroin, morphine, and cocaine. The fetus might be born addicted, presenting a typical withdrawal syndrome. Patients on neuroleptics may deliver children with tardive dyskinesia.

Complicated labor and delivery can be caused not only by malformation of the fetus or drug presence in the fetus, but also by the action of psychotropics on the mother. Drugs modify the normal physiology of the pregnant woman, affecting the mechanics and homeostasis of labor and delivery.

Proven teratogeneic drugs:

- thalidomide
- lithium salts
- anticonvulsants

Diazepam has also been reported to have teratogenic effects; however, the issue is questionable for some psychopharmacologists.

If the patient is already pregnant, give as little medication as possible. Keep in mind that the fetus is most vulnerable to defects during the first trimester. For this reason, stop the medication in the first trimester and restart treatment in the fourth month.

If the patient wants to become pregnant, consult with an experienced pharmacologist and an expert in birth defects, and work in close relationship with the patient's obstetrician. It is also a good idea to draw legal documents to waive yourself from ulterior responsibility (the jury may disagree in case of a malpractice suit).

Seizure Disorders

A seizure is the result of a histological and/or biochemical cerebral lesion. Consequently, the lesion increases the excitatory bombardment or causes an inhibitory discharge at the synapse. The biochemical pathogenesis seems to involve the GABA-ergic system, pyridoxal 5'phosphate deficiency, the adrenergic system, and the serotonergic system. As we know, these systems are intimately related, and hence affected by psychotropics. When considering psychotropic medication for patients with OCD presenting an epileptic variant or subset, special emphasis should be placed in the treatment outline; an association between obsessionality and epilepsy has been noted. In centerencephalic and temporal lobe epilepsy, a continuous state of obsessiveness may be observed. Seizure and OCD associations have been reported in complex stereotyped automatism, Tourette's, epileptoid personality, scrupulosity syndrome, organic orderliness, and moral hypertrophy (Yaryura-Tobias & Neziroglu, 1997).

Should a patient with OCD and grand mal seizure disorder be medicated? The patient should be medicated, preferably with SSRIs in addition to the anticonvulsant. Clomipramine presents a higher incidence of seizure when given at a higher dose (over 250 mg/po/day). Our personal experience with hundreds of patients does not show this side effect, even in doses beyond 250 mg. Nonetheless, the prescriber should avoid CMI use. Other TCAs may also induce seizures.

Psychiatric symptoms of the seizure disorder appear before the onset of seizure (preictal period) or following a seizure (posictal period). There are some theoretical possibilities to explain the occurrence of psychiatric symptoms. The preictal period is an interval of variable time. The time frame shows the possibility of a psychiatric continuum, that is, a dormant symptom or disorder inserted within the epileptic context, which flares up as a consequence of the epileptic discharge. The other possibility is a transient psychiatric episode.

Mental Retardation

OCD may be associated with mental retardation without constituting a comorbid condition. Several syndromes with a predominant high cortical function deficit present phenomenology compatible with simple obsessionality and compulsiveness. These conditions include the Lesh-Nyhan syndrome, the Cornelia de Lange syndrome, the Prader-Willi syndrome, and other nonspecific pervasive disorders.

The main symptoms to treat are motor compulsions, notably, auto-aggression or the urge to self-harm. On many occasions, patients present, besides aggressiveness, psychotic symptoms interspersed with obsessions and compulsions.

Psychotropic medication in mental retardation is mostly used to control misbehaviors that are severely disruptive or may endanger others or the patient. Therefore, neuroleptics, anxiolytics, anticonvulsants, TCAs, and SSRIs are prescribed. Many of these patients are receiving drugs for other medical conditions (e.g., epilepsy, hormone therapy), so the prescriber must face a polypharmacy regimen with its inherent drug interaction problems.

Dosage, as seen in this chapter for other groups, is gradually administered in small increments. Patients should be closely supervised for medical side effects.

Conclusion

Pharmacotherapy for special groups requires the intervention of a specialist knowledgeable in medication dosage, drug interaction, side effects, and various disorders on the OCD spectrum. Three concepts should be kept in mind: Dosages for children and the elderly are almost the same; pregnant patients may not be routinely medicated; and mentally retarded patients may present a very individual and distinct ability to metabolize drugs, and they may also respond to drug treatment paradoxically.

8

Treatment for the
Obsessive-Compulsive Spectrum

THE OBSESSIVE-COMPULSIVE SPECTRUM is a series of major psychiatric disorders manifesting obsessions and/or compulsions with enough intensity to be considered by the clinician as an interface with OCD or a concomitant OCD syndrome. The spectrum encompasses both related disorders and comorbid conditions.

Related disorders refer to disorders that are very similar to OCD in symptomatology, treatment response, and family history. Comorbidity is the coexistence of two conditions apparently at the same time. However, our preliminary studies have shown that the shared phenomenology is the manifestation of a continuum emerging as a sequential event in time and space within the OCD context. In other words, although the OCD nucleus remains stable, parallel conditions may emerge over time, overlapping with OCD's mainstream pathophysiology.

Regardless of the theoretical position for defining and studying the spectrum, the clinician must medicate a condition presenting protean symptomatology. The condition may not respond to classical OCD pharmacotherapy, but it may respond to polypharmacy management.

For the sake of clarity we may assume the following conditions to be related disorders or comorbid conditions under the spectrum:

- body dysmorphic disorder
- hypochondriasis
- Gilles de la Tourette's syndrome

The following are related disorders:

- schizophrenia
- mood disorders
- major depressive disorder
- manic-depressive illness or bipolar disorder
- eating disorders
- self-mutilation

- drug and alcohol dependence
- mental retardation

Trichotillomania is also considered a comorbid disorder by many practitioners; however, we consider it a separate disorder. This issue is addressed at the end of the chapter.

Body Dysmorphic Disorder

Body dysmorphic disorder (BDD) is an intense preoccupation, obsession, overvalued idea, or delusion pertaining to body shape. We purposefully define BDD as such, because there is no consensus to identify BDD as OCD, a delusional syndrome, a somatoform disorder, or a symptom drifting among other psychiatric disorders. The current trend suggests classifying the illness as a variant of OCD.

For treatment organization, we will focus on BDD as a disorder of the thought and somatosensorial systems. The thought disorder is manifested by a faulty belief; the somatosensorial disorder, by a body-image dysperception. Two cognitions are clearly demonstrated: "I perceive myself as ugly" and "I believe I am ugly."

In our opinion, patients perceive themselves as ugly when they are not because of a distorted somatosensorial mechanism in the brain. A visual misperception causes them to hold strongly to their feelings of ugliness. Conversely, if patients have a normal somatosensorial input, then their belief in their ugliness is based solely on cognitions, that is, strictly a thinking process.

BDD patients are far from being ugly. Nonetheless, they may consult a plastic surgeon to have their body features modified. We presume that more patients with BDD consult a plastic surgeon than a psychiatrist or a psychologist. In order of frequency, patients are concerned with their facial features (e.g., nose, lips, hairline), skin, breasts, buttocks, thighs, and penis. Note that patients are mostly concerned with facial features. We consider this region "social sensitive" because it is constantly visually exposed to the criticism of others.

Paradoxically, patients with skin dysmorphia may constantly pick and dig into their skin to remove marks, moles, or blemishes, to the point that plastic surgery may be needed.

Differential diagnoses entail depression, schizophrenia, psychosis, monosymptomatic hypochondriasis, eating disorders, and personality disorders.

Drug Therapy

Lack of diagnostic criteria for BDD has created a schism between American and European schools of psychiatry, affecting the availability of methodologically sound research. Few controlled studies have been done, and most reports are anecdotal.

Medications prescribed are neuroleptics, TCAs, or SSRIs. Four drugs have been used: clomipramine, fluoxetine, pimozide, and lithium. Some patients require polypharmacy.

Overall, treatment results are unsatisfactory. Patients do not improve or they improve for a while and then relapse. Our experience has been negative; analyzing refractory patient treatment outcome in the long term, we conclude that

1. patients lack motivation for therapy in general,
2. patients lack motivation for drug therapy in particular, and
3. patients are reluctant to take medication.

This fluctuating and uneven response to treatment may indicate: (a) that the presence of various BDD types (obsessional, overvalued ideas, delusional) does not necessarily respond to identical symptomatic treatment, (b) the somatosensorial system is disturbed and medication is ineffective, and (c) that borderline personality or histrionic features are indirectly "sabotaging" treatment outcome.

Behavioral Treatment

There are very few controlled behavioral treatment outcome studies. Most are case studies with before- and after-treatment reports. Behavior therapy for BDD consists primarily of exposure and response prevention and cognitive therapy. During the exposure part of the therapy patients expose their defect. As mentioned above, the misperceived defect may be the hairline, complexion, nose, eyes, or any other body part. Ordinarily, patients either avoid exposing these defects to others (passive avoidance) or try to camouflage them (active avoidance), for example, by using excessive makeup, wearing hats or caps, wearing baggy clothes at all times, allowing only a certain profile to be seen, etc. During exposure and response prevention, patients are prevented from engaging in either active or passive avoidance. Although they initially feel anxious, their anxiety lessens over time, until they no longer feel anxious. In addition, they are instructed not to check the mirror, an urge they frequently have in order to determine if the defect has magically disappeared. A few patients get to a point where looking into the mirror causes more anxiety/discomfort than not looking, and so they avoid looking at themselves—these patients are told to look in the mirror. The concept of behavior therapy with BDD is to have patients face their discomforts until they no longer feel uneasy. Below is an excerpt from a therapy session in which John is exposed to his "large nose."

Therapist: John, I would like you to show me exactly what you don't like about your nose.

John: Well, it is flat and bumpy right at the tip [points] and the bumpiness seems to be more on the right side. I hate it when someone sits to my right because not only can they see the bumpiness but also my nose seems so much bigger.

Therapist: What do you do about that?

John: For the bumpiness I use coverup makeup to fill in the indentations and I try never to sit on someone's left. Of course I don't have to worry much about that any longer because for the most part I avoid going out.

Therapist: Do you go out at all?

John: I go to school but I have been missing a lot of classes and I was thinking about withdrawing.

Therapist: We are going to develop an anxiety hierarchy. What this entails is setting up situations that you currently avoid or face with difficulty. I am going to ask you to tell me situations that would evoke an anxiety of 20 to 30 SUDs. SUDs stands for subjective units of discomfort—it's a way of subjectively rating your anxiety level from 0 to 100. Zero means no anxiety, total relaxation, and 100 means a panic state. Now, tell me how anxious you would feel if you did not use any coverup makeup and went to class.

John: I think that would be about an 80. Worse than that would be to actually go out with a girl.

Therapist: Okay, what about not wearing coverup and going to an empty restaurant with me?

John: I would not like it but I think I could probably do it, about a SUD of 50.

Therapist: How much anxiety would you feel walking down the street at night with no camouflage makeup?

John: That would be about a 30 or 40.

Therapist: What about if we walked into a waiting room and you had no makeup on and sat to the left of someone? And if you sat on the right?

John: Sitting on the left would be exposing my bad profile and therefore my anxiety would probably would be about 60 without makeup and 45 with makeup. However, if I were to expose my less bumpy side, my anxiety or SUD as you call it would be 50 without makeup and 30 with it.

Therapist: Do you see that you feel less anxious in certain situations and more in others?

John: Yeah, but I can't do anything about it.

Therapist: You can't or you won't? Cognitive therapy will teach you how to differentiate between the can'ts and won'ts.

John: I don't think any of this is going to work because I don't really care what others think of me. The only thing that matters to me is what I feel and think.

Therapist: I realize that, but the way you will change the way you feel and think is by going through this therapy. We will start by slowly having you not wear coverup. In fact, what I would like you to do is bring all the makeup you have at home and leave it in my office.

John: I can't—or as you would say, won't—do that: I will freak out!

Therapist: Okay, what we will do is have you rub off some of the makeup you have on. Will you do that right now? Then we will go out for a walk, and if you feel comfortable with that, we will talk to people in this office while facing them with your bad profile.

John: I can't believe you are asking me to do this.

At this point, the therapist helps the patient rub off some his makeup and then begins to expose John's bad profile to people within the office. The therapist tells John that while he makes small talk with office personnel, exposing his bad profile, he should think that everyone is noticing how ugly he is and feeling really repulsed by him.

John: Did you notice how Maryann (the receptionist) looked at me? She knew I looked different.

Therapist: She might have noticed you looked different but what makes you think that she thought you looked ugly? Different doesn't mean ugly you know.

John: I know, but I can tell she noticed the bumps on my nose and she must have been wondering where they came from.

Therapist: John, every time you notice someone looking at you and you think that she is noticing how ugly you are, I want you to "flood" yourself. In other words, tell yourself that she is noticing your big bumpy nose and thinking, "How could he have gone out in public like that?" In fact, think of her telling family members about you at night and describing you with disgust. [The therapist continues to exaggerate the point until the patient sees it as ridiculous.]

John: I'll try but I can't promise you anything. Some things I know I will never do.

Therapist: Let's not worry about what you won't do. Let's just concentrate on whatever we work on in the session.

The therapist and patient would continue along these lines until every item on the anxiety hierarchy had been practiced. John's anxiety hierarchy is shown in table 8.1.

TABLE 8.1   Anxiety hierarchy for BDD (nose)

Situation	SUD*
walk down street at night/no makeup	30
sit in waiting room on someone's right/with makeup	30
sit in waiting room on someone's left/with makeup	45
sit in waiting room on someone's right/no makeup	50
sit in waiting room on someone's left/no makeup	60
dine with the therapist in an empty restaurant/no makeup	50
attend class/no makeup	80
go on a date	95

*subjective unit of discomfort

Cognitive therapy for BDD would consist of challenging some faulty cognitions. Some common faulty cognitions observed in BDD patients are:

- I must be noticed.
- I must be perfect.
- I must be outstanding.
- Being average is being a loser.
- One must always strive to be better than others and if one is not then one is worthless.

Table 8.2 depicts cognitive therapy with someone who thinks his nose is too big.

TABLE 8.2   Cognitive restructuring for BDD (nose)

A. *Activating event: being with others*

B. *Beliefs*
   1. I am ugly/unattractive.
   2. My nose is big.
   3. I can't tolerate the anxiety.
   4. I need to be noticed.
   5. I need to have a perfect nose.
   6. I need the approval of others.

C. *Consequences*
   1. Emotional: anxiety
   2. Behavioral: mirror checking

D. *Disputing beliefs*
   1. Where is the evidence you are ugly?
   2. Where is the evidence your nose is too big?
   3. Where is the evidence you can't tolerate anxiety?
   4. Why must you be noticed?
   5. Is it feasible for you to be perfect?
   6. Is if feasible for you to be approved by everyone?

E. *Effect of disputing beliefs*
   1. There is no evidence I am ugly.
   2. There is no evidence my nose is too big except for my own perception.
   3. I don't like the anxiety but I can tolerate it.
   4. I would like to be noticed but I don't have everything I want.
   5. There is no perception of life.
   6. It is not possible for everyone to approve of me.

Hypochondriasis

Hypochondriasis (HC) is characterized by a strong preoccupation with having a serious physical illness based in misinterpreting bodily cues or symptoms. HC became known to the medical profession about 2,000 years ago, when Galen skillfully described it and suggested melancholia as its pathogenesis. Because the patient complains strictly of physical symptoms, treatment is sought in emergency rooms or general practitioners' or primary care physicians' offices, with the complete exclusion of psychiatrists or psychologists. However, HC symptoms are usually identified with psychiatric disorders, including OCD, borderline personality disorder, major depression, somatic syndromes (e.g., conversion hysteria), schizophrenia, generalized anxiety disorders, body dysmorphic disorder, and mostly monosymptomatic delusion. The major symptoms are: pain, concern with having a deadly illness (e.g., cancer, heart disease), muscleskeletal complaints, and gastrointestinal problems. Systematic studies of this population yields the presence of illness phobia and fear of dying. Overall, HC appears as a cognitive complex with a two-tier track: a false belief and a misperception. Whether HC is a symptom, a syndrome, or a disorder has yet to be determined.

Drug Treatment

Most patients come to a psychiatric consult once the pilgrimage to hospitals and general medicine offices has been exhausted. HC treatment is target-oriented. The major psychiatric symptoms are: depression, obsessions, compulsions, depressions, and phobias.

Pharmacotherapy includes the classical antidepressants, anti-obsessive-compulsive agents, and anxiolytics. When psychotoform symptoms are observed, small doses of antipsychotic medications may be prescribed.

Behavioral Treatment

The psychological approach includes psychoanalysis, psychotherapy, cognitive therapy, and behavior therapy. Traditionally, the intervention employed is supportive or "reassurance-based." This technique involves a physician reassuring the patient that no physical etiology for his presenting problem has been identified. Medical tests and specialized exams are employed as a means of allaying the patient's fears. This type of intervention helps only temporarily, if at all, as the health concerns return shortly. Although reassurance may temporarily decrease hypochondriasis, in the long run it tends to increase it.

Currently, cognitive and behavior therapy is indicated in the treatment for HC. Behavioral therapies such as systematic desensitization, implosion, and exposure and response prevention have been used. Exposure and response prevention is conducted in a manner similar that employed with OCD patients. Patients are gradually exposed to cues that evoke fear and anxiety. In other words, somatic sensations are recreated in the office and patients are told they are developing or have the illness they fear. Cognitive therapy is used to correct faulty cognitions and beliefs inherent in HC, such as catastrophic thinking (e.g., "I have a headache. I must have a tumor") and overgeneralization (e.g., "My friend had a heart attack. I will have a heart attack and die").

It is extremely difficult to convince patients that they have an emotional illness. It is important to spend a lot of time developing rapport and reducing their anger at the medical profession for not having found their physical illness. Because patients rarely go to a mental health facility, knowledge of HC is limited, and thus treatment outcome seriously suffers.

Gilles de la Tourette's Syndrome

Gilles de la Tourette's syndrome (GT) has a childhood onset, but may commence during adolescence. It is characterized, by tics, motor stereotypia, echolalia, echokinesis, self-mutilation, obsessions, compulsions, and aggressive behavior. A major component of GT is OCD. Therefore, the appearance or insertion of OCD into GT and vice versa is common.

A male-female ratio of 3:1 is the accepted sexual distribution, with a high incidence of relatives having GT or OCD. In fact, certain studies indicate a common genetic pathway for both OCD and GT (Pauls, 1992; Pauls & Leckman, 1986).

Tourette's syndrome appears to have organic correlates (e.g., basal ganglia) and a biochemical involvement affecting the serotonergic-dopaminergic balance. These correlates may determine the treatment outline for GT.

Drug Therapy

Overall, pharmacotherapy utilizes serotonin and/or dopamine blockers. The most utilized drug is haloperidol in doses of 0.5 to 4 mg/day/po. Other drugs associated with the catecholaminergic pathway are pimozide, risperidone, and fluphenazine. Clomipramine and SSRIs (fluoxetine, paroxetine, sertraline) have been given in doses similar to those for children with OCD (see chapter 7). Clonidine, an alpha adrenergic agonist, in doses of 0.1 to 0.3/day/po, is an alternative treatment for GT. A specific drug for GT treatment is still unavailable.

The use of phenothiazine (e.g., haloperidol) therapy may cause cognitive impairment, manifested by a drop in academic achievement, decreased concentration, lack of motivation, poor memory, and difficulties with concentration. Discontinuation of the medication causes a complete reversal of these side effects.

Behavioral Treatment

Psychotherapy has been unsuccessful in treating this condition. Where the OCD symptomatology is outstanding, behavior and cognitive intervention may help. The research in this area is limited because until very recently GT was considered a neurological disorder. In the past 20 years some advances have been made with habit reversal, a behavioral technique used to control the tics. Habit reversal involves teaching patients to utilize and tighten the opposite muscles to those involved in the tic. For example, a patient who has a shoulder tic would be instructed to pull down hard on the shoulder and tighten it up whenever the urge to tic is felt. Although habit reversal is somewhat effective in reducing the tics, it is not effective in eliminating them.

Cognitive therapy may be used to deal with the secondary negative effects of Tourette's syndrome. For example, patients who suffer embarrassment from the movements or experience anxiety in interpersonal relationships may be helped with cognitive therapy. Their faulty cognitions (e.g., "Everyone is staring at me and I can't stand it. I am the center of attention and it's awful. It's horrible to have tics") may be challenged. Challenging these thoughts will assist the patient in reducing secondary anxiety, which can indirectly increase the frequency of the tics. However, more research is needed to develop techniques to directly reduce the tics.

Schizophrenia

The clinical interaction between OCD and schizophrenia was recognized in the early 1900s. Historically, both OCD and schizophrenia seem to share interfaces in their clinical course. For instance, OCD may be prodromal to schizophrenia, both conditions may replace each other like a back-and-forth mechanism, or they may coexist in harmony. Recent interest in the research of OCD and schizophrenia, notably their comorbidity, demands a brief review on their interaction, and how this interaction may affect the therapeutic approach.

Inspecting both OCD and schizophrenia, we find points of coincidence regarding thought mechanisms, perception, motor impairment, and perhaps anatomical and neurotransmitter parameters.

OCD and schizophrenia share a gray area of symptoms that fluctuate back and forth, making it difficult to establish a correct diagnosis. Typical examples are OCD cases presenting overvalued ideas, doubtful beliefs, or poor insight. Those cases are certainly not primary or classical OCD, but atypical forms that may develop into psychotic forms. We feel that OCD and schizophrenia are two distinct entities, although they may affect, to some degree, the same cerebral regions and physiological mechanisms.

Anatomical morphology, including cerebral lobes, brain-ventricular ratio, and cerebral metabolic alterations, points toward organic involvement in both OCD and schizophrenia, otherwise considered "functional" by many schools of thought.

Certainly neurotransmitters could not remain excluded from speculations on the pathogenesis of OCD and schizophrenia. A serotonin (5-HT) disturbance for OCD and a dopamine disturbance for schizophrenia have drawn the interest of investigators. The discovery of receptors and subreceptors for these neurotransmitters and further research findings in this area indicate that both 5-HT and dopamine may mediate the neurochemical disturbance in both conditions. Therefore, accepting a priori that both OCD and schizophrenia pathology are influenced by the same neurotransmitters, it is tempting to combine medication acting on 5-HT and dopamine pathways. These concepts require understanding drug therapy interaction when medicating OCD-schizophrenia comorbidity.

Drug Treatment

The concomitant presence of OCD and schizophrenia leads to conflicts. Will an antipsychotic agent aggravate OCD? Will an AOCA aggravate schizophrenia?

The presence of obsessions and compulsions in patients with schizophrenia has been empirically proven as a mechanism of defense that keeps the psychosis under control. Therefore, a combination of an antipsychotic with an AOCA is recommended to prevent a flare-up.

Many years ago, we tried clomipramine in patients with schizophrenia. The rationale was to break the paranoid nucleus, since clomipramine worked well in the obsessional nucleus. Regrettably, out of ten patients four had to be hospitalized and the others were clinically unchanged or worse. Conversely, haloperidol was prescribed to break the obsessional nucleus, but results were equivocal.

As usual, the treatment should be individually tailored. The main task is to isolate the major symptoms and target them. A standardized approach to medicating this patient population seems to fail. Research done in patients with schizotypal personality disorder shows a high rate of treatment failure. Many pharmacological combinations for the treatment of OCD-schizophrenia have been reported anecdotally. As stated above, an acceptable treatment is to combine anti-obsessive-compulsive and antipsychotic agents (table 8.3 lists medications commonly used with patients with OCD with psychotic features). This approach is based on our experience, as well as that of others, investigating OCD and schizophrenia (Yaryura-Tobias, Campisi, McKay, & Neziroglu, 1995).

Keep in mind that the priority is to treat:

- symptom intensity
- symptom frequency
- primary symptoms
- secondary symptoms

TABLE 8.3   Medications for obsessive-compulsive disorder
and schizophrenia

clomipramine
fluphenazine
fluvoxamine
haloperidol
pimozide
risperidone
trifluoperazine

Neuroleptics

Neuroleptics with sedative qualities may be given in small doses. They act like anxiolytics, antiemetics, and antiallergics, and potentiate analgesic action. They may induce sleep at treatment onset. In patients with aggression or impulsiveness, we look for sedative neuroleptics. In patients with OCD-schizophrenia, it is common to see a tendency toward impulsive and aggressive behavior. This clinical compulsive phenomenon, and the likelihood of a subclinical epileptic form, should be assessed. If positive, neuroleptics with a high threshold for seizures should be prescribed.

Neuroleptics with sedative properties include:

- chlorpromazine
- chlorprothixene
- clozapine
- levomepromazine
- promethazine
- properciazine

Neuroleptics with nonsedative qualities are faster in action and do not cause sedation, allowing a better performance during daytime. These drugs include:

- fluphenazine
- haloperidol
- penfluridol
- perphenazine
- pimozide
- prochlorperazine
- sulpiride
- thioridazine
- thiothixene
- trifluoperazine

Atypical Antipsychotics

Atypical antipsychotics are clozapine and risperidone. They present a different side-effect profile and receptor affinity, with the following pharmacological characteristics:

- mild extrapyramidal side effects
- sporadic tardive dyskinesia
- mild action on prolactin levels
- action on the autonomous nervous system
- antagonic activity on serotonin (5-HT2) and dopamine (DA2)

Clozapine needs blood control to prevent agranulocytosis.

These two antipsychotics are prescribed for the negative symptoms of schizophrenia, although this classification has not been widely validated. Their administration in OCD with or without schizophrenic symptomatology is still a research issue.

Mood Disorders

The relationship between mood disorders and OCD has long preoccupied phenomenologists. Research on the association between OCD and other major psychiatric disorders has concluded that major depressive disorder is perhaps the main interacting disorder with OCD. These researchers view OCD as a form of an affective disorder, rejecting the notion of OCD as a form of anxiety or as an independent disorder. This concept is based on the conspicuous presence of depression in OCD and OCD's response to antidepressant medication. Nowadays, this idea is obsolete, yet the association between OCD and major affective disorder does exist.

Major Depressive Disorder

One problem in differentiating the various forms of depression is the mixture of endogenous and exogenous symptoms coexisting in the same individual. The additional problem of separating OCD from major depressive disorder is compounded by the conspicuous presence of secondary depression. Because OCD is an emotionally and economically devastating illness, it is highly likely that a patient will develop secondary depression.

In France, in 1866, Morel described clinical variants of both conditions. A major depressive episode has been reported in 56.9% of patients with OCD (Karno et al., 1988), and for many OCD with major depressive disorder is the most common form of comorbidity. Conversely, our experience indicates that, although there is comorbid OCD-major depressive disorder, most symptoms of depression in patients with OCD are secondary to the primary symptomatology. In fact, a review of the current literature assessing OCD and comorbid depression indicates several limitations: (1) insufficient number of patients, (2) lack of reliability and sensitivity in the instruments used to assess the disorder, and (3) diagnostic discrepancies in the definition of major depression. We have estimated that 90% of our OCD population (N = 2,500) suffers from secondary depression. Nonetheless, this emotional "transgression" is accompanied by others, such as fear or anxiety or anger (Yaryura-Tobias & Neziroglu, 1983).

Anatomical and other neurobiological parameters of these conditions may converge, explaining the association between OCD and major depressive disorder. Greater understanding of frontal lobe circuitry and the hypothalamic and basal ganglia connections may elucidate the hypothetical link.

Further, research into catecholamines, indolamines, pyridoxal phosphate, tertrahydrobiopterines, and amino acid byproducts, reported to be affected in various ways in OCD and major depression, may advance our knowledge of both conditions. Fortunately, the incipient field of neurohistochemistry is slowly opening new inroads in the pathogenesis of these conditions.

For the time being, practitioners have to resort to the therapeutic tools known to them. The drugs that we use in the treatment of OCD and major depression are listed in table 8.4.

One favorable event in the combined treatment is that some antidepressant and anti-obsessive-compulsive agents have therapeutic action for both conditions. Remember that OCD requires higher doses of these agents. This difference in dosage suggests distinctive neurobiochemical involvement.

TABLE 8.4   Treatment for obsessive-compulsive disorder and major depressive disorder

Generic Name	Dosage Range
clomipramine	50–250 mg/day
fluoxetine	20–80 mg/day
sertraline	50–200 mg/day
fluvoxamine	50–300 mg/day
paroxetine	10–50 mg/day
venlafaxine	37.5–225 mg/day
D-l phenylalanine	1000 mg/day
tyrosine	10000 mg/day
L-tryptophan	1–3 gm/day
methylphenidate	5–30 mg/day

Manic-Depressive Illness (Bipolar Disorder)

With a manic-depressive illness comorbid OCD usually affects the manic phase. This observation was made in 1912, and since then several reports have been published (e.g., McKay, Yaryura-Tobias, & Neziroglu, 1994; Yaryura-Tobias & Neziroglu, 1983). Sometimes these patients developed a full manic phase, which replaces the obsessive-compulsive symptomatology. Further, the spontaneous extinction of the manic phase may be succeeded by obsessions and compulsions. These clinical observations are far from being exact. Overall, milder symptoms of either condition are covered by the intense symptoms of the predominant phase.

In the presence of this nosology, and if the patient is receiving antidepressant medication, notably TCAs, consider the diagnosis of a hypomanic side effect. We recommend that during the diagnostic interview the practitioner look for changes in sleep pattern (evidenced by the patient's comment, "I don't need to sleep"), excessive increase in mental and physical energy, and loss of appetite ("I don't feel hungry").

Drug Treatment

Pharmacological therapy is tailored to the patient's symptom intensity, frequency, and duration, drug side effects, and drug interaction.

Overall, AOCAs and mood stabilizers are the two main groups of medications used. Because AOCAs have already been discussed in chapter 6, this chapter will present mood stabilizers.

Lithium
The most important pharmacological activities of lithium are:

- diminishes sensitivity to neurotransmitter receptors
- delays norepinephrine sensitive adenylate cyclase
- acts on the calcium, sodium, and potassium channels
- has a bioavailability of 100%

Lithium doses range from 900 to 1500 mg/day; plasma levels determine the optimal dose. There are many side effects; table 8.5 lists the most common. Measuring lithium levels at regular intervals may prevent serious side effects.

Table 8.5   Lithium: common side effects

tremors	weight gain
slowed mentation	hypothyroidism
forgetfulness	polyuria
nausea	polydipsia
diarrhea	rashes

Carbamazepine

Carbamazepine is an anticonvulsant, with specific action on partial and generalized seizures and trigeminal neuralgia. It is also administered for aggression and for bipolar disorders. Its oral daily dose ranges between 200 and 600 mg. The most common medical side effects at the initiation of therapy are dizziness, drowsiness, unsteadiness, nausea, and vomiting. The prescriber must also be aware of the possibility of the development of agranulocytosis and aplastic anemia.

Three major symptoms will concern the prescriber: obsessionality, manic symptoms, and aggressiveness. In the OCD manic subset, aggression can be observed in either OCD or manic-depressive illness, and it should be concomitantly treated. These symptoms should be considered as a total unit for treatment purposes; therefore, combining drugs to affect a wider pharmacological spectrum is advisable. The combination of clomipramine and lithium may control these three symptoms. The starting dose should be small for the less predominant symptoms. If the obsessive-compulsive phase has been substituted by the manic phase, lithium should be the primary drug.

Another symptom is racing of the mind without becoming manic. Sometimes racing of the mind is accompanied by the inability to sit still. This complaint brings memories of hyperactive behavior, a familiar symptom of many patients with OCD who suffered from attention-deficit/hyperactive disorder during childhood. Once again, when treating OCD it is important to consider the wide range of phenomenological parameters that may modify treatment selection.

Eating Disorders

Eating disorders comprise three major groups: primary anorexia nervosa (PAN), bulimia nervosa (BN), and obesity. Major characteristics of an eating disorder include:

- compulsion to eat or rejection of the urge to eat
- hypothalamic pathology in PAN
- obsession with body shape based on social expectations
- interface with OCD
- occurs in response to anxiety and depression

Primary Anorexia Nervosa

Primary anorexia nervosa (PAN) is characterized by (1) a refusal to eat or a compulsion to avoid food, (2) obsessiveness with food and body image, and (3) compulsive rituals pertaining to food shopping and preparation and table setting. Actually, PAN is a misnomer in that the patient is hungry but will not eat.

Clinical Features

Onset: before age 25
Male: female ratio: almost exclusively female
Weight loss: more than 25% of the original weight
Menstrual cycle: amenorrhea or dysmenorrhea
Skin: lanugo, yellowish tint (caused by hypercarotinemia)
Joints: hypertrophy of hand joints
Heart: bradycardia
Teeth: caries, enamel dissolution due to vomiting

Mental Symptoms

Personality: rigid, inner or outer aggressiveness, obstinacy, hysteroid features, intermittent hyperactivity
Major psychiatric features: OCD
Weight loss is also caused by several practices such as vomiting, cathartics or laxatives, amphetamines or other anorexigens, jogging, dancing, or any kind of exercising.

Laboratory Findings

The physical status is certainly important in that a patient may need nonpsychiatric medical assistance to restore enough weight to prevent serious medical complications, including death.

A specific laboratory profile is not pathognomonic, and simply reveals the nutritional category. Alteration in glucose metabolism (hypoglycemia), hypothyroidism, hypoproteinemia, hypovitaminosis, notably vitamin A, and hypopotassemia are common findings. Low potassium may cause muscular twitches and cardiac alterations such as hypotension and T wave flattening.

Hypoproteinemia causes loss of muscular mass, including the heart muscle, and brain atrophy (remember this for cognitive therapy!).

Researchers have observed 5-HT as a major factor in PAN neurochemistry. Nonetheless, undernutrition sets the pace in pathological findings and masks the heuristic biological elements causing PAN.

Differential Diagnoses
Differential diagnoses include:

- secondary anorexia
- cancer
- hypopituitarism
- immunodeficiencies
- schizophrenia, catatonic types
- major depressive disorder, severe type

Treatment
An evaluation before treatment will help the clinician to dispense the right medication without further jeopardizing the physical status of the patient. The evaluation should include a physical examination and assessment of nutritional status. The patient should be asked about the use of purgatives or laxatives, diuretics, and enemas, as well as drug abuse.

Fundamental to a successful behavioral and cognitive program is the establishment at the onset of treatment of:

- awareness of illness
- rapport with therapist
- acceptance of illness to modify the maladaptive behavior

When the patient's weight is extremely low, cyproheptadine in doses of 4 to 12 mg/day seems efficacious. Cyproheptadine has four important actions: It antagonizes serotonin, stimulates appetite, enhances protein deposit, and is antihistaminic. Once the body gains an acceptable weight (about 90 pounds or more), TCAs or AOCAs may be administered.

Common medications used for PAN include:

- antidepressants/anti-obsessive-compulsives
- amitriptyline
- clomipramine
- fluoxetine
- anabolics
- insulin
- steroids
- chlorpromazine

Prognosis
Poor prognosis is determined by:

- onset in early teens
- chronicity
- severe symptomatology
- prevalent hysteroid features
- inner or outer anger
- need to sabotage

Good prognosis is determined by:

- onset in late teens
- shorter period from onset of illness to treatment
- bulimia
- obsessoid features

These prognosis determinants are subject to many other variables, making prediction of outcome very difficult. Our experience is relatively negative; a lasting good outcome is uncommon. Although the obsessive-compulsive symptoms are controllable, the patient's personality and unstable relationship with her family and therapist affect treatment outcome. The most difficult patients to treat are those suffering from self-mutilation. Finally, patients with PAN sometimes manifest a very deep, well hidden desire to die. This chronic suicidal ideation is manifested by their starving themselves to death. In fact, mortality rates range between 7 and 21%.

Bulimia Nervosa

Bulimia nervosa (BN) is characterized by episodic eating binges. Major characteristics include:

- eating large qualities of food
- lack of control while eating
- decreased satiation point
- impulsive onset of the binging episode
- eat-vomit-eat cycle
- use of laxatives, cathartics

Mental Symptoms
The patient with BN needs social approval for her body shape. Contemporary Western culture demands a slim figure, and disapproves of overweight. The highest prevalence of BN is found among wealthy families.

Personality traits include obsessionality, perfectionism, and depression. Patients obsess about body image, food intake, and social acceptance. BN and PAN share many symptoms and behaviors.

Differential Diagnoses
Differential diagnoses include:

- other eating disorders
- anxiety
- major depressive disorder
- obsessive-compulsive disorder
- substance abuse
- personality disorders

Treatment
The pharmacotherapy of BN is based on its depressive and obsessive-compulsive substratum. Therefore, the treatment emphasizes the use of AOCAs or TCAs. Psychotherapeutic choices are supportive and insight therapy and cognitive-behavioral therapy. In general, the results are inconclusive, and for the time being there is not a specific treatment modality.

Obesity

Obesity is the willing or unwilling accumulation of fat, accompanied by large volumes of food intake in a chronic and systematic way.

Three types of obesity are distinguished: mild (over 20 to 40% of body weight), moderate (over 40 to 100% of body weight), and severe (over 100%). Although these figures may be arbitrary, moderate and severe obesity are considered morbid. Therefore, morbid obesity is classified under medical conditions without the need for a psychiatric diagnosis.

Contributing Factors
In today's world of opposites, notably overeating and famine, the etiology of obesity cannot be pointed to one single or multiple cause, but rather it may reflect any combination of the following:

- social factors (lower class and poor immigrants)
- cultural factors (certain African and Middle Eastern countries view obesity as a sign of beauty)
- learned behavior (family history of obesity)
- stress
- chronic anxiety

- sexual abuse, rape, severe marital disturbance (to establish a corporeal "off limits" boundary
- genetic factors
- endocrine and metabolic factors
- developmental factors (excessive amount of fat cells)
- hypothalamic pathology
- physical inertia, sedentary behavior

Treatment

Like any other eating disturbance, treatment of obesity requires a biopsychosocial strategy. Treatment consists of two tracks: medical and psychological. The medical approach focuses on psychiatric factors (e.g., anxiety control) that are modifiable by medication. The use of specific anorexigenic substances, such as amphetamines, fenfluramine, and penthermine, may provide, in the short term, visible weight loss.

However, anorexigenic side effects can be harmful. The following have been reported: mental and physical hyperactivity, nervousness, anger, mood swings, impaired judgement, hallucinations, delusions, and addiction. If OCD components are present, AOCAs may be tried. Fluoxetine in doses higher than 80 mg/day seem to curtail the appetite.

Overall, patients interested in long-term results are better off adhering to a corrective diet, a structured behavioral food management program, and an intensive physical exercise program. As reinforcement, a program to manage food intake and maladaptive behavior will fulfill the long-term therapeutic needs.

Psychological therapy consists of cognitive and behavior therapy, focusing on the analysis of false beliefs about body weight, esthetics of body image, and physical damage caused by overeating.

Self-Mutilation

Self-mutilation is an objective symptom present in several conditions:

- psychosis
- malingering in prison inmates
- borderline personality
- aggressive behavior
- eating disorders
- mental retardation
- trichotillomania
- compulsive orectic mutilative syndrome

We shall now focus on one disorder with strong or overt obsessive-compulsive symptomatology, where self-harm is part of a compulsive ritual.

Compulsive Orectic Mutilative Syndrome

This syndrome was established in the 1970s during our research in OCD. It affects pubescent females and is characterized by:

- obsessions
- compulsions
- an eating disorder
- dysmenorrhea
- self-mutilation
- aggressive behavior
- insomnia
- an elevated pain threshold
- family disturbances

The syndrome is symptomatologically divided into two phases: early, or puberal, and late, or postpubertal. The early phase consists of PAN. Patients refuse to eat, become amenorrheic, aggressive, and may suffer from binges of eating.

The late phase follows appetite restoration, although bulimic behavior may be noticed, and restitution of the menstrual cycle. This phase marks the overt aggressive behavior and self-harm.

All along, patients present obsessive-compulsive symptoms.

Physical and sexual abuse is reported in about 70% of the patients.

The act of self-mutilation is ritualistic, meticulous, symmetrical, and painful. The painlessness suggests an increased pain threshold, ecstasy, depersonalization, or endorphin-serotonin dysregulation. These are heuristic possibilities.

Patients can harm themselves in the following locations: skin, oral mucosa, vagina, dorsal aspects of the arms to avoid vessels' trajectory, and the body in general, with the exception of the face. Instruments used are broken glasses, razor blades, knives, and scissors.

Forty percent present with nonspecific EEGs, and 60% present an abnormal 5-hour oral glucose tolerance response, described as hypoglycemic (Yaryura-Tobias & Neziroglu, 1983).

Treatment

Most patients seek treatment for PAN or OCD. Patients rarely come for the treatment of self-harm. The symptoms are well hidden and certainly embarrassing. It is important to perform a physical examination to find self-harm. Because psychiatrists rarely perform a physical exam the syndrome often goes undetected. A reasonable treatment includes a physical examination, laboratory testing, the control of biological features similar to PAN and OCD, psychosocial aspects such as being physically or sexually abused, and serious family constellation disturbances. Patients are usually educated in fear, with strong parental authoritarian figures. Consequently, oppositional behavior, arguments, lack of praising, and abuse further ignite the already established self-harm pathology.

Drug and Alcohol Dependence

The treatment management of drug and alcohol addiction superimposed to OCD requires that the patient first be detoxified. Without previous or concomitant detoxification, any attempt to control OCD will be futile and failure will ensue. Detoxification as the priority issue is based on the biochemical need to avoid mixing in the system illegal drugs with anti-obsessive-compulsive agents. Interactions between these drugs may interfere with the therapeutic program by causing unwanted side effects and toxic reactions, or by neutralizing a drug's therapeutic effects. To avoid this problem, it is advisable to hospitalize the patient. In a controlled environment, the patient will have to adhere to the treatment program. OCD treatment can then be concomitantly implemented.

There is a tendency to classify an addiction as another form of OCD. This may not be so. It must be clearly established that the addiction is distinct from a compulsion. The urge of the patient with an addiction is to seek out pleasure. Conversely, the urge of a patient with a compulsion is to reduce anxiety and unpleasantness. Studies of the prevalence of OCD among patients with alcoholism, compared to the general population, show a range between 6 and 12% (Eisen & Rasmussen, 1989). OCD symptoms were found in patients who used alcohol, heroin, codeine, morphine, and cocaine (Fals-Stewart & Schafer, 1992).

We could not find specific literature for the treatment of these dual conditions, but we feel that each condition should be treated with the medication suggested for that condition. The potential for drug interaction should be considered. Overall, the coexistence of OCD with alcohol and/or drug dependence is difficult to treat. Perhaps the drug user's inability to live without drugs and craving for instant pleasure are the major obstacles to successful treatment.

Mental Retardation

For the treatment of mental retardation see chapter 6.

Trichotillomania

A diagnosis of trichotillomania, as currently defined in the *DSM-IV* (APA, 1994), requires that the patient engage in the recurrent pulling of hair resulting in noticeable hair loss, experience an increasing sense of tension immediately before pulling out the hair or when attempting to resist the behavior, and pleasure, gratification, or relief upon hair pulling. For many patients, this condition may be accompanied by inspection of the hair root, hair twirling, pulling the strand between the teeth, or trichophagia (the ingestion of hair).

Although trichotillomania is presently characterized as an impulse disorder, some researchers believe that it fits into the obsessive-compulsive model (Jenike, Baer, & Minichiello, 1990; Philippopoulos, 1961; Primeau, & Fontaine, 1987; Swedo et al., 1989; Tynes et al., 1990). The patient typically experiences an increasing sense of tension immediately prior to hair pulling or when attempting to resist hair pulling. Some patients report an urge to pull. Immediately after pulling, the patient experiences a positive change in affect and often reports feeling soothed. A patient with OCD typically experiences a reduction in anxiety after performing a compulsion but does not necessarily feel soothed. In fact, the performance of the compulsion is often annoying, frustrating, and unpleasant. The experience of pleasure reported by many patients after hair pulling differentiates these individuals from those with OCD, who typically experience no pleasure while performing compulsions. This would suggest that hair pulling is shaped, strengthened, and maintained as a function of negatively reinforcing consequences (i.e., reduction in unpleasant affect) as well as positive reinforcement.

Other differentiating features reported by these researchers are the lower incidence of obsessions and compulsions and lower levels of anxiety and depression reported by patients with trichotillomania relative to those with OCD. The experiential differences and the lack of other compulsions in trichotillomania have led some researchers to believe it is not a variant of OCD (Christenson et al., 1991; Stanley, Swann, & Bowers, 1992; Winchel et al., 1992).

Some researchers postulate it is a separate syndrome (Delgado & Mannino, 1969; Greenberg & Sarner, 1965), similar to other maladaptive habits such as thumb sucking, nail biting, and nose picking (Azrin, Nunn, & Frantz, 1980).

Behavioral Treatment

The first reported behavioral intervention for trichotillomania described a program of self-monitoring with response chain interruption (Taylor, 1963). This entailed instruction in behavioral self-monitoring coupled with verbal instructions to their hands to "stop." Other interventions reported include: counting and recording hair pulls (Saper, 1971) and contingent punishment. Researchers investigating the latter intervention strategy have utilized denial of privileges and the application of eye drops (Epstein & Peterson, 1973), aversive self-stimulation with a rubber band (Mastellone, 1974; Mathew & Kumaraiah, 1988; Stevens, 1984), and punishment via sit-ups whenever a pull attempt is made (MacNeil & Thomas, 1976). Except for Saper's study (1971), patients reported zero hair pulling rates at the end of treatment.

Other behavior therapies reported to have resulted in at least moderate improvement include covert desensitization (Levine, 1976), attention reflection and response prevention by cutting hair close to the scalp (Massong et al., 1980), attention reflection combined with contingent punishment (Altman et al., 1982), facial screening with a soft terry cloth upon an attempt to pull (Barmann & Vitali, 1982), and a multicomponent treatment package with self-monitoring, hair collection, goal setting, relaxation, and stimulus control (Bornstein & Rychtarik, 1978).

The most successful behavioral treatment in the remediation of hair pulling is known as "habit reversal training." First introduced by Azrin and Nunn (1973) as a self-management treatment for nervous habits (e.g., tics, thumb sucking, stuttering), this protocol includes 13 components: (1) *Competing response training* focuses on teaching the patient a behavioral response which precludes the performance of the hair pulling response. A typical strategy requires the patient to clench the fists together and to keep his arms locked and firmly buttressed against his sides. (2) *Habit awareness training* teaches the patient to be aware of the specific bodily movements involved in the hairpulling. (3) *Self-monitoring techniques* and daily records help to make the patient aware of rate, frequency, and intensity of the hair pulling, and to assist the patient in (4) *identifying response precursors* (e.g., face touching, hair straightening or twirling) and (5) *identifying habit-prone situations* (e.g., sedentary activities such as watching television, studying, and being alone, as well as stress-inducing situations related to work, family, and social functioning). (6) *Relaxation training* is taught to assist in the management of urges and anxiety. (7) *Response prevention* (e.g., practicing a competing response for 3 minutes when a response precursor and/or habit-prone situation has been identified) and (8) *habit interruption* (e.g., engaging in the competing response to interrupt hair pulling) are designed to allow the patient's experience of urges and anxiety to dissipate in the absence of hair pulling in a manner consistent with most ERP-based treatment approaches. The authors further recommend the use of (9) *positive attention/overcorrection* (e.g., positive hair care), (10) *practicing competing responses* in front of a mirror in order to ensure inconspicuousness of the response, and (11) *solicitation of social support* (e.g., praise from significant others for behavioral success). Finally, it is recommended that treatment be concluded with (12) *a habit inconvenience review* (i.e., a discussion of the ways in which the patient's condition interferes with life functioning) and (13) *a display of improvement.* The latter component stresses deliberate and prolonged exposure to situations previously avoided. Azrin et al. (1980) replicated their original work in a study comparing habit-reversal training to negative practice in 34 hair pullers. Negative practice requires the patient to enact and exaggerate the hair pulling response with great frequency, while refraining from actually pulling hair from the scalp. The theoretical rationale posits that continued responding (hair pulling) in the absence of reinforcement (urge reduction) will ultimately result in extinction. Results indicated that patients engaged in 90% less hair pulling with habit reversal, compared to 50% with negative practice.

Conclusion

The treatment for and management of the OCD spectrum poses a great challenge. To treat more than one psychiatric condition in one person requires skill and a good dose of magic, as one disease causes multiple responses, mobilizing all of the bodily subsystems. The biobehavioral program is an integral approach to this situation, targeting several considerations: the brain's complexity, electrohistochemical mapping, medication specificity, behavioral and cognitive techniques, the patient's emotional world and family network, and socioeconomic determinants.

The treatment of the OCD spectrum demands personalized and continuous attention, including very close supervision and the active participation of a multidisciplinary staff and the patient's family members.

9

Adjunct Therapies

A S WE HAVE DISCUSSED in previous chapters, OCD is very complex and difficult to treat because its pathology is multivariate: It includes anatomy, biochemistry, heredity, learning behavior, family interaction, and social factors. To obviate the several hindrances encountered in the treatment of OCD, we must go beyond the classical pharmacological and behavioral techniques and also include adjunct therapies. These therapies respond to the need to treat the psychosocial variables afflicting the patient.

Family Intervention

Family intervention is valuable in that it fulfills two important needs: (1) the patient's need for a strong emotional and economic network, and (2) the requirement for an accessible, nearby "cotherapist," that is, a family member.

As one patient said, "Living with OCD is hell." A patient with OCD will benefit greatly from emotional bonds with others; love, understanding, and companionship will help him or her cope with such an invasive illness. However, an emotional bond is difficult to establish because the patient needs to be in control and cannot share. These two features undermine any emotional exchange; the patient takes without giving anything in return.

Eventually, as the disease progresses, the patient is incapable of holding a job. The care of OCD is expensive and unless the patient is reasonably wealthy, good treatment becomes only a dream.

There is sufficient well-documented research (e.g., Mehta, 1990) establishing that family participation is conducive to a better treatment outcome. Family intervention emphasizes the importance of the patient's own resources to cope with the illness by utilizing family systems and object-relations approaches.

The Family

A family is a group of people who live together to be loved and to love, to be cared for and to care. Family members also give each other shelter, food, clothing, and upbringing.

A healthy family is interdependent. The amount of dependency varies within the family structure and is related to age, gender, education, economic status, and the degree of dominance. More dominant family members are less dependent on the family.

Normal dependency changes with biological growth, economic freedom, and psychological equilibrium. The dependency increases when one suffers from a physical or mental disorder. In OCD, a paradoxical phenomenon occurs: The patient tends to dominate, while becoming extremely dependent.

The following is a series of guidelines that the therapist may find useful to share with the patient's family.

1. Keep cool at home. Use a quiet manner.
2. Lower expectations temporarily—compare progress this month to last month rather than last year. Observe the patient's progress with the disorder; do not compare his behavior to anyone else's.
3. Overlook rituals and checking; see them as coping strategies. Do not participate in rituals.
4. Do not judge the behavior. Accept it as the best the patient can do right now.
5. Do not pressure the patient to verbalize anxiety (it only makes matters worse).
6. Help channel the patient's energy into activities, such as jogging, swimming, dancing, etc. Activity is more likely to calm the patient than will talking about the obsessive-compulsive behavior.
7. Allow verbal expressions of rage and anger. Listen to what is said. If you are the target of the anger outburst, try not to be defensive.
8. Help the patient develop confidence in his own decisions and choices by allowing him enough time to make them. Never make decisions for the patient; however, if the patient is a very young child, help him make decisions.
9. Do not confront the patient's words or actions; simply reflect the feelings behind them and allow further discussion.
10. Do not pressure the patient to perform the "therapeutic homework," but stick to the time allotted by the therapist. If he is not in therapy, slowly cut back the compulsive activity time.
11. Always explain the behavioral changes the patient has to do—make only reasonable demands.

12. Calmly set limits and be sure everybody knows what the rules are. Limit the amount of time spent talking about obsessional topics and iterative questions to ten minutes or less; conversations pertaining to obsessive-compulsive topics of more than ten minutes may not be productive because they will reinforce the symptoms rather than weaken them. Do not arbitrarily decide to restrict rituals or their duration on your own—ask the therapist.
13. Ignore what you cannot change. Let some things slide. But never ignore violence or suicidal threats.
14. Say what you have to say clearly, calmly, and in a positive way.
15. Be sure the patient takes only medication prescribed by his or her doctor.
16. Be sure the patient does not use street drugs or alcohol; they worsen symptoms.
17. Encourage the patient to carry on life as usual, to reconnect with friends, hobbies, and family routine.
18. Pick up on early changes and signs; consult with the therapist.
19. Solve problems step by step. Make changes gradually. Work on one thing at a time.
20. If the patient is on a behavior modification program, help him follow assignments, allowing time and space in which to do them. Do not get involved unless the patient is a child.

Symptoms that are frequent and intense and cannot be hidden by the patient result in outstanding problem areas. They are outstanding because they are visible and may affect the interaction between the patient and family members. These symptoms demand family participation because the patient is unable to handle them alone. Examples of these problem areas include:

- iterative questioning (one answer is hardly enough)
- doubting (leads to inability to make decisions)
- inability to make decisions (calls for dependency)
- self-centeredness (the patient is always first, and cannot share)
- self-absorption (concentrates on his obsessions)
- aggressiveness (may be outwardly directed)
- bizarre rituals (may ask others to help with his or her rituals)

Behavioral Management with Family Intervention

Awareness, understanding, and acceptance of the disorder by both the patient and family are conducive to practicing home-oriented behavior therapy. The benefits of this approach are reflected in improvements in the following:

- anxiety
- depression
- obsessionality
- compulsions
- verbal and physical hostility
- social adjustment
- work and household duties
- behavior and academic performance in school or college

Family Attitudes and Behaviors toward the Illness and the Patient

Patients with OCD or the spectrum neither enjoy life nor manifest a need for dreaming or coming up with short- or long-term projects. They basically live within their obsessionality to the exclusion of the outside and matters unrelated to OCD.

Family participation brings the present and the reality of everyday life into the patient's focus. Nonetheless, one has to consider the individual pathology of family members. It has been reported (Neziroglu, Yaryura-Tobias, Lemli, et al., 1994) that approximately 50% of family members of patients with OCD suffer from some sort of a major psychiatric disorder; in fact, 8 to 10% of the parents also suffer from OCD. These figures reflect the importance of hereditary factors and learned behaviors affecting treatment outcome in various ways. Furthermore, the therapist's awareness of relatives with OCD living with the patient requires therapeutic intervention to prevent reinforcement of maladaptive behavior.

The family's attitude is fundamental to the patient's management of his condition. Careful scrutiny of patient-family interaction is relevant. Years of disease may have washed away tolerance, hope, and the dream of a better future. Positive and negative interactions must be considered and discussed (table 9.1).

Psychoeducation for all family members living with the patient enhances treatment outcome. It has been our experience that active family intervention in therapeutic procedures is a great improvement factor. Therefore, we consider it a must to bring to the family understanding and acceptance of the disorder and tolerance of the patient's suffering.

Understanding OCD includes explaining the medical and psychological mechanism that is causing the thought pathology and abnormal behaviors. The most important factor that we insist be well understood is the *patient's inability to control symptoms or to function with the family's absolute denial of his having a serious condition.*

Family members are prone to deny the presence of OCD because of the social stigma around mental illness. Denial is a way to reject the illness and

TABLE 9.1 Family attitudes: positive and negative prognostic indicators

Positive Interactions

understanding the illness
cooperating with the treatment
strongly supporting the patient's needs

Negative Interactions

skepticism
frustration
criticism
anger
indifference
emotional overinvolvement

avoid acceptance. Without acceptance, family intervention as cotherapist is prone to failure. But acceptance alone, without a substantial amount of tolerance for the patient's abnormal thinking and behavior, is useless.

The family must distinguish between the normal attitude and behavior of the patient and the attitude and behavior affected by OCD. The family has to know that not all thoughts and behaviors are direct consequences of OCD pathology, but a great number of them are. This knowledge facilitates the application of behavioral therapy at home, and is certainly conducive to accepting and tolerating the patient within an integral frame of reference.

Self-Help Group

The self-help group is a therapeutic modality geared to offer psychoeducational information, emotional support, an opportunity to share OCD experiences, and a way to socialize with an understanding peer group.

A few research papers have been published describing techniques and results of self-help group sessions. For example, the Iowa model is usually patient-generated, and is used for a variety of disorders including OCD (Black, Noyes, Goldstein, & Blum 1992). The model emphasizes patient education and support. A similar group, exclusively for family members, is also described. Overall, these groups report improvement in social management of the illness and in sharing experiences.

For over 15 years, our institute, the Institute for Bio-Behavioral Therapy and Research, has been conducting self-help groups lead by a psychologist. The presence of other persons manifesting similar symptoms and discussions of how they handle those symptoms and what effect OCD has had on their lives make for a provocative and stimulating exchange. We encourage patients to bring in family members. The results are positive in that patients become more aware of OCD, its implications, and various methods for dealing with the condition.

Group Therapy

Several proposals for group treatment have been advanced. Overall, these projects are quite similar to self-help groups in that both models emphasize support and psychoeducational training. However, some group therapy approaches apply specific cognitive and behavioral instructions (Hafner, 1992; Tynes et al., 1990). Although the therapeutic gains were small, patients improved in the following nonspecific areas:

- enhanced mood
- increased sense of hope
- reduction in disabling effects causing by the illness
- better understanding of the disorder
- more control over obsessions/compulsions

As a result, a significant reduction of obsessionality and compulsions, depression, and anxiety occurs.

Occupational Therapy

The goal of occupational therapy is to make the patient more functional. The worse scenario for a patient with OCD is to remain idle. Giving the patient a daily list of activities is important; he or she must get up in the morning looking forward to the new day. In this way, he will have less free time to engage in repetitive and unproductive thinking and performance of compulsions and rituals. Planned activities will also give the patient opportunities to escape the chronic routine of behaviors that keeps him in a vicious cycle throughout the day.

When the pathological routine cycle is broken, the patient can become involved in a healthier schedule. One way to move in that direction is to use the Model of Human Occupation (Bavaro, 1991), which helps to identify major disruptions in habituation and to asses volition, and thus to evaluate the patient's ability to perform and his or her capacity to adjust to the environment.

Art Therapy

At the psychiatric unit of Winthrop University Hospital, Mineola, New York, we have used a model incorporating free drawing followed by reading poetry of published authors as well as patients. Sessions revolve around a given theme; the drawings and poetry are not analyzed, but used to express inner and outer perceptions. Although symptoms remained basically unchanged in participants with OCD, during the three-hour sessions they were able to act symptom-free, perhaps because they were able to concentrate exclusively on the sessions. Once the sessions finished, their behaviors reverted back to the old pattern. We think this model will operate well in a long-term program. Unfortunately, short hospitalization admissions are not conducive to implementing this therapy on a lomg-term basis. To conclude, not much research has been done in art therapy for OCD. This seems to be a new therapeutic area to be explored.

Meditation

Meditation is an exercise in self-reflection. Actually, meditation is the act of deep thinking, which requires time to practice and a time out from activities. Although meditation is often associated with spirituality or religiosity, it is not necessary to subscribe to any particular set of beliefs. One need simply accept the existence of a soul consciousness and a body consciousness in order to reap the benefits of meditation. In this manner, meditation becomes more effective, for meditation is a lifestyle and is therefore an important coadjuvant treatment choice.

There is no formal information on the action of meditation on OCD, and we are not aware of any published methodologically designed research in this regard. Recently, a few papers have been presented at scientific meetings, and the conclusions of their observations are few and equivocal. We have explored meditation for OCD in a very anecdotal manner, that is, without following a strict methodology. We are currently designing a research protocol to study the effects of meditation on OCD. Meanwhile, we would like to share some ideas that we communicate to our patients.

Some of the living values or set of norms that some schools of meditation include in their lifestyle seem to be oppositional to some pathological attitudes and beliefs held by patients with OCD (table 9.2). If the patient adopts some of these beliefs, we may expect to see an improvement in symptomatology.

Treatment

If possible, the patient should always meditate in the same room. Preferably it should be softly lighted and quiet. The patient may sit in the lotus position or in any other position that is comfortable. If desired, a candle or incense can be placed at a reasonable distance so that she can focus on the light of the candle or the burning incense. The aroma of the incense adds an additional feature to set the mood for relaxation and concentration.

Patients with OCD face three major obstacles to the practice of meditation: inability to sit still, obsessionality, and poor concentration. Severe

TABLE 9.2 Attitudes and beliefs related to OCD and its treatment

Patients with OCD	Opposing Values
constricted	carefree
fearful	reassuring
worried, dependent	moderately detached
unable to make decisions	courageous
self-centered	generous
restless	patient
low self-esteem	self-confident
complex	simple
intolerant	accepting

anxiety and the need to perform compulsive acts or rituals prevent the patient from being still and able to concentrate. Obsessionality and concentration go hand in hand, because obsessions prevent normal thought from emerging. Consequently, patients with OCD cannot concentrate as they wish. The obsessive thought forces its way into the brain with unusual force and endurance, and refuses to go away. This intrusive thinking is overwhelming and sends the patient into despair. The inability to function is the result of severe symptomatology and is difficult to minimize and certainly to eradicate.

The purpose of meditation is to gradually interfere with the continuity or perseverance of the same useless obsessive thought. Obsessive thoughts storm the brain at the beginning of the meditation session, but then leave very fast. Skillful practitioners of meditation are able to dismiss those thoughts very rapidly and reach a deeper meditative state that allows them to focus on one major thought of their choice. Further, in higher levels of consciousness, some people are able to erase their thoughts completely, achieving a highly spiritual trance, that is, one beyond thought. However, the OCD patient should be happy to be able to moderately control the amount of obsessive thinking. To sit still, to concentrate better, and to decrease the intensity and frequency of obsessions are remarkable accomplishments.

Nutrition

Nutrition is one of the many biobehavioral tools used to correct, as much as possible, any deviation from the norm. Good nutrition is important since nutrients manufacture neurotransmitters, coenzymes, hormones, and other elements, to make the body a healthy functioning system. Patients with OCD or its associated conditions may also suffer from biochemical imbalances related to nutrition.

As an example let's look at several biochemical reactions that seem to play an important role in the pathogenesis of OCD. One is the metabolism of the amino acid tryptophan, the precursor of serotonin, a neurotransmitter that seems to mediate OCD pathology. Another one is vitamin B6, as the coenzyme pyridoxal phosphate, required to convert tryptophan to serotonin. A third one is glucose, a major factor for brain metabolism. Cerebral and peripheral glucose metabolism seems altered in OCD, as shown in positron emission tomography or during a 5-hour oral glucose tolerance test (Yaryura-Tobias, 1988).

A deficit of or a dependency on (the individual needs higher levels of a vitamin) vitamins of the B complex has been related to OCD (Hermesh et al., 1988).

Needless to say, eating disorders cause a chaotic nutritional problem, either by the severe decrease in food intake in anorexia or an increase of intake in compulsive obesity.

The patient with bulimia also has nutritional problems, which are aggravated by vomiting (affecting electrolytes and blood pH) or the use of laxatives, which affect the absorption of nutrients and minerals from the intestines. For those who severely deprive themselves of proteins, an aggravation of OCD may ensue, since l-tryptophan is lacking. Furthermore, hypoproteinemia may lead to brain atrophy—a diagnosis to be considered in those special cases. Restoration of food intake reverses the atrophy.

Food allergies may affect not only the skin and the respiratory tract, but also the gastrointestinal system and the brain. Indirectly, allergy symptomatology of the brain may manifest symptoms such as fatigue, headaches, irritability, and somnolence. These characteristics are commonly seen in allergic patients in general. The pharmacological profile of antihistamines must correlate with the anti-obsessive-compulsive agent, since both drugs can be incompatible with Cytochrome P450 (see chapter 6), which may interfere negatively with some drug interactions.

Traditionally diets have been prescribed for different ailments: There are diets for hypertension, kidney disorders, allergies, high cholesterol—the list is extensive. Unfortunately, there is no specific diet for OCD and its spectrum. But perhaps some recommendations extracted from empirical or anecdotal knowledge can be useful. Patients with OCD may benefit by eating foods rich in tryptophan (e.g., milk, turkey) or even in serotonin (e.g., pineapple). Certainly the amounts consumed are far from pharmacological doses. Patients who are overstimulated, irascible, or nervous may do better by reducing foods with psychomotor stimulant properties. Refraining from coffee, alcohol, chocolate, and refined sugars may be helpful. For patients who require a calming effect because they are continuously angry, a vegetarian diet with a little white meat or fish will have a positive effect in a long-term program.

Patients who are very anxious and irritable can control some of their symptoms by avoiding refined carbohydrates (sugars, candies, pastries) and substituting a complex carbohydrate diet and fruits for the sweet tooth.

Physical Exercise

"A healthy mind in a healthy body" is a valid axiom for today's society. Patients suffering with OCD or its associated conditions present symptoms that can benefit from regular exercises adjusted to the patient's physical fitness.

- Anxiety, panic, and stress can be helped by stretch exercises, low impact aerobics, and calisthenics.
- Breathing exercises, as used in meditation techniques, are a good companion throughout the day, if one dedicates a few moments to stretch out and do breathing exercises. Breathing will help patients who hyperventilate due to panic or anger.
- A very complete exercise, that is, one that works on the muscular and respiratory systems, is jogging or brisk walking. Aerobics stimulate the production of endorphins, helping the patient with depression by boosting the mood. Swimming is also a complete exercise; in addition, swimming has soothing hydrotherapeutic effects.
- Horseback riding has been reported to improve low self-esteem, feelings of inadequacy, or exaggerated fear, such as in phobias.
- Sports in general, where concentration is a requirement, may reduce the intensity and frequency of obsessive-compulsive symptoms.

Social Skills Training

Social skills training is a therapeutic modality that is useful to remedy patients' social deficits. This training has been utilized in schizophrenia, depression, alcoholism, and other major psychiatric disorders affecting patients' functioning. Social skill remedial techniques seem to assist in symptom control, in shaping up appropriate responses, and in extinguishing inappropriate or socially maladaptive behaviors (see table 9.3).

OCD is an enslaving disease that forces patients to cater for years to their symptoms. Consequently, patients cannot keep or gain friends, may be unable to date or become emotionally involved, and cannot handle business relations or cope with school pressure or demands.

A patient who is interested in moving into the social mainstream needs to behave like any normal individual. He or she has to practice social ease, mutual respect, understanding, a compromising attitude, self-awareness,

TABLE 9.3   Behavior domains for social skills interventions

---

conversation skills

introductions

selecting a topic for conversation

staying on topic / changing topics

starting / ending conversations

identifying nonverbal cues associated with a listener's
    maintaining or losing interest

ending conversations / cues associated with ending social
    interaction

appropriate facial expressions

appropriate eye-contact

appropriate distance from listener

reciprocity (turn-taking)

---

sacrifice for others, loyalty, awareness of others, moderate detachment, and thoughtfulness.

OCD symptoms and behaviors that cause social deficits include dependence, glueiness (severe dependence), lack of social judgment, inadequate social manners, logorrhea, loss of capacity to shift topics, self-centeredness, speech speed, verboseness, and circumstantiality.

Patients are unable to converse about a theme, relate an event, or engage in focused conversation. They tend to branch out, diverging from the topic or simply detouring from the main line of the conversation.

Dependence

Patients have a strong need to rely on others to function. Dependence stems from two symptoms that work together: doubting and inability to make decisions. Of course, there is a great degree of variability associated to symptom severity. Not every patient is continuously dependent. Some patients may need someone to make decisions for them in matters they consider beyond their capacity to decide; some count on others to cope with life responsibilities.

Some patients present a special feature characterized by the need to be very close to another person, usually a family member living in the same house. This person has to be always in view or nearby. To be left alone causes unsurmountable stress or even anger. This highly close relationship may be willingly accepted by the involved family member. In this case, a symbiotic relationship develops. When this occurs, any attempt to break the pathological binding will be rejected. Moreover, symbiosis will sabotage treatment outcome, because either the patient or the family member will persevere in order to preserve the gains. Glueiness is also a symptom of the epileptic personality, notably seen in major seizure disorders such as temporal lobe epilepsy (TLE). Note that OCD symptoms are commonly observed in TLE.

Inadequate Social Manners

Severe intensity and frequency of symptoms interferes with the learning of social manners. Early onset of OCD in children may show these deficits over time. As the illness becomes chronic and obsessions and compulsions cause maladaptive behaviors, the social deficits become more obvious and less acceptable by the surrounding milieu. Common social inadequacies include:

- how to greet another person
- how to shop
- how to eat in public
- poor eating manners
- how to date
- how to behave during a job interview

These basic social behaviors can be extremely difficult to implement. Patients who are homebound, living in isolation, or have obvious bizarre behaviors will find it difficult to modify old patterns of behaviors. These behaviors establish a barrier between patients and society, preventing them from having a normal life even if symptoms are under control. As a consequence, patients cannot study or work, and they are unable to be loved and to have their own family.

Lack of Social Judgment

Patients with OCD usually tend to judge others under an obsessive-compulsive perspective. This view reflects rigidity, questioning of right and wrong, order, meticulosity, and cleanliness. These parameters become hypertrophied in the patient's mind, and in time such standards create social conflicts. As patients state, "People don't live up to my standards."

Logorrhea

Logorrhea is defined as pathological talkativeness, which is at times incoherent. Logorrhea is observed in psychomotor excitation, hypomania, hyperactivity, manic-depressive illness, and OCD. Patients with OCD suffering from logorrhea usually complain of mind racing and thoughts coming up faster than words to express them. Logorrhea is uncommon in OCD, and if observed will not only lead the diagnostician to a better diagnosis, but also indicate the need to explore the possibility that the patient's social life is affected by logorrhea.

Loss of Capacity to Shift Topics

In chapter 2, we mentioned that patients with OCD cannot shift from one topic to the next unless the topic is finished, nor can they be interrupted from tasks they are performing—to do so would create aggravation. In any school or work situation there are a reasonable number of interruptions during the day; patients have to become aware of this "problem" that goes unnoticed by most. Patients see these interruptions as rude behaviors, and they resent them. They fail to realize that interruptions are part of sharing a given activity.

Self-Centeredness

One characteristic that permeates through the OCD profile is self-centeredness. This negative quality sets the pace for establishing a good or bad interrelationship between patients and others. Patients are immersed in their own selves and their own lives and OCD absorbs them continuously. Therefore, they automatically reject events, problems, or any other life circumstance affecting those close to them. Patients with OCD come across as selfish and indifferent individuals who are only concerned with their problems. Further, since they are quite dependent on others to be able to cope with life, friction, quarrels, and tension determine the family interaction. They don't understand that life is a give-and-take proposition.

Moving from egocentric attitudes to generosity might be the way to minimize egocentricity, making the patient more likable.

Speech Slowness

The manner in which we address others, the speed of our speech, and the way we present the content of our conversations determine the effect we have on others and whether we obtain what we want from our conversation. Some patients with OCD suffer from an atypical form of speech known as slowness, which is manifested by slow thinking and slow speech. This form seems to be the result of several causes: (a) hesitation to form a sentence, (b) need for accuracy in the statement to be made, (c) need to pause with equal timing between words or sentences, and (d) interest in perfect diction to prevent misunderstandings. All of these requirements need time to implement them. Patients with slow speech jeopardize their ability to converse, making the interlocutor restless and bored. Subsequently, the conversation may be abruptly ended.

Target Areas for Social Skills Training

A series of 12 sessions may suffice to train a patient with OCD. Sessions are once a week for 45 minutes, with a total duration of three months. Individual role playing and corrective feedback are conducted for 30 minutes, and the other 15 minutes are spent training the patient to use the technique.

Conversation Skills
Conversation skills to target include:

- introduction
- selecting a topic for conversation
- staying on topic and changing topics
- starting and ending conversation
- identifications of nonverbal cues associated with a listener's maintaining or losing interest
- ending conversations/cues associated with ending social interaction
- appropriate facial expressions
- appropriate eye-contact
- distance from listener
- taking turns, reciprocity

Treatment consists of cognitive and behavioral techniques including exposure and response prevention.

House Chores Training
Patients often have difficulty carrying out domestic chores because they have lost their sense of priority. In milder forms of OCD, patients retain their priorities and are able to prepare a list of daily activities. Other symptoms interfering with house chores are double-checking, perfectionism, obsessions with order or symmetry, and fear of contamination.

Some patients need to constantly double-check their work, others demand perfection in their chores, and still others need to place everything in an exact and predetermined order. Those who suffer from a fear of contamination or an ongoing urge to clean will spend hours sanitizing and cleaning. Many patients will work through the late hours of the night, with little sleep, in order to finish their chores.

Eating Manners
Patients with OCD may be concerned with their eating. Problem areas:

- swallowing rather than chewing
- slow eating (hours to finish a meal)
- picking or rejecting food items from the meal placed in front of them
- avoidance of eating in front of others
- need to prepare their meal alone, so that food preparation follows a predetermined ritual
- fears of choking on food

Dating
OCD with early onset may suppress sexual curiosity and the desire to establish an emotional relationship with another person. Therefore, the patient may have foregone adolescent and early adult dating. When the patient feels ready to socialize, it is often much later than the norm. Consequently, the patient needs to be trained in courtship, using attitudes and behaviors compatible with his or her age. Certainly, it is difficult to "catch up" with lost years of emotional fulfillment.

Shopping
Shopping for food, clothing, or anything else is an insurmountable ordeal for those who suffer from severe doubting and cannot make decisions. These patients end up delegating these tasks to others or asking someone to accompany them. A cotherapist may go shopping with the patient and clock the amount of time it takes the patient to select and pay for a very few items. Gradually, time and numbers of items are increased.

Posture
Hypervigilance, anxiety, depression, and thought rigidity mold the body posture of a patient with OCD. This rigid posture is also observable in the face, where expressions are kept to a minimum, quite similar to Parkinson's "poker face." Remedies for a better posture include exercises, yoga, dancing, and facial exercises in front of a mirror. The therapist should

remember that patients treated with neuroleptics may present facial and postural symptoms as side effects.

Conclusion

Adjunct therapies, although not essential to directly target the OCD nucleus, facilitate the patient's recovery. Once improvement is achieved, it is then time to habilitate and/or rehabilitate the patient. The patient's family is the most important factor during the patient's course of the illness. Because the family is a network of interdependence, the patient's strong tendency to depend on others may impair treatment outcome, which requires the ability to make decisions and resources to be self-sufficient. Self-help groups bring into focus the intimacy of illness, which is usually preserved by the patient's modesty. This forum, run by patients, helps to remove the mystery of the illness. Here symptoms are shared; patients feel better just by knowing they are not alone in their misery. Meetings also provide an opportunity to discuss medications and its side effects as well as tips to tackle specific problems, annoying symptoms, insomnia, etc.

Group therapy, occupational therapy, and art therapy are additional aids that when properly applied may enhance the overall treatment approach.

Meditation opens the door for the patient to the art of reducing the superficial thinking process to a slow and in-depth thought process. This technique may help the patient to regulate the intensity and frequency of the obsessional thinking.

Once the patient has improved, social skills training may be in order, because most patients have serious difficulties interacting socially. Although not very popular with managed care companies, social skills training is a fundamental tool that will promote the welfare of the patient with OCD.

10

Prognosis

MEDICINE, AND CERTAINLY PSYCHIATRY, is a combination of science and art. To limit psychiatric studies to a strict scientific paradigm is arguable, because psychiatry encompasses biopsychosocial parameters that may not respond to the application of scientific methodology. The intuition and experience of the practitioner coupled with a dash of creativeness are important for a better treatment outcome.

It is very difficult to treat OCD while excluding other concomitant parameters. Therefore, all those factors need to be considered for treatment purposes, and certainly for prognostic indicators. Finally, weak knowledge of OCD, limited *DSM-IV* classification scope, and dubious methodology to assess symptoms, both their severity and improvement, certainly create hesitations to endorse a priori a successful outcome. We feel the protean symptomatology of OCD requires a classification revision to offer wider diagnostic capability and therapeutic flexibility.

Prognosis is one of the most trying aspects of OCD. Prognosis depends not only on the natural course of the disease but also on many intertwining variables. If proper treatment is instituted, the likelihood of success is considerable, but of course this is subject to a number of psychosocial and psychiatric variables that may alter treatment outcome.

Psychosocial Variables

Major psychosocial outcome modifiers include:

- lack of motivation
- patient's secondary gains
- family's secondary gains
- lack of support systems
- psychiatric family pathology
- prior level of functioning
- procrastination

Motivation is the most important factor that keeps everybody fit to function and cope with life for years to come. Unmotivated patients are prone to failure, even if they adhere to some form or aspect of treatment (e.g., pharmacotherapy). Failure is the result of our complex brain that operates in unison with several biopsychosocial factors dealing with OCD. These factors have been discussed in chapter 6, and they comprise all the parameters used to assess and treat OCD or its spectrum.

Motivation must be addressed with patients and their families. Before starting therapy, patients should be able to state their reasons for seeking treatment. If they cannot, the therapist should assist them to find at least one. The will to improve is not enough; it must be accompanied by the willingness to pursue a given goal.

A factor often ignored by the therapist, who is mostly absorbed by the severity of the symptoms, is the *patient's gains by remaining ill*. In chronic patients under the care of their families, dependency is very strong and difficult to uproot. Patients feel very comfortable relinquishing their responsibilities and letting someone else make decisions. As we know, an inability to make decisions is one of the core OCD symptoms.

We recommend that therapists acquaint themselves with the family's living arrangements. Many patients refuse to shop or do any household chores under the excuse of having incapacitating symptoms. Others refuse to be left alone, out of unreasonable fears (e.g., agoraphobia). And although some explanations might be valid, others are quite false.

Family gains, perhaps, transpire more pathology than expected. There may be a family member who has dedicated his or her life to caring for the patient. The person involved is usually a female, mother or spouse, who makes this activity the reason for her life. These devoted persons have a hidden need to keep the patient so they will continue to have a purpose in life. What used to be, at the onset of OCD, a meritory disposition to care for the patient's needs, has become with the passage of time, paradoxically, a means to fulfill their own personal needs.

The therapist will be able to detect family gains by observing family dynamics and asking the appropriate questions.

Support networks infuse therapy with strength and endurance. Patients who do not have such networks are left to their own emotional turmoil, indecisiveness, and doubting and will fare badly in outcome. A structured life program that complements behavioral intervention will regulate the patient's daily activities, medication adherence, and behavioral homework.

Family psychiatric pathology plays a direct influence on outcome by affecting psychosocial areas of family interaction. These family members (1) do not understand OCD, (2) cannot distinguish normal from abnormal behavior, (3) reinforce OCD symptomatology, (4) indirectly approve maladaptive behaviors, (5) are preoccupied with their own illness, and (6) have no time for the patient with OCD.

Considering that 50% of family members present a psychiatric illness, of which 8% are parents of patients with OCD who also suffer from OCD (Neziroglu et al., 1994), poor prognosis in these cases should not surprise anyone.

The patient's *prior level of functioning* is an important determinant in outcome. We have reached the conclusion, after reviewing many charts, that good outcome is correlated with good functioning before becoming ill. Conversely, patients unable to attain school or academic degrees, who do not have steady jobs, or who fail in their emotional endeavors do poorly in treatment outcome.

Those whose conditions have an early onset present a substantial lack of knowledge, insufficient skills, and poor coping mechanisms. These patients require extra efforts to compensate for the many social deficits undoubtedly affecting prognosis. The procrastinator is an indifferent, lazy, or self-destructive person who avoids responsibilities. This characteristic certainly interferes with the patient's adherence to the therapeutic program. Procrastination in patients with OCD seems related to inner anger and self-destructive behavior in terms of destroying social relations, school or work performance, etc. Psychotherapy directed at modifying procrastination must precede OCD treatment; otherwise treatment is prone to failure.

Psychiatric Variables

Major psychiatric outcome modifiers include:

- other coexisting psychiatric disorders
- overvalued ideas
- delusions
- personality disorders
- brain anatomical changes
- childhood onset of illness
- lapse between onset of illness and beginning of treatment
- severity and frequency of symptoms

Psychiatric disorders, whether coexisting, grafted, or inserted in an ongoing OCD process, may interfere with the evolution of OCD, affecting its outcome. This is caused by symptoms alien (pertaining to other major psychiatric disorders) to the main OCD core that are refractory to the pharmacological or psychotherapeutic intervention directly geared toward OCD symptomatology. These symptoms are abnormal thought disorders excluding obsessionality, somatosensorial dysperception (e.g., eating disorders, body dysmorphic disorder), self-harm, and catatonic-like motor impairment, including slowness. When these symptoms are present, the therapist must tailor the treatment to the special symptomatological needs of the patient. Keep in mind that severe depression may prevent the patient from engaging in any form of therapy. "I feel like doing nothing" is a typical answer when the patient is questioned. In this instance, cognitive therapy may be a powerful ally.

An *overvalued idea* is a strong conviction or belief that is extremely difficult to eradicate. This symptom is observed in four major psychiatric entities: body dysmorphic disorder, eating disorders, hypochondriasis, and atypical OCD. Overvalued ideas are difficult to treat. Perhaps the best approach is to use a combination of cognitive therapy and medication. Overall outcome is uncertain.

Delusions are another group of symptoms pathognomonic of psychosis. Nonetheless, in atypical forms of OCD (e.g., atypical OCD psychosis), schizophrenia with obsessive components, OCD with psychotic components, schizoaffective disorder with obsessive-compulsive symptoms, and paranoid disorders in general with OCD features, an imbrication occurs, posing therapeutic problems that are difficult to resolve. These problems are: (1) the irreversible belief of the thought process, (2) the distrust and fear of threat that prevents adherence to pharmacological intervention or psychological suggestions, and (3) an inability to commit to a therapeutic contract.

Personality disorders are overall a serious modifier of OCD therapeutic outcome. Obsessive premorbid personality disorder or any other type of personality disorder hinders treatment outcome.

Brain anatomical changes may induce OCD atypical forms that resist treatment. Brain lesions such as tumors, cerebrovascular accidents, atrophies, cysts, or degenerative processes will determine treatment outcome. Patients with OCD and anatomical changes are basically indifferent to their illness, do not report anxiety, and are subsequently hesitant to engage in a treatment program. Their concrete thought process blocks their ability to participate in a behavioral and cognitive program. Adherence to treatment is almost nil.

Onset of illness also plays a considerable role in determining treatment outcome. The early onset of either the "full" illness (the classical OCD presentation) or obsessional and/or phobic symptoms during childhood are poor prognosis predictors.

The lapse between the onset of illness and the first consult and treatment may set the pace of recovery. The average lapse ranges between seven and ten years. Longer lapses may delay or prevent recovery. However, recent renewed interest in neuron plasticity, an indicator of functional restitution, may transform a chronic condition into a reversible state (Yaryura-Tobias & Neziroglu, 1997).

Symptom severity and frequency are two variables that influence outcome. Severely ill patients are unable to take care of themselves, fail to take medication, cannot engage in behavioral therapy, and cannot concentrate enough to participate in cognitive therapy. Patients are devastated by their symptoms, report strong feelings of hopelessness, and have serious family disturbance situations. Hospitalization is then a proposal to consider.

Exogenous and Endogenous Factors

In addition to psychosocial and psychiatric variables, exogenous and endogenous factors also influence prognosis. Exogenous factors influencing a psychiatric disorder are social upbringing, family education, social interaction, academic and working conditions, economic status, cultural and spiritual values, political regime, and the natural environment with its stable and seasonal variables.

Endogenous factors as contributors of psychiatric treatment are heretogenetic factors, anatomo-electro-biochemical make-up, nutrition, stress, infections, other medical conditions, and side effects of medication for other medical conditions.

Neurosurgery

The prognosis of treatment with neurosurgery depends on the severity of the symptomatology, the type of OCD, and the procedure employed. The literature is not very optimistic, yielding figures of improvement that range between 30 and 80% (Pato et al., 1988). However, there is no long-term follow-up. Recent studies on neurosurgery speak of a 30 to 40% improvement rate (Mindus et al., 1994). In general, the obsessive-compulsive symptomatology follows a brief period of improvement with a subsequent relapse. Suppression of anxiety, blunting of the affect, and indifference toward the illness are common postsurgical clinical observations.

In addition, we have observed a postsurgical syndrome, which is transient but often present for a prolonged time. This syndrome may have the following features: personality changes, regression to primitive behavioral states (e.g., fetal position), depression, psychotic bouts, and suicide.

Malignant Form

Certain forms of OCD follow a fluctuating course of improvement and worsening, with a gradual decline, similar to the course of multiple sclerosis. This is not a rare form, although systematic studies in this regard are unavailable. Throughout the years of our commitment to the study of OCD, we have been baffled by the presence of distinct forms of OCD courses that, despite cyclic improvement, gradually fall into decline. Effective medications or behavior techniques promising in typical OCD forms do not have a positive effect in the malignant form. We usually consider neurosurgery for this subgroup. Further, this form is classified therapeutically as refractory; nosologically it is not always classified as malignant. The analogy of malignant OCD with terminal cancer is acceptable. Not enough investigation has been dedicated to pursue the origins and mechanisms of the malignant form.

Conclusion

Because OCD etiology has not yet been determined, well-defined treatment programs are nonexistent. This statement applies to all forms of therapy, whether administered individually or in combined form. This observation is corroborated by current findings reporting an improvement rate of about 50% (Yaryura-Tobias & Neziroglu, 1997). The other 50% consists of refractory cases or treatment failures. Searching for a better improvement rate, we began to explore other avenues of treatment modalities. At the Institute for Bio-Behavioral Treatment and Research we believe that a biopsychosocial model for OCD may enlighten other therapeutic avenues. As we have outlined in this book, our multidisciplinary approach focuses on the medical and psychological aspects of OCD, within a family and social context. A patient's lifestyle, nutritional status, physical exercise activities, ability for self-introspection, faculty to interact with others, and capacity to adjust to a changeable world are all variables to explore.

Appendix: Assessment Scales

Behavior Measurement Chart

Instructions

Please record the actual number of minutes you spend on Ritual A and Ritual B on the attached sheet. In the box titled "Activity or Thought that Evokes the Ritual," write a very *brief* description of what caused you to do your rituals. In the box titled "Discomfort," record how you felt at that moment on a 0-to-100 scale (0 means completely calm and 100 means extremely upset or disturbed.).

For washing or cleaning rituals, record how many minutes or seconds that you spent washing your hands, bathing, or cleaning things around you. Record the time you start this activity and the time you are done with it. *For checking rituals,* record how many minutes or seconds you spend checking. Record the time you start to check a particular item and the time you finish checking that item and leave the situation.

Example

Ritual A ___Washing___   Ritual B ___Checking___

Time of Day	Activity or Thought that Evokes the Ritual	Discomfort (0–100)	Number of Minutes Spent on Rituals	
			A	**B**
6:00 – 6:30 AM				
9:00 – 9:30				
9:30 – 10:00	Took out garbage	70	4 min.	
11:30 – 12:00 PM	Bathroom — urination	80	5 min. 25 sec.	
12:00 – 12:30	Unplugged iron	40		6 min.
6:30 – 7:00	Checked stove after dinner	60		10 min.

Self-Monitoring of Rituals

Name _____   Date _____

Ritual A _____   Ritual B _____

In the second column of the table below please describe the activity or thought that evokes the ritual. In the third column record the anxiety / discomfort level (0–100). In the fourth column write the number of minutes you spend performing the rituals during the time stated in column 1.

Time of Day	Activity or Thought that Evokes the Ritual	Discomfort (0–100)	Number of Minutes Spent on Rituals	
			A	B
6:00 – 6:30 AM				
6:30 – 7:00				
7:00 – 7:30				
7:30 – 8:00				
8:00 – 8:30				
8:30 – 9:00				
9:00 – 9:30				
9:30 – 10:00				
10:00 – 10:30				
10:30 – 11:00				
11:00 – 11:30				
11:30 – 12:00				
12:00 – 12:30 PM				
12:30 – 1:00				
1:00 – 1:30				
1:30 – 2:00				

Time of Day	Activity or Thought that Evokes the Ritual	Discomfort (0–100)	Number of Minutes Spent on Rituals	
			A	B
2:00 – 2:30				
2:30 – 3:00				
3:00 – 3:30				
3:30 – 4:00				
4:00 – 4:30				
4:30 – 5:00				
5:00 – 5:30				
5:30 – 6:00				
6:00 – 6:30				
6:30 – 7:00				
7:00 – 7:30				
7:30 – 8:00				
8:00 – 8:30				
8:30 – 9:00				
9:00 – 9:30				
9:30 – 10:00				
10:00 – 10:30				
10:30 – 11:00				
11:00 – 11:30				
11:30 – 12:00				
1:30 – 6:00 AM				
TOTAL				

Beck Depression Inventory

Date: _____

Name: _____   Marital Status: ___ Age: ___ Sex: ___

Occupation: _____   Education: _____

Instructions

This questionnaire consists of 21 groups of statements. After reading each group of statements carefully, circle the number (0, 1, 2, or 3) next to the one statement in each group that **best** describes the way you have been feeling the **past week, including today.** If several statements within a group seem to apply equally well, circle each one. **Be sure to read all the statements in each group before making your choice.** [Note that the following two items are representative examples of the inventory.]

1.   **0**   I do not feel sad.

      1   I feel sad.

      2   I am sad all the time and I can't snap out of it.

      3   I am so sad or unhappy that I can't stand it.

2.   **0**   I am not particularly discouraged about the future.

      1   I feel discouraged about the future.

      2   I feel I have nothing to look forward to.

      3   I feel that the future is hopeless and that things cannot improve.

Beck Anxiety Inventory

Name: _____   Date: _____

Instructions

Below is a list of common symptoms of anxiety. Please carefully read each item in the list. Indicate how much you have been bothered by each symptom during the PAST WEEK, INCLUDING TODAY, by placing an X in the corresponding space in the column next to each symptom. [Note that the following two items are representative examples of the inventory.]

	Not at all	Mildly It did not bother me much	Moderately It was very unpleasant, but I could stand it	Severely I could barely stand it.
7. Heart pounding or racing.				
14. Fear of losing control.				

Self-Evaluation Questionnaire

Name: _____ Date: _____

Age: _____ Sex: M ___ F ___

Instructions

A number of statements that people have used to describe themselves are given below. Read each statement and then blacken the appropriate circle to the right of the statement to indicate how you feel right now, that is, at this moment. There are no right or wrong answers. Do not spend too much time on any one statement but give the answer that seems to best describe your present feelings. [Note that the following five items are representative examples of the State-Trait Anxiety Inventory, developed by Charles D. Spielberger in collaboration with R. L. Gorsuch, R., Lushene, P. R. Vagg, and G. A. Jacobs.]

	Not at all	Somewhat	Moderately so	Very much so
7. I am presently worrying over possible misfortunes	①	②	③	④
17. I am worried	①	②	③	④
25. I feel like a failure	①	②	③	④
34. I make decisions easily	①	②	③	④
40. I get in a state of tension or turmoil as I think over my recent concerns and interests	①	②	③	④

Rational Emotive Therapy Homework Sheet

How I Make Myself Upset

A. *Activating Event.* Describe in one sentence the event about which you became upset.

_____

_____

C. *Consequence.* Describe how you felt, or your *emotional reactions* to the above situation.

_____

_____

B. *Belief.* The thoughts you were having and/or the things you were telling yourself about A. Write them down here if they are exaggerated, unrealistic, or cannot be proven (e.g., "should" statements, "I can't stand . . .", It's awful that . . .").

_____

_____

_____

D. *Disputing.* Question and challenge the irrational belief (B). Ask yourself if there is real evidence for these beliefs. If there is none, provide a more rational alternative belief.

Evidence: _____

_____

_____

Rational Alternative: _____

_____

_____

This homework sheet is provided by the Institute for Bio-Behavioral Therapy & Research; 935 Northern Boulevard, Suite 102; Great Neck, New York 11021; (516) 487-7116

YBOCS Symptom Checklist

Instructions

Generate a *Target Symptoms List* from the *YBOCS Symptom Checklist* by asking the patient about specific obsessions and compulsions. Check all that apply. Distinguish between current and past symptoms. Mark principal symptoms with a "p." These will form the basis of the *Target Symptoms List*. Items marked "*" may or may not be OCD phenomena.

Aggressive Obsessions

Current Past

_____	_____	Fear might harm self
_____	_____	Fear might harm others
_____	_____	Violent or horrific images
_____	_____	Fear of blurting out obscenities or insults
_____	_____	Fear of doing something else embarrassing*
_____	_____	Fear will act on unwanted impulses (e.g., to stab friend)
_____	_____	Fear will steal things
_____	_____	Fear will harm others because not careful enough (e.g., hit/run motor vehicle accident)
_____	_____	Fear will be responsible for something else terrible happening (e.g., fire, burglary)
_____	_____	Other _____

Contamination Obsessions

_____	_____	Concerns or disgust with bodily waste or secretions (e.g., urine, feces, saliva)
_____	_____	Concern with dirt or germs
_____	_____	Excessive concern with environmental contaminants (e.g., asbestos, radiation, toxic waste)
_____	_____	Excessive concern with household items (e.g., cleansers, solvents)
_____	_____	Excessive concern with animals (e.g., insects)
_____	_____	Bothered by sticky substances or residues
_____	_____	Concerned will get ill because of contaminant

Current Past

_____ _____ Concerned will get others ill by spreading contaminant (Aggressive)

_____ _____ No concern with consequences of contamination other than how it might feel

_____ _____ Other _____

Sexual Obsessions

_____ _____ Forbidden or perverse sexual thoughts, images, or impulses

_____ _____ Content involves children or incest

_____ _____ Content involves homosexuality*

_____ _____ Sexual behavior towards others (Aggressive)*

_____ _____ Other _____

Hoarding/Saving Obsessions

(Distinguish from hobbies and concern with objects of monetary or sentimental value)

_____ _____ _____

Religious Obsessions (Scrupulosity)

_____ _____ Concerned with sacrilege and blasphemy

_____ _____ Excess concern with right/wrong, morality

_____ _____ Other _____

Obsession with Need for Symmetry or Exactness

_____ _____ Accompanied by magical thinking (e.g., concerned that another will have accident unless things are in the right place)

_____ _____ Not accompanied by magical thinking

Miscellaneous Obsessions

_____ _____ Need to know or remember

_____ _____ Fear of saying certain things

_____ _____ Fear of not saying just the right thing

_____ _____ Fear of losing things

Current Past

_____ _____ Intrusive (nonviolent) images

_____ _____ Intrusive nonsense sounds, words, or music

_____ _____ Bothered by certain sounds/noises*

_____ _____ Lucky/unlucky numbers

_____ _____ Colors with special significance

_____ _____ Superstitious fears

_____ _____ Others _____

Somatic Obsessions

_____ _____ Concern with illness or disease*

_____ _____ Excessive concern with body part or aspect of appearance (e.g., dysmorphophobia)*

_____ _____ Other ___

Cleaning/Washing Compulsions

_____ _____ Excessive or ritualized handwashing

_____ _____ Excessive or ritualized showering, bathing, toothbrushing, grooming, or toilet routine

_____ _____ Involves cleaning of household items or other inanimate objects

_____ _____ Other measures to prevent or remove contact with contaminants

_____ _____ Other _____

Checking Compulsions

_____ _____ Checking locks, stove, appliances, etc.

_____ _____ Checking that did not/will not harm others

_____ _____ Checking that did not/will not harm self

_____ _____ Checking that nothing terrible did/will happen

_____ _____ Checking that did not make mistake

_____ _____ Checking tied to somatic obsessions

_____ _____ Other _____

Current Past

Repeating Rituals

_____	_____	Rereading or rewriting
_____	_____	Need to repeat routine activities (e.g., in/out door, up/down from chair)
_____	_____	Other _____

Counting Compulsions

_____ _____ _____

Ordering/Arranging Compulsions

_____ _____ _____

Hoarding/Collecting Compulsions

[Distinguish from hobbies and concern with objects of monetary or senti-mental value (e.g., carefully reads junk mail, piles up old newspapers, sorts through garbage, collects useless objects)]

_____ _____ _____

Miscellaneous Compulsions

_____	_____	Mental rituals (other than checking/counting)
_____	_____	Excessive listmaking
_____	_____	Need to tell, ask, or confess
_____	_____	Need to touch, tap, or rub*
_____	_____	Rituals involving blinking or staring*
_____	_____	Measures (not checking) to prevent: harm to self ____; harm to others ____; terrible consequences _____
_____	_____	Ritualized eating behaviors*
_____	_____	Superstitious behaviors
_____	_____	Trichotillomania*
_____	_____	Other self-damaging or self-mutilating behaviors*
_____	_____	Other _____

YBOCS TOTAL (add items 1–10) ☐

Patient Name _____　　Date _____

Patient ID _____　　Rater _____

	None	Mild	Moderate	Severe	Extreme
1. Time spent on obsession	0	1	2	3	4

1b. Obsession-Free Interval (do not add to subtotal or total score)	No symptoms	Long	Moderately Long	Short	Extremely short
	0	1	2	3	4

	None	Mild	Moderate	Severe	Extreme
2. Interference from obsessions	0	1	2	3	4
3. Distress of obsessions	0	1	2	3	4

	Always resists				Completely yields
4. Resistance	0	1	2	3	4

	Complete control	Much control	Moderate control	Little control	No control
5. Control over obsessions	0	1	2	3	4

OBSESSION SUBTOTAL (add items 1–5) ☐

	None	Mild	Moderate	Severe	Extreme
6. Time spent or compulsions	0	1	2	3	4

6b. Compulsion-Free Interval (do not add to subtotal or total score)	No symptoms	Long	Moderately Long	Short	Extremely short
	0	1	2	3	4

	None	Mild	Moderate	Severe	Extreme
7. Interference from compulsions	0	1	2	3	4
8. Distress from compulsions	0	1	2	3	4

	Always resists				Completely yields
9. Resistance	0	1	2	3	4

	Complete control	Much control	Moderate control	Little control	No control
10. Control over compulsions	0	1	2	3	4

COMPULSION SUBTOTAL (add items 6–10) [ ]

	Excellent				Absent
11. Insight into O-C symptoms	0	1	2	3	4

	None	Mild	Moderate	Severe	Extreme
12. Avoidance	0	1	2	3	4
13. Indecisiveness	0	1	2	3	4
14. Pathological responsibility	0	1	2	3	4
15. Slowness	0	1	2	3	4
16. Pathological doubting	0	1	2	3	4

17. Global severity	0	1	2	3	4	5	6
18. Global improvement	0	1	2	3	4	5	6

19. Reliability	Excellent = 0	Good = 1	Fair = 2	Poor = 3

Overvalued Ideas Scale

First name and last initial, or full name: _____

Phone number: _____

Date: _____

To the patient: "Answer the following questions about obsessions and/or compulsions that you experienced in the past week."

List three (3) of the *main* beliefs that the patient has had in the last week (e.g., I am unattractive, my nose is misshapen, my complexion is full of pimples, I will get AIDS if I do not wash properly, my house may burn down if I do not check the stove before leaving the house, etc.) Rate each belief separately. Put a number next to each belief number that best describes your response to the question. **Only list beliefs related to obsessive-compulsive disorder. Rate all items as if the patient were stating the strength of his belief, according to your evaluation.**

1) _____

2) _____

3) _____

1) How strong is the belief?

1	2	3	4	5	6	7	8	9	10
Not very strong									**Very strong**

    Belief #1 Rating _____

    Belief #2 Rating _____

    Belief #3 Rating _____

2) How reasonable is the belief?

| 1 | 2 | 3 | 4 | 5 | 6 | 7 | 8 | 9 | 10 |

Not very reasonable   **Very reasonable**

   Belief #1 Rating   _____

   Belief #2 Rating   _____

   Belief #3 Rating   _____

3) In the last week, what was the *lowest* rating for these beliefs?

| 1 | 2 | 3 | 4 | 5 | 6 | 7 | 8 | 9 | 10 |

Completely unreasonable   **Completely reasonable**

   Belief #1 Rating   _____

   Belief #2 Rating   _____

   Belief #3 Rating   _____

4) In the last week, what was the *highest* rating for these beliefs?

| 1 | 2 | 3 | 4 | 5 | 6 | 7 | 8 | 9 | 10 |

Completely unreasonable   **Completely reasonable**

   Belief #1 Rating   _____

   Belief #2 Rating   _____

   Belief #3 Rating   _____

5) How inaccurate is the belief?

| 1 | 2 | 3 | 4 | 5 | 6 | 7 | 8 | 9 | 10 |

Completely inaccurate   **Completely accurate**

   Belief #1 Rating   _____

   Belief #2 Rating   _____

   Belief #3 Rating   _____

6) How likely is it that others have the same belief?

| 1 | 2 | 3 | 4 | 5 | 6 | 7 | 8 | 9 | 10 |

Completely unreasonable   **Completely reasonable**

   Belief #1 Rating _____

   Belief #2 Rating _____

   Belief #3 Rating _____

7) If other people do not have these beliefs, to what do is this attributed?

| 1 | 2 | 3 | 4 | 5 | 6 | 7 | 8 | 9 | 10 |

They know it is absurd   **They are ignorant/lack information**

   Belief #1 Rating _____

   Belief #2 Rating _____

   Belief #3 Rating _____

8) How effective are the compulsions/ritualistic behaviors in
    preventing negative consequences?

| 1 | 2 | 3 | 4 | 5 | 6 | 7 | 8 | 9 | 10 |

Not very effective   **Very effective**

   Belief #1 Rating _____

   Belief #2 Rating _____

   Belief #3 Rating _____

9) Compared to others, how unusual is the belief?

| 1 | 2 | 3 | 4 | 5 | 6 | 7 | 8 | 9 | 10 |

Completely unusual   **Not at all unusual**

   Belief #1 Rating _____

   Belief #2 Rating _____

   Belief #3 Rating _____

Suggested Readings

Chapter 1

Hollander, E., Zohar, J., Marazziti, D., & Olivier, B. (Eds.). (1994). *Current insights in obsessive-compulsive disorder*. New York: Wiley.

Jenike, M. A., Baer, L., & Minichiello, W. E. (1990). *Obsessive-compulsive disorders: Theory and management*. St. Louis: Mosby Year Book.

Rasmussen, S. A., & Eisen, J. L. (1992). The epidemiology and clinical features of obsessive-compulsive disorder. *Psychiatric Clinics of North America, 14*(4), 743-758.

Ruiloba, J. V., & Berrios, G. E. (1995). *Estados obsesivos* [Obsessive states]. Madrid: Masson.

Yaryura-Tobias, J. A., & Neziroglu, F. A. (1983). *Obsessive-compulsive disorder: Pathogenesis, diagnosis, and treatment*. New York: Marcel Dekker

Yaryura-Tobias, J. A., & Neziroglu, F. A. (1997). *Obsessive-compulsive disorder and its spectrum*. Washington, DC: American Psychiatric Press.

Chapter 2

Beck, A. T., Epstein, N., Brown, G., & Steer, R. A. (1988). An inventory for measuring anxiety: Psychometric properties. *Journal of Consulting and Clinical Psychology, 56*, 893-897.

Beck, A. T., Ward, C. H., Mendelsohn, M., Mock, J., & Erbaugh, J. (1961). An inventory for measuring depression. *Archives of General Psychiatry, 4*, 561-571.

Behar D., Rapoport, J. L., Berg, C. J., et al. (1984). Computerized tomography and neuropsychological test measures in adolescents with obsessive compulsive disorder. *American Journal of Psychiatry, 141*, 336-369.

Insel, T. R., Donnelly, E. F., Lalakea, M. L., et al. (1983). Neurological and neuropsychological studies of patients with obsessive-compulsive disorder. *Biological Psychiatry, 18*, 741-751.

Jenike, M. A., Baer, L., & Minichiello, W. (Eds.). (1990). *Obsessive-compulsive disorders: Theory and management*. St. Louis: Mosby Year Book.

McKay, D., Danyko, S. J., Neziroglu, F., & Yaryura-Tobias, J. A. (1995). Factor structure of the Yale Brown obsessive-compulsive scale: A two-dimensional measure. *Behaviour, Research, and Therapy, 33,* 865-869.

Neziroglu, F., McKay, D., Yaryura-Tobias, J. A., Steven, K., & Todaro, J. (1996). The overvalued ideas scale: Development, reliability, and validity in obsessive-compulsive disorder. Manuscript submitted for publication.

Chapter 4

Cottraux, J., Mollard, E., Bouvard, M., et al. (1990). A controlled study of fluvoxamine and exposure in obsessive-compulsive disorder. *International Clinical Psychopharmacology, 5*(1), 7-30.

Foa, E. B, & Chambless, D. L. (1978). Habituation of subjective anxiety during flooding in imagery. *Behaviour Research and Therapy, 16,* 391-399.

Foa, E. B., Steketee, G. S., Grayson, J. B., & Doppelt, H. G. (1983). Treatment of obsessive-compulsives: When do we fail? In E. B. Foa, & P. M. G. Emmelkamp (Eds.), *Failures in behavior therapy* (pp. 10-34). New York: Wiley.

Foa, E. B., & Steketee G. S. (1979). Obsessive-compulsives: Conceptual issues and treatment interventions. In M. Hersen, R. M. Eisler, & P. M. Miller (Eds.), *Progress in behavior modification* (Vol. VII, pp. 71-51). New York: Academic.

Mavissakalian, M. R., Jones, B., Olson, S., et al. (1990). Clomipramine on obsessive-compulsive disorder: Clinical response and plasma levels. *Journal of Clinical Psychopharmacology, 10*(4), 261-268.

Neziroglu, F., & Yaryura-Tobias, J. A. (1995). *Over and over again: Understanding obsessive compulsive disorder.* Boston: Lexington.

Rachman, S., & Hodgson, R. (1980). *Obsessions and compulsions.* Englewood Cliffs, NJ: Prentice Hall.

Steketee, G. (1993). *Treatment of obsessive compulsive disorder.* New York: Guilford.

Turner, S. M., & Beidel, D. C. (1988). *Treating obsessive compulsive disorder.* New York: Pergamon.

Wernicke, C. (1900). Grundisse der psychiatrie [Foundations of psychiatry]. Leipzig: F. Barth.

Yamagami, T. (1971). The treatment of an obsession by thought stopping. *Journal of Behavioral Therapy and Experimental Psychiatry, 2,* 133-135.

Chapter 6

Austin, L. S., Lydiard, R. B., Fossey, M. D., Zealberg, J. J., Laraia, M. T., & Ballenger, J. C. (1990). Panic and phobic disorders in patients with obsessive compulsive disorder. *Journal of Clinical Psychiatry, 51*(11), 456-458.

Baer, L., Rauch, S. L., Ballanine, H. T., Martuza, R., Cosgrove, R., Cassem, E., Giriunas, I., Manza, P. A., Dimino, C., & Jenike, M. (1995). Cingulotomy for intractable obsessive compulsive disorder. *Archives of General Psychiatry, 52,* 384-392.

Baker, R. W., Chengappa, K. N. R., Baird, J. W., Steingard, S., Christ, M. A. G., & Schooler, N. R. (1992). Emergence of obsessive compulsive symptoms during treatment with clozapine. *Journal of Clinical Psychiatry, 53*(12), 439-442.

Brochier, T., & Hantouche, E. (1989). Analyse critique des etudes pharmacoolgiques [Critical analysis of pharmacological studies]. *Encephale, 15*(3), 325-333.

Browne, M. et al. (1993). The benefits of clomipramine-fluoxetine combination in obsessive compulsive disorder. *Canadian Journal of Psychiatry, 38*(5), 242-243.

Christensen, H., Hadzi-Pavlivic, D., Andrews, G., & Mattick, R. (1987). Behavior therapy and tricyclic medication in the treatment of obsessive compulsive disorder: A quantitative review. *Journal of Consulting and Clinical Psychology, 55*(5), 701-711.

Cottraux, J., Mollard, E., Bouvard, M., Marks, I., Sluys, M., Nury, A. M., Douge, R., & Cialdella, P. (1990). A controlled study of fluvoxamine and exposure in obsessive compulsive disorder. *International Clinical Psychopharmacology, 5,* 17-30.

Fals-Stewart, W., & Schafer, J. (1992). The treatment of substance abusers diagnosed with obsessive compulsive disorder: An outcome study. *Journal of Substance Abuse Treatment, 9*(4), 365-370.

Goodman, W. K., McDougle, C. J., Barr, L. C., Aronson, S. C., & Price, L. H. (1993). Biological approaches to treatment-resistant obsessive compulsive disorder. *Journal of Clinical Psychiatry, 54*(Suppl.), 16-26.

Goodman, W. K., McDougle, C. J., & Price, L. H. (1992). Pharmacotherapy of obsessive compulsive disorder. *Journal of Clinical Psychiatry, 53*(4)(Suppl.), 29-37.

Grady, T. et al. (1993). Double-blind study of adjuvant buspirone for fluoxetine-treated patients with obsessive compulsive disorder. *American Journal of Psychiatry, 150*(5), 819-821.

Greist, J. H. (1992). An integrated approach to treatment of obsessive compulsive disorder. *Journal of Clinical Psychiatry, 53*(Suppl.), 38-41.

Greist, J. H., Jefferson, J. W., Kobak, K. A., Katzelnick, D. J., & Serlin, R. C. (1995). Efficacy and tolerability of serotonin transport inhibitors in obsessive compulsive disorder. *Archives of General Psychiatry, 52,* 53-60.

Grimsley, S. R., & Jann, M. W. (1992). Paroxetine, sertraline, and fluvoxamine: New selective serotonin reuptake inhibitors. *Clinical Pharmacy, 11,* 930-957.

Hewlett, W. A. (1993). The use of benzodiazepines in obsessive compulsive disorder and Tourette's syndrome. *Psychiatric Annals, 23*(6), 309-316.

Holland, E., DeCaria, M., Franklin, R., Schneier, F. R., Schneier, H. A., Liebowitz, M. R., & Klein, D. F. (1990). Fenfluramine augmentation of serotonin reuptake blockade antiobsessional treatment. *Journal of Clinical Psychiatry, 51* (3), 119-123.

Hollander, E., Zohar, J., Marazziti, D., & Olivier, B. (Eds.). (1994). *Current insights in obsessive compulsive disorder.* New York: Wiley.

Husain, M. M., Lewis, S. F., & Thornton, W. L. (1993). Maintenance ECT for refractory obsessive compulsive disorder. *American Journal of Psychiatry, 150,* 1899-1900.

Jacobsen, F. M. (1992). Fluoxetine-induced sexual dysfunction and an open trial of yohimbine. *Journal of Clinical Psychiatry, 53* (4), 119-122.

Jefferson, J. W., & Greist, J. H. (1996). The pharmacotherapy of obsessive compulsive disorder. *Psychiatric Annals, 26*(4), 202-209.

Jenike, M. A. (1993). Augmentation strategies for treatment-resistant obsessive compulsive disorder. *Harvard Review Psychiatry, 1,* 17-26.

Jenike, M. A., Baer, L., Ballantine, H. I. T., et al. (1991). Cingulotomy for refractory obsessive compulsive disorder: A long-term follow-up of 33 patients. *Archives of General Psychiatry, 48,* 548-555.

Jenike, M., et al. (1991). Buspirone augmentation of fluoxetine in obsessive compulsive disorder. *American Journal of Psychiatry, 52,* 13-14.

Klein, D. F. (1994). The utility of guidelines and algorithms for practice. *Psychiatric Annals, 24*(7), 362-367.

Leach, A. M. (1995). The psychopharmacotherapy of eating disorders. *Psychiatric Annals, 25*(10), 628-633.

Maletzky, B., McFarland, B., & Burt, A. (1994). Refractory obsessive compulsive disorder and ECT. *Convulsive Therapy, 10*(1), 34-42.

Markowitz, P. et al. (1990). Buspirone augmentation of fluoxetine in obsessive compulsive disorder. *American Journal of Psychiatry, 147,* 798-800.

Marks, I., & O'Sullivan, G. (1988). Drugs and psychological treatments for agoraphobia / panic and obsessive compulsive disorders: A review. *British Journal of Psychiatry, 153,* 650-658.

Maxmen, J. S., & Ward, N. G. (1995). *Psychotropic Drugs: Fast Facts* (2nd ed.). New York: Norton.

Mellman, L. A., & Gorman, J. M. (1984). Successful treatment of obsessive compulsive disorder with ECT. *American Journal of Psychiatry, 141,* 596-597.

Mesaros, J. (1993). Fluoxetine for primary enuresis. *Journal of the American Academy of Child and Adolescent Psychiatry, 32*(7), 877-878.

Miller, N. S. (1995). Pharmacological management of major comorbid psychiatric disorders in drug and alcohol addictions. *Psychiatric Annals, 25*(10), 621-627.

Mindus, P., Rauch, S. L., Nyman, H., Baer, L., Edman, G., & Jenike, M. A. (1994). Capsulotomy and cingulotomy as treatments for malignant obsessive compulsive disorder: An update. In E. Hollander, J. Zohar, D. Marazziti, & B. Olivier (Eds.), *Current insights in obsessive compulsive disorder* (pp. 245-276). New York: Wiley.

Murdoch, D., & McTavish, D. (1992). Sertraline: A review of its pharmacodynamic and pharmacokinetic properties, and therapeutic potential in depression and obsessive compulsive disorder. *Drugs, 44*(4), 602-624.

Neziroglu, F., & Neuman, J. (1990). Three treatment approaches for obsessions. *Journal of Cognitive Psychotherapy, 4*(4), 377-392.

Opler, L. A., & Hwang, M. Y. (1994). Schizophrenia: A multidimensional disorder. *Psychiatric Annals, 24*(9), 491-495.

Riley, A. J., Goodman, R. E., Kellett, J. M., & Orr, R. (1989). Double blind trial of yohimbine hydrochloride in the treatment of erection inadequacy. *Sexual and Marital Therapy, 4*(1), 17-26.

Sandyk, R. (1992). L-tryptophan in neuropsychiatric disorders: A review. *International Journal of Neuroscience, 1*(4), 127-144.

Schatzberg, A. F., & Cole, J. O. (1991). *Manual of clinical psychopharmacology* (2nd ed.). Washington: American Psychiatric Press.

Simeon, J. et al. (1990). Treatment of adolescent obsessive compulsive disorder with a clomipramine-fluoxetine combination. *Psychopharmacology Bulletin, 26,* 285-290.

Stein, D. J., Hollander, E., Anthony, D. T., Schneier, F. R., Fallon, B. A., Liebowitz, M. R., & Klein, D. F. (1992). Serotonergic medications for sexual obsessions, sexual addictions, and paraphilias. *Journal of Clinical Psychiatry, 53*(8), 267-271.

Stein, D. J., Hollander, E., Mullen, L. S., DeCaria, C. M., & Liebowitz, M. R. (1992). Comparison of clomipramine, alprazolam and placebo in the treatment of obsessive compulsive disorder. *Human Psychopharmacology, 7,* 389-395.

Towbin, D. E., Leckman, J. F., & Cohen, D. J. (1987). Drug treatment of obsessive compulsive disorder: A review of findings in the light of diagnostic and metric limitations. *Psychiatric Developments, 1,* 25-50.

Warneke, L. (1989). Intravenous chlorimipramine therapy in obsessive compulsive disorder. *Canadian Journal of Psychiatry, 34,* 853-859.

Wisner, K. et al. (1995). Serum clomipramine and metabolite levels in four nursing mother-infant pairs. *Journal of Clinical Psychiatry, 56*(1), 17-20.

Yaryura-Tobias, J. A., & Neziroglu, F. A. (1983). Biological therapy. In J. A. Yaryura-Tobias & F. A. Neziroglu (Eds.), *Obsessive-compulsive disorders: Pathogenis, diagnosis, and treatment* (pp. 173-194). New York: Marcel Dekker.

Zitterl, W., Lenz, G., Mairhofer, A., & Zapotoczky, H. G. (1990). Obsessive Compulsive disorder: Course and interaction with depression. A review of the literature. *Psychopathology, 23*(2)\R\, 73-80.

Zohar, J., Zohar-Kadouch, R. C., & Kindler, S. (1992). Current concepts in the pharmacological treatment of obsessive compulsive disorder. *Drugs, 43*(2), 210-218.

Chapter 7

Arrindell, W. A., Emmelkamp, P. M., & Bast, S. (1983). The Maudsley marital questionnaire (MMQ): A further step towards its validation. *Personality and Individual Differences, 4*(5), 457-464.

Arrindell, W. A., Emmelkamp, P. M., Monsma, A., & Brilman, E. (1983). The role of perceived parental rearing practices in the aetiology of phobic disorders: A controlled study. *British Journal of Psychiatry, 143,* 183-187.

Black, D. W., & Blum, N. S. (1992). Obsessive compulsive disorder support groups: The Iowa model. *Comprehensive Psychiatry, 33*(1), 65-71.

Emmelkamp, P. M. G. (1982). *Phobic and obsessive compulsive disorders.* New York: Plenum.

Emmelkamp, P. M., & de-Lange, I. (1983). Spouse involvement in the treatment of obsessive compulsive patients. *Behaviour Research and Therapy, 21*(4), 341-346.

Emmelkamp, P. M., Van-Dyck, R., Bitter, M., Heins, R., et al. (1992). Spouse-aided therapy with agoraphobics. *British Journal of Psychiatry, 160*, 51-56.

Enright, S. J. (1991). Group treatment for obsessive compulsive disorder: An evaluation. *Behavioural Psychotherapy, 19*(2), 183-192.

Fals-Stewart, W., & Lucente, S. (1994). Behavioral group therapy with obsessive compulsives: An overview. *International Journal of Group Psychotherapy, 44*(1), 35-51.

Flament, J. F., Rapoport, J. L., Berg, C. J., Sceery, W., Kilts, C., Mellstrom, B., & Linnoila, M. (1985). Clomipramine treatment of childhood obsessive compulsive disorder: A double-blind controlled study. *Archives of General Psychiatry, 42*, 977-983.

Gadow, K. D. (1991). Clinical issues in child and adolescent psychopharmacology. *Journal of Consulting & Clinical Psychology, 59*(6), 842-852.

Hafner, R. J. (1988). Obsessive compulsive disorder: A questionnaire survey of a self-help group. *International Journal of Social Psychiatry, 34*(4), 310-315.

Hafner, R. J. (1992). Anxiety disorders and family therapy. *Australian and New Zealand Journal of Family Therapy, 13*(2), 99-104.

Jenike, M. A., Baer, L., & Minichiello, W. E. (1990). *Obsessive Compulsive Disorders: Theory and Management* (2nd ed.). St. Louis: Mosby.

Krone, K. P., Himle, J. A., & Nesse, R. M. (1991). A standardized behavioral group testament program for obsessive compulsive disorder: Preliminary outcomes. *Behaviour Research and Therapy, 29*(6), 627-631.

Lavy, E. H., van Oppen, P., & van den Hout, M. A. (1994). Selective processing of emotional information in obsessive compulsive disorder. *Behaviour Research and Therapy, 32*(2), 243-246.

Leonard, H., Swedo, S., Rapoport, J. L., Coffey, M., & Cheslow, D. (1988). Treatment of childhood obsessive compulsive disorder with clomipramine and desmethylimipramine: A double-blind crossover comparison. *Psychopharmacology Bulletin, 24*(1), 93-95.

Piacentini, J., Jaffer, M., Gitow, A., Graae, F., Davies, S.O., Del Bene, D., & Liebowitz, M. (1992). Psychopharmacologic treatment of child and adolescent obsessive compulsive disorder. *Psychiatric Clinics of North America, 15*(1), 87-107.

Rapoport, J. L. (1986). Antidepressants in childhood attention deficit disorder and obsessive compulsive disorder. *Psychosomatics, 27*(Suppl. 11), 30-36.

Rapoport, J. L. (1989). *The body who couldn't stop washing.* New York: Dutton.

Riddle, M. A., Schaill, L., King, R. A., Hardin, M. T., Anderson, G. M., Ort, S. I., Smith, J. C., Leckman, J. F., & Cohen, D. J. (1992). Double-blind, crossover trial of fluoxetine and placebo in children and adolescents with obsessive compulsive disorder. *Journal of the American Academy of Child & Adolescent Psychiatry, 31*(6), 1062-1069.

Simeon, J. G., Thatte, S., & Wiggins, D. (1990). Treatment of adolescent obsessive compulsive disorder with a clomipramine-fluoxetine combination. *Psychopharmacology Bulletin, 26*(3), 285-290.

Stekette, G., & White, K. (1990). *When once is not enough*. Oakland, CA: New Harbinger.

Turner, S. M., & Beidel, D. C. (1988). *Treating obsessive compulsive disorder*. New York: Pergamon.

Tynes, L. L., Salins, C., Skiba, W., Winstead, D. K., et al. (1992). *Comprehensive Psychiatry, 33*(3), 197-201.

van Oppen, P., & Arntz, A. (1994). Cognitive therapy for obsessive compulsive disorder. *Behaviour Research and Therapy, 32*(1), 79-87.

Chapter 8

Adam, B. S., & Kashani, J. H. (1990). Trichotillomania in children and adolescents: Review of the literature and case report. *Child Psychiatry & Human Development, 20*(3), 159-163.

Angulo, M. (1992). Growth hormone evaluation and treatment in Prader-Will Syndrome. *NATO ASI, 461*, 171-174.

Baer, L. (1992). Behavior therapy for obsessive-compulsive disorder and trichotillomania: Implications for Tourette's syndrome. In T. N. Chase, A. J. Friedhoff, & D. J. Cohen (Eds.), *Advances in Neurology* (pp. 333-340). New York: Raven.

Barsky, A. J. (1992). Hypochondriasis and obsessive-compulsive disorder. *Psychiatric Clinics of North America, 15*(4), 791-801.

Buvat, J., & Buvat-Herbaut, M. (1978). Dysperception of body image and dysmorphobobias in mental anorexia: A propos of 114 cases involving both sexes. I. Altered mechanism of perception in mental anorexia. *Annals of Medical Psychology, 136*(4), 547-561.

de Leon J., Bott A., & Simpson G. M. (1989). Dysmorphophobia: Body dysmorphic disorder or delusional disorder, somatic symptom? *Comprehensive Psychiatry, 30*, 457-472.

Deckert D. W., & Malone D. A. (1990). Treatment of psychotic symptoms in OCD patients. *Journal of Clinical Psychiatry, 51*(6), 259.

Fallon, B. A., Javitch, J. A., Hollander, E., et al. (1991). Hypochondriasis and obsessive-compulsive disorder: Overlaps in diagnosis and treatment. *Journal of Clinical Psychiatry, 52*(11), 457-460.

Fenton, W. S., & McGlashan T. H. (1986). The prognostic significance of obsessive compulsive symptoms in schizophrenia. *American Journal of Psychiatry, 143*, 437-441.

Gross, G., Huber, G., & Armbruster, B. (1986). Schizoaffective psychoses-long term prognosis and symptomatology. In A. Marneros, & M. T. Tsuang (Eds.), *Schizoaffective psychoses* (pp. 188-203). Berlin-Heidelberg: Springer-Verlag.

Gross, G., Huber, G., & Schuttler, R. (1986). Long-term course of Schneiderian schizophrenia. In A. Marneros & M. T. Tsuang (Eds.), *Schizoaffective psychoses* (pp. 164-178). Berlin-Heidelberg: Springer-Verlag.

Hermesh, H., Hoffnung, R. A., Aizenberg D., et al. (1989). Catatonic signs in severe obsessive compulsive disorder. *Journal of Clinical Psychiatry, 50*, 303-305.

Hollander, E., Neville, D., Frenkel, M., et al. (1992). Body dysmorphic disorder: Diagnostic issues and related disorders. *Psychosomatics, 33*(2), 156-165.

Hollander, E., & Phillips, K. A. (1993). Body image and experience disorders. In E. Hollander (Ed.), *Obsessive-compulsive related disorders* (pp. 17-48). Washington, DC, American Psychiatric Press.

Jenike, M. A., Baer L., Minichiello, W. E., et al. (1986). Concomitant obsessive-compulsive disorder and schizotypal personality disorder. *American Journal of Psychiatry, 143*(4), 530-532.

Leonhard, K. (1968). *Le psicosi edogene* [Endogenous psychoses]. Milan: Feltrinelli.

McKay, D., & Neziroglu, F. (1993). *Hypochondriases: Common pathways to obsessive-compulsive disorder.* Symposium presented at 27th annual meeting of Association for Advancement of Behavior Therapy, Atlanta.

Modell, J. G., Glaser, F. B., Mountz, J. M., et al. (1992). Obsessive and compulsive characteristics of alcohol abuse and dependence quantification by a newly developed questionnaire. *Alcoholism, 162*(2), 266-271.

Neziroglu, F. (1994). Complexities and lesser known aspects of obsessive-compulsive and related disorders. *Cognitive and Behavioral Practice, 1*, 133-156.

Neziroglu, F., Hoffman, J., & Yaryura-Tobias, J. A., (1996). Current issues in behavior and cognitive therapy for obsessive-compulsive disorder. *CNS Spectrums, 1*, 47-54.

Neziroglu, F., & Yaryura-Tobias, J. A. (1993). Exposure, response prevention, and cognitive therapy in the treatment of body dysmorphic disorder. *Behavior Therapy, 24*, 431-438.

Neziroglu, F., & Yaryura-Tobias, J. A. (1993). Body dysmorphic disorder. Phenomenology and case descriptions. *Behavioural Psychotherapy, 21*, 27-36.

Philips, K. A., McElroy, S. L., Keck, P. E., et al. (1993). Body dysmorphic disorder: 30 cases of imagined ugliness. *American Journal of Psychiatry, 150*, 302-308.

Salkovskis, P. M., & Warwick, H. M. C. (1986). Morbid preoccupations, health anxiety and reassurance: A cognitive behavioral approach to hypochondriasis. *Behaviour Research & Therapy, 24*, 597-602.

Senjo, M. (1989). Obsessive-compulsive disorder in people that abuse codeine. *Acta Psychiatrica Scandinavica, 79*(6), 619-620.

Turner, S. M., Jacob, R. G., & Morrison, R. (1984). Somatoform and Factitious Disorders. In H. E. Adams, & P. B. Sutker (Eds.), *Comprehensive Handbook of Pyschopathology* (pp. 307-345). New York: Plenum.

Vaughan, M. (1976). The relationships between obsessional personality obsessions in depression, and symptoms of depression. *British Journal of Psychiatry, 129*(7), 36-39.

Yaryura-Tobias, J. A., Patito, J. A., Mizrahi, J., et al. (1974). The action of pimozide on acute psychosis. *Acta Psychiatrica Belgica, 74,* 421-429.

Chapter 9

Bellodi, L., Scuito, G., Diaferia, G., Ronchi, P., et al. (1992). Psychiatric disorders in the families of patients with obsessive compulsive disorder. *Psychiatry Research, 42*(2), 111-120.

Clark, D. A., & Bolton, D. (1985). Obsessive compulsive adolescents and their parents: A psychometric study. *Journal of Child Psychology & Psychiatry & Allied Disciplines, 26*(2), 267-276.

Ehiobuche, I. (1988). Obsessive compulsive neurosis in relation to parental child-rearing patterns amongst the Greek, Italian, and Anglo-Australian subjects. *Acta Psychiatrica Scandinavica—Supplementum, 344,* 115-120.

Emmelkamp, P. M., de Haan, E., & Hoogduin, C. A. (1990). Marital adjustment and obsessive compulsive disorder. *British Journal of Psychiatry, 156,* 55-60.

Frost, R. O., Steketee, G., Cohn, L., & Griess, K. E. (1991, November). *Familial and background characteristics of nonclinical compulsives.* Paper presented at the 25th annual convention of the Association for the Advancement of Behavior Therapy, New York.

Hafner, J. R. (1982). Marital interaction in persisting obsessive compulsive disorders. *Australian and New Zealand Journal of Psychiatry, 16*(3), 171-178.

Hafner, J. R. (1988). Obsessive compulsive disorder: A questionnaire survey of a self-help group. *The International Journal of Social Psychiatry, 34*(4), 310-315.

Hafner, R. J. (1992). Anxiety disorders and family therapy. *Australian and New Zealand Journal of Family Therapy, 13*(2), 99-104.

Hibbs, E. D., Hamburger, S. D., Lenane, M., Rapoport, J. L., et al. (1991). Determinants of expressed emotion in families of disturbed and normal children. *Journal of Child Psychology and Psychiatry and Allied Disciplines, 32*(5), 757-770.

Hoover, C. F., & Insel, T. R. (1984). Families of origin in obsessive compulsive disorder. *Journal of Nervous and Mental Disease, 172*(4), 207-215.

Insel, T. R., Hoover, C., & Murphy, D. L. (1983). Parents of patients with obsessive compulsive disorder. *Psychological Medicine, 13*(4), 807-811.

Khanna, S., Rajendra, P. N., & Channabasavanna, S. M. (1988). Social adjustment in obsessive compulsive disorder. *International Journal of Social Psychiatry, 34*(2), 118-122.

Knolker, U. (1983). Obsessive compulsive disorders in children and adolescents: Pathogenetic aspects in the context of family background. *Zeitschrift fur Kinder und Jungendpsychiatrie, 11*(4), 317-327.

McKeon, P., & Murray, R. (1987). Familial aspects of obsessive compulsive neurosis. *British Journal of Psychiatry, 151,* 528-534.

Nicoloni, H. (1991). Birth order effect in the family type of obsessive compulsive disorder. *Salud Mental, 14*(1), 44-47.

Oppenheim, S., & Rosenberger, J. (1991). Treatment of a case of obsessional disorder: Family systems and object relations approaches. *American Journal of Family Therapy, 19*(4), 327-333.

Simoni, P. S. (1991). Obsessive compulsive disorder. The effect of research on nursing care. *Journal of Psychosocial Nursing & Mental Health Services, 29*(4), 19-23.

Tyness, L. L., Salins, C., & Winstead, D. K. (1990). Obsessive compulsive patients: Familial frustration and criticism. *Journal of the Louisiana State Medical Society, 142*(10), 28-29.

Chapter 10

Baer, L., Jenike, M. A., Black, D. W., Treece, C., Rosenfeld, R., & Greist, J. (1992). Effect of axis II diagnoses on treatment outcome with clomipramine in 55 patients with obsessive compulsive disorder. *Archives of General Psychiatry, 49*, 862-866.

Jenike, M. A. (1990). Approaches to the patient with treatment-refractory obsessive compulsive disorder. *Journal of Clinical Psychiatry, 51*(2), 15-21.

Leonard, H. et al. (1993). A 2- to 7-year follow-up study of 54 obsessive compulsive children and adolescents. *Archives of General Psychiatry, 50*, 429-439.

McKay, D., Todaro, J. F., Neziroglu, F., & Yaryura-Tobias, J. A. (1996). Evaluation of a naturalistic maintenance program in the treatment of obsessive compulsive disorder: A preliminary investigation. *Journal of Anxiety Disorders, 10*(3), 211-217.

O'Sullivan, G., Noshirvani, H., Marks, I., Monteiro, W., & Lelliott, P. (1991). Six-year follow-up after exposure and clomipramine therapy for obsessive compulsive disorder. *Journal of Clinical Psychiatry, 52*(4), 150-155.

References

Adams, G. (1994). Social competence of adolescents with obsessive-compulsive disorder. *OCD Newsletter, 8*(5), 3-4.

Altman, K., Grahs, S., & Friman, P., et al. (1982). Treatment of unobserved trichotillomania by attention reflection and punishment of an apparent covariant. *Journal of Behavioral Therapy and Experimental Psychiatry, 13,* 337-340.

American Psychiatric Association. (1994). *Diagnostic and statistical manual of mental disorders* (4th ed.). Washington, DC: Author.

Azrin, N. H., & Nunn, R. G. (1973). Habit reversal: A method of eliminating nervous habits and tics. *Behaviour Research and Therapy, 11,* 619-628.

Azrin, N. H., Nunn, R. G., & Frantz, S. E. (1980). Treatment of hairpulling (trichotillomania): A comparative study of habit reversal and negative practice training. *Journal of Behavioral Therapy and Experimental Psychiatry, 11,* 13-20.

Baer, L., & Minichiello, W. E. (1990). Behavior therapy for obsessive-compulsive disorder. In M. A. Jenike, L. Baer, & W. E. Minichiello (Eds.), *Obsessive-compulsive disorders: theory and management* (pp. 203-232). Boston: Mosby Year Book.

Barmann, B. C., & Vitali, D. L. (1982). Facial screenings to eliminate trichotillomania in developmentally disabled persons. *Behavior Therapy, 13,* 735-742.

Baum, M. (1966). Rapid extinction of an avoidance response following a period of response prevention in the avoidance apparatus. *Psychological Report, 18,* 55-64.

Bavaro, S. M. (1991). Occupational therapy and obsessive-compulsive disorder. *American Journal of Occupational Therapy, 45,* 456-458.

Baxter, L. R., Phelps, M. E., Mazziotta, J. C., et al. (1987). Local cerebral glucose metabolic rates in obsessive-compulsive disorder: A comparison with rates in unipolar depression and in normal control. *Archives of General Psychiatry, 44,* 211-218.

Baxter, L. R., Schwartz, J. M., Bergman, K. S., et al. (1992). Caudate glucose metabolic rate changes with both drug and behavior therapy for obsessive-compulsive disorder. *Archives of General Psychiatry, 49,* 681-689.

Beck, A. T., Rush, A. J., Shaw, B. F., & Emery, G. (1979). *Cognitive therapy of depression.* New York: Guilford.

Black, D. W., Noyes, Jr., R., Goldstein, R. B., & Blum, N. (1992). A family study of obsessive-compulsive disorder. *Archives of General Psychiatry, 49,* 362-368.

Bornstein, P. H., & Rychtarik, R. G. (1978). Multi-component behavioral treatment of trichotillomania: A case study. *Behaviour Research and Therapy, 16,* 217-220.

Broadbent, D., Cooper, P., Fitzgerald, P., et al. (1982). The cognitive failures questionnaire (CFQ) and its correlates. *British Journal of Clinical Psychology, 21,* 1-16.

Carr, A. T. A. (1974). Compulsive neurosis: A review of the literature. *Psychological Bulletin, 81*, 311-318.

Catapano, F., Monteleone, P., Fuschino, A., Maj, M., & Kemali, D. (1992). Melatonin and cortisol secretion in patients with primary obsessive-compulsive disorder. *Psychiatry Research, 44*(3), 217-225.

Chiocca, E. A, & Martuza, R. L. (1990). Neurosurgical therapy of obsessive-compulsive disorder. In M. Jenike, L. Baer, & W. Minichiello (Eds.), *Obessive-compulsive disorders: Theory and management* (pp. 283-294). Boston: Mosby.

Christensen, H., Hadzi-Pavlovic, D., Andrews, G., et al. (1987). Behavior therapy and triyclic medication in the treatment of obsessive-compulsive disorder: A quantitative review. *Journal of Consulting and Clinical Psychology, 55*, 701-11.

Christenson, G. A., Mackenzie, T. B., Mitchell, J. E., et al. (1991). A placebo controlled, double blind crossover study of fluoxetine in trichotillomania. *American Journal of Psychiatry, 148*, 1566-1571.

Clomipramine Collaborative Study Group (1991). Clomipramine in the treatment of patients with obsessive compulsive disorder. *Archives of General Psychiatry, 48*, 730-738.

Conde-López, V., de la Gandara Martin, J. J., Blanco Lozano, M. I. (1990). Minor neurological signs in obsessive-compulsive disorder. *Actas Luso Españolas de Neurologia, Psiquiatriay Ciencias Afines, 18*, 143-164.

Cottraux, J., Mollard, E., Bouvard, M., et al. (1990). A controlled study of Fluvoxamine and exposure in obsessive-compulsive disorder. *International Clinical Psychopharmacology, 5*(1), 17-30.

Delgado, R. A., & Mannino, F. V. (1969). Some observations on trichotillomania in children. *Journal of American Academic Child Psychiatry, 81*, 229-246.

Dollard, J., & Miller, N. E. (1950). *Personality and psychotherapy: An analysis in terms of learning, thinking, and culture.* New York: McGraw Hill.

Eisen, J. L., & Rasmussen, S. A. (1989). Coexisting obsessive-compulsive disorder and alcoholism. *Journal of Clinical Psychiatry, 50*(3), 96-98.

Ellis, A. (1962). *Reason and emotion in psychotherapy.* New York: Lyle Stuart.

Emmelkamp, P. M. G., & Beens, H. (1991). Cognitive therapy with obsessive-compulsive disorder: A comparative evaluation. *Behaviour Research and Therapy, 29*(3), 293-300.

Emmelkamp, P. M. G., Van der Helm, M., Van Zanten, B. L., et al. (1980). Contributions of self-instructional training to the effectiveness of exposure in-vivo: A comparison with obsessive-compulsive patients. *Behaviour Research and Therapy, 18*, 61-66.

Emmelkamp, P. M. G., Visser, S., & Hoekstra, R. J. (1988). Cognitive therapy vs. exposure in vivo in the treatment of obsessive compulsives. *Cognitive Therapy Research, 12*, 103-114.

Epstein, L. H., & Peterson, G. L. (1973). The control of undesired behavior by self-imposed contingencies. *Behavior Therapy, 4*, 91-95.

Fals-Stewart, W., & Lucente, S. (1994). Treating obsessive-compulsive disorder among substance abusers: A guide. *Psychology of Addictive Behaviors, 8*(1), 14-23.

Fals-Stewart, W., & Schafer, J. (1992). The treatment of substance abusers diagnosed with obsessive-compulsive disorder: An outcome study. *Journal of Substance Abuse Treatment, 9*(4), 365-370.

Flor-Henry, P. (1983). *Cerebral basis of psychopathology.* Boston: John Wright.

Foa, E. B., & Steketee, G. S. (1984). [Reply to letter to the editor]. *Archives of General Psychiatry, 41*, 107.

Freeston, M. H., Ladouceur, R., Gagnon, F., & Thibodeau, N. (1993). Belief about obsessional thought. *Journal of Psychopathology Assessment, 15,* 1-21.

Garber, H. J., Ananth, J. V., Chiu, L. C., et al. (1989). Nuclear magnetic resonance study of obsessive-compulsive disorder. *American Journal of Psychiatry, 146,* 1001-1005.

Goodman, W. K., Price, L. H., Rasmussen, S. A., Mazure, C., Fleischman, R. L., Hill, C. L. Heninger, G. R., & Charney, D. S. (1989). The Yale Brown Obsessive Compulsive Scale: 1. Development, use and reliability. *Archives of General Psychiatry, 46,* 1006-1011.

Grady, T. A., Pigott, T. A., L'Heureux F., et al. (1993). Double-blind study of adjuvant buspirone for fluoxetine treated patients with obsessive compulsive disorder. *American Journal of Psychiatry, 150,* 819-821.

Greenberg, H. R., & Sarner, C. A. (1965). Trichotillomania: A review. *Comprehensive Psychiatry, 26,* 123-128.

Greist, J. H. (1992). An integrated approach to treatment of obsessive-compulsive disorder. *Journal of Clinical Psychiatry, 53*(4), 38-40.

Griesinger, W. (1965). Mental pathology and therapeutics. (E. H. Ackerknecht, Trans.). New York: Hafner. (Original work published 1867).

Groves, P. M., & Lynch, G. S. (1972). Mechanisms of habituation in the brain stem. *Psychology Review, 79*(3), 237-244.

Hafner, R. J. (1992). Anxiety disorders and family therapy. *Australian and New Zealand Journal of Family Therapy, 13,* 99-104.

Hall, R. C. (Ed.). (1980). *Psychiatric presentations of medical illness: Somatapsychic disorders.* New York: Spectrum.

Hermesh, H., Weizman, A., Shahar, A., et al. (1988). Vitamin B12 and folic acid serum levels in obsessive-compulsive disorder. *Acta Psychiatrica Scandinava, 78,* 8-10.

Hersen, M., & Bellack, A. S. (1977). Assessment of social skills. In A. R. Ciminero, K. S. Calhoun, & H. E. Adams (Eds.), *Handbook of Behavioral Assessments* (pp. 509-554). New York: Wiley.

Hewlett, W. A., Vinogradov, S., & Agras, W. S. (1990). Clonazepam treatments of obsessions and compulsions. *Journal of Clinical Psychiatry, 51,* 158-161.

Hiss, H., Foa, E. B., Kozak, M. J. (1994). Relapse prevention program for treatment of obsessive-compulsive disorder. *Journal of Consulting and Clinical Psychology, 62*(4), 801-808.

Hoehn-Saric, R., & Benkelfat, C. (1994). Structural and functional brain imaging in obsessive compulsive disorder. In E. Hollander, J. Zohar, D. Marazziti, & B. Olivier (Eds.), *Current insights in obsessive compulsive disorder* (pp. 183-211). New York: Wiley.

Hollander, E., Liebowitz, M. R., Winchel, R., Klumker, A., & Klein, D. (1989). Treatment of body dysmorphic disorder with serotonin reuptake blockers. *American Journal of Psychiatry, 146*(6), 768-770.

Hollander, E., Schiffman, E., Cohen, B., et al. (1990). Signs of central nervous system dysfunction in obsessive compulsive disorder. *Archives of General Psychiatry, 47,* 27-32

Hollander, M. (1994). Post-treatment considerations of quality-of-life issues, psychological growth, and social skills training. *OCD Newsletter, 8*(6), 4-5.

James, I. A. & Blackburn, I. (1995). Cognitive therapy with obsessive-compulsive disorder. *British Journal of Psychiatry, 166,* 444-450.

Janet, P. (1903). *Les obsessions et la psychasthenie* [Obsessions and psychasthenia]. Paris: Alcan.

Jenike, M. A., Baer, L., & Minichiello, W. E. (Eds.) (1990). *Obessive-compulsive disorders: Theory and management.* Boston: Mosby.

Karno, M., Goldin, J. M., Soreman, S. B., et al. (1988). The epidemiology of obsessive-compulsive disorder in five U.S. communities. *Archives of General Psychiatry, 45,* 1094-1099.

Kirk, J. W. (1983) Behavioral treatment of obsessive-compulsive patients in clinical practice. *Behaviour Research and Therapy, 21,* 57-62.

Kozak, M. J., & Foa, E. B. (1994). Obsessions, overvalued ideas, and delusions in obsessive compulsive disorder. *Behaviour Research and Therapy, 32,* 343-353.

LeBoeuf, A. et al. (1974). An automated aversion device in the treatment of a compulsive handwashing ritual. *Journal of Behavior Therapy and Experimental Psychiatry, 5,* 267-270.

Levine, B. A. (1976). Treatment of trichotillomania by covert sensitization. *Journal of Behavioral Therapy and Experimental Psychiatry, 7,* 75-75.

Liberman, R. P., Kopelowicz, A., & Young, A. S. (1994). Bio-behavioral treatment and rehabilitation of schizophrenia. *Behavior Therapy, 25,* 89-108.

MacNeil, J., & Thomas, M. R. (1976). Treatment of obsessive-compulsive hair pulling (trichotillomania) by behavioral and cognitive contingency manipulation. *Journal of Behavioral Therapy and Experimental Psychiatry, 7,* 391-392.

Maier, N. R. F. (1949). *Frustration: The study of behavior without a goal.* New York: McGraw-Hill.

Malloy, P. (1987). Frontal lobe dysfunction in obsessive-compulsive disorder. In E. Perecman (Ed.), *The frontal lobes revisited* (pp. 75-89). New York: IRBN.

Mallya, G. K., White, K., Waternaux, C., et al. (1992). Short-and long-term treatment of obsessive-compulsive disorder with fluvoxamine. *Annals of Clinical Psychiatry, 4,* 77-80.

Marks, I. M., Stern, R. S., Mawson, D., Cobb, J., & McDonald, R. (1980). Clomipramine and exposure for obsessive-compulsive rituals. *British Journal of Psychiatry, 136,* 1-25.

Massong, S. R., Edwards, R. P., & Range-Sitton, L., et al. (1980). A case of trichotillomania in a three-year-old boy treated by response prevention. *Journal of Behavioral Therapy and Experimental Psychiatry, 11,* 223-225.

Mastellone, M. (1974). Aversion therapy: A new use for the old rubber band. *Journal of Behavioral Therapy and Experimental Psychiatry, 5,* 311-312.

Mathew, A., & Kumaraiah, V. (1988). Behavioral intervention in the treatment of trichotillomania. *Indian Journal of Pediatrics, 55,* 451-453.

Mavissakalian, M., Turner, S. M., & Michelson, L. (1985). Future directions in the assessment and treatment of obsessive-compulsive disorder. In M. Mavissakalian, S. M. Turner, & L. Michelson (Eds.), *Obsessive-compulsive disorder: Psychological and pharmacological treatment* (pp. 213-228). New York: Plenum.

McFall, M. .E., & Wollershein, J. P. (1979). Obsessive-compulsive neurosis: A cognitive-behavioral formulation and approach to treatment. *Cognitive Therapy Research, 3,* 333-348.

McKay, D., & Neziroglu, F. (1996) Social skills training in a case of obsessive-compulsive disorder with schizotypal personality disorder. *Journal of Behavior Therapy and Experimental Psychiatry, 27,* 189-194

McKay, D. R., Yaryura-Tobias J. A., Neziroglu, F. A. (1994). Obsessive compulsive disorder and bipolar disorder: Preliminary outcome data. *Biological psychiatry 35,* 615-747.

Mehta, M. (1990). A comparative study of family-based and patient-based behavioural management in obsessive-compulsive disorder. *British Journal of Psychiatry, 157,* 133-135.

Meyer, V. (1966). Modification of expectations in cases with obsessional rituals. *Behaviour Research and Therapy, 4,* 273-280.

Mindus, P., Rauch, S. L., Nyman, H., Baer, l., Edman, G., & Jenike, M. A. (1994). Capsulotomy and cingulotomy as treatments for malignant obsessive compulsive disorder: An update. In E. Hollander, J. Zohar, D. Marazziti, & B. Olivier (Eds.), *Current insights in obsessive compulsive disorder* (pp. 245-276). New York: Wiley.

Mowrer, O. H. (1960). *Learning theory and behavior.* New York: Wiley.

Neziroglu, F. (1979). A combined behavioral-pharmacotherapy approach to obsessive-compulsive disorders. In J. Obiols, C. Ballus, E. Gonzales-Monclus, & J. Pujol (Eds.), *Biological psychiatry today* (pp. 591-596). Amsterdam: Elsevier.

Neziroglu F., Anemone, R., & Yaryura-Tobias, J. A. (1992). Onset of obsessive compulsive disorder in pregnancy. *American Journal of Psychiatry, 149*(7), 947-950.

Neziroglu, F., McKay, D., Yaryura-Tobias, J. A., Stevens, K., & Todaro, J. (1996). The overvalued ideas scale: Development, reliability and validity in obsessive-compulsive disorder. Manuscript submitted for publication.

Neziroglu, F., & Neuman, J. (1990). Three treatment approaches for obsessions. *Journal of Cognitive Psychotherapy, 4,* 377-392.

Neziroglu, F. A., Steel, J., Yaryura-Tobias, J. A., Hitri, A., Diamond, B. (1990). Effect of behavior therapy on serotonin level in obsessive-compulsive disorder. In C. N. Stefanis, A. D. Rabavilas, & Soldatos, C. R. (Eds.), *Psychiatry: A world perspective* (pp. 707-710). New York: Elsevier.

Neziroglu F. A., & Yaryura-Tobias J. A. (1980). Follow-up study on obsessive-compulsive patients on clorimipramine and behavior therapy. *Pharmaceutical Medicine, 1*(2), 170-173.

Neziroglu, F., & Yaryura-Tobias, J. A. (1991). *Over and over again: Understanding obsessive-compulsive disorder.* New York: Lexington.

Neziroglu, F., & Yaryura-Tobias, J. A. (1992). Body dysmorphic disorder phenomenology and case descriptions. *Behavioral Psychotherapy, 21,* 27-36.

Neziroglu, F., & Yaryura-Tobias, J. A. (1993). Exposure, response prevention and cognitive therapy in the treatment of body dysmorphic disorder. *Journal of Behavior Therapy, 24,* 431-438.

Neziroglu, F., & Yaryura-Tobias, J. A. (1994). Obsessive compulsive disorder. In J. L. Juday, W. V. Ornum, & N. Stilllwell (Eds.), *The counseling sourcebook: A practical reference on contemporary issues* (pp. 425-436). New York: Crossroad.

Neziroglu, F. A., Yaryura-Tobias, J. A., Lemli, J. M., et al (1994). Estudio demografico del trastorno obseso compulsivo [Demographic study of the obsessive-compulsive disorder]. *Acta Psiquiatrica Psicologica de America Latina, 40,* 217-223.

Okasha, A., & Raafat, M. (1990). Neurophysiological substrate of obsessive-compulsive disorder: An evidence from topographic EEG. *Egypt Journal of Psychiatry, 13,* 97-106.

O'Sullivan, G., Noshirvani, H., Marks, I., et al. (1991). Six-year follow-up after exposure and clomipramine therapy for obsessive-compulsive disorder. *Journal of Clinical Psychiatry, 52*(4), 150-5.

Pato, M. T., Hill, J. L., & Murphy, D. L. (1990). A clomipramine dosage reduction study in the course of long-term treatment of obsessive-compulsive disorder patients. *Psychopharmacology Bulletin, 26,* 211-214.

Pato, M. T., & Zohar, J. (Eds.). (1991). *Current treatments of obsessive-compulsive disorder.* Washington: American Psychiatric Press.

Pato, M. T., Zohar-Kadouch, R., Zohar, J., et al. (1988). Return of symptoms after discontinuation of clomipramine in patients with obsessive-compulsive disorder. *American Journal of Psychiatry, 145,* 1521-1525.

Pauls, D. L. (1992). The genetics of obsessive compulsive disorder and Gilles de la Tourette's syndrome. *Psychiatric Clinics of North America, 15,* 759-766.

Pauls, D. L., & Leckman, J. F. (1986). The inheritance of Gilles de la Tourette's syndrome and associated behaviors: Evidence for autosomal dominant transmission. *New England Journal of Medicine, 315,* 993-997.

Philippopoulos, G. S. (1961). A case of trichotillomania (hairpulling). *Acta Psiquiatrica y Psicologica de America Latina, 9,* 304-312.

Philips, K. A. (1991). Body dysmorphic disorder: The distress of imagined ugliness. *American Journal of Psychiatry, 148*(9), 1138-1148.

Primeau, F., & Fontaine, R. (1987). Obsessive disorder with self-mutilation: A subgroup responsive to pharmacotherapy. *Canadian Journal of Psychiatry, 32,* 699-701.

Rachman, S., & Hodgson R. (1980). The theory and practice of modifying obsessions. In J. Jenkins, W. Mischel, & W. Hartup (Eds.), *Obsessions and compulsions* (pp. 165-187). New Jersey: Prentice-Hall, Inc.

Riggs, D. S., & Foa, E. B. (1994). Obsessive-compulsive disorder. In D. Barlow (Ed.), *Clinical Handbook of Psychological Disorders* (pp. 189-239). New York: Guilford.

Rimm, D. C., & Masters, J. C. (1974). *Behavior therapy: Techniques and empirical findings.* New York: Academic.

Rubin, R. D., & Merbaum, M. (1971). Self-imposed punishment versus desensitization. In A. A. Lazarus, & C. M. Franks (Eds.), *Advances in behavior therapy* (pp. 184-207). New York: Academic.

Salkovskis, P. M. (1985). Treatment of an obsession. *British Journal of Clinical Psychology, 22,* 311-313.

Salkovskis, P. M., & Warwick H. M. C. (1985). Cognitive therapy of obsessive-compulsive disorder: Treating treatment failures. *Behavioural Psychotherapy, 13,* 243-255.

Salkovskis, P. M., Westbrook, D. (1989). Behaviour therapy and obsessional ruminations: Can failure be turned into success? *Behaviour Research and Therapy, 27*(2), 149-160.

Sandyk, R. (1992). Does melatonin mediate the therapeutic effects of 5-HT reuptake inhibitors in obsessive-compulsive disorder? *International Journal of Neuroscience, 64*(1-4), 221-223.

Saper, B. (1971). A report on behavior therapy with outpatient clinic patients. *Psychiatric Quarterly ,45,* 209-215.

Sher, K. J., Frost, R. O., Otto, R. (1983). Cognitive deficits in compulsive checkers: An exploratory study. *Behavior, Research, and Therapy, 21,* 357-363.

Solyom, L. (1969). A case of obsessive neurosis treated by aversion relief. *Canadian Psychiatric Assocation Journal, 14,* 623-626.

Solyom, L., & Sookman, D. (1977). A comparison of clomipramine hydrochloride (Anafranil) and behavior therapy in the treatment of obsessive neurosis. *Journal of International Medical Research, 5*(5), 49-61.

Stahl, S. M. (1992). Serotonin neuroscience discoveries usher in a new era of novel drug therapies for psychiatry. *Psychopharmacology Bulletin, 28*(1), 3-8.

Stanley, M. A., Swann, A. C. Bowers, T. L., (1992). A comparison of clinical features in trichotillomania and obsessive-compulsive disorder. *Behavioral Research and Therapy, 30,* 39-44.

Steketee, G. S., Foa, E. B., Grayson, J. B. (1982). Recent advances in the treatment of obsessive-compulsives. *Archives of General Psychiatry, 39,* 1365-1371.

Sternberg, D. E. (1986). Testing for physical illness in psychiatric patients. *Journal of Clinical Psychiatry, 47*(1), 3-9.

Stevens, M. J. (1984). Behavioral treatment of trichotillomania. *Psychological Report, 55,* 987-990.

Swedo, S. E., Rapoport, J. L., et al. (1989). A double-blind comparison of clomipramine and desipramine in the treatment of trichotillomania (hair-pulling). *New England Journal of Medicine, 321,* 497-501.

Taylor, J. G. (1963). A behavioral interpretation of obsessive compulsive neurosis. *Behavioral Research and Therapy, 1,* 237-244.

Turner, S. M., Jacob, R. G., & Morrison, R. (1994). Somatoform and factitious disorders. In H. E. Adams (Ed.), *Comprehensive handbook of psychopathology* (pp. 307-345). New York: Plenum.

Tynes, L. L., White, K., Steketee G. S., et al., (1990). Toward a new nosology of obsessive-compulsive disorder. *Comprehensive Psychiatry, 31,* 465-480.

van Oppen, P., & Arntz, A. (1994). Cognitive therapy for obsessive compulsive disorder. *Behavioral Research and Therapy, 32,* 79-87.

van Oppen, R., De Hann, E., van Balkom, A., Spinhoven, P., Hoogduin, K., & van Dyke, R. (1995). Cognitive therapy and exposure in vivo in the treatment of obsessive-compulsive disorder. *Behaviour Research and Therapy, 33,* 379-390.

Watsky, E. J., & Salzman, C. (1991). Psychotropic drug interactions. *Psychopharmacology, 42*(3), 247-256.

Wernicke, C. (1900). *Grundisse der psychiatrie* [Foundations of psychiatry]. Leipzig, Germany: F. Barth.

Winchel, R. M., Jones, J. S., Stanley, B., et al. (1992). Clinical characteristics of trichotillomania and its response to fluoxetine. *Journal of Clinical Psychiatry, 53,* 304-308.

Wolpe, J. (1973). *The practice of behavior therapy* (3rd ed.). New York: Pergamon.

Wolpe, J. (1990). *The practice of behavior therapy* (4th ed.). Needham Heights, MA: Allyn & Bacon.

Yaryura-Tobias, J. A. (1988). Desorden obseso-compulsivo primario: Aspectos bioquimicos [Obsessive-compulsive disorder: Biological aspects]. In J. Ciprian-Ollivier (Ed.), *Psiquiatria biológica* [Biological psychiatry], Vol 12. (pp. 120-127). Buenos Aires: Cientifica, Inter Americana.

Yaryura-Tobias, J. A., Campisi, T. A., McKay, D., & Neziroglu, F. A. (1995). Schizophrenia and obsessive-compulsive disorder: Shared aspects of pathology. *Neurology, Psychiatry, and Brain Research, 3,* 143-148.

Yaryura-Tobias, J. A., & Neziroglu, F. A. (1983). *Obsessive-compulsive disorders: Pathogenesis, diagnosis, and treatment.* New York: Marcel Dekker.

Yaryura-Tobias, J. A., & Neziroglu, F. A. (1997). *Obsessive-compulsive disorder spectrum.* Washington, DC: American Psychiatric Press.

Yaryura-Tobias, J. A., Neziroglu, F., & Bergman, L. (1976). Chlorimipramine for obsessive-compulsive neurosis: An organic approach. *Current Therapeutic Research, 20*(4), 542-549.

Yaryura-Tobias, J. A., Neziroglu, F., & Kaplan, S. (1995). Self-mutilation, anorexia, and dysmenorrhea in obsessive-compulsive disorder. *International Journal of Eating Disorders, 17*(1), 33-38.

Index